Society and Education: An Outline of Comparison

Society and Education: An Outline of Comparison explores the relation of society to education in Europe, as well as its comparative perspective towards overseas societies and their institutions. It is an enquiry into the social-historical institution of education and cross-cultural studies in Europe.

Elaborating on the Castoriadian ontology, the book delves into the magma of social imaginary significations that characterise and associate pivotal epochs of the continent's history, Classical Greece and Modernity, and exemplifies their incarnation in educational systems and in the formation of the European and, in general, the Western comparative gaze. With a particular focus on our epoch, Postmodernity and globalisation, the study traces the pervasive dominance of capitalist significations in social institutions, forms and activities, as well as in education and the way it is compared across countries. Nevertheless, as Moutsios suggests, the European tradition, notwithstanding its ideological usage by much of social sciences, contains an indissoluble critical and self-reflective dimension, which needs to be sustained and advanced in education and its cross-cultural comparison, perhaps more than ever before.

The book demonstrates the embeddedness of education in its cultural context and should, therefore, be of great interest to academics, researchers and post-graduate students who are involved with comparative education, the sociology and history of education, education policy and European studies.

Stavros Moutsios is an Associate Professor of International Comparative Education Policy at Aarhus University (DPU, Copenhagen). He studied at the University of London and the Aristotle University of Thessaloniki, where he also worked as a Lecturer, and he has been a visiting scholar at the University of Auckland and a research fellow at Berlin Humboldt University.

Society and Education

An Outline of Comparison

Stavros Moutsios

Routledge
Taylor & Francis Group
LONDON AND NEW YORK

First published 2018
by Routledge
2 Park Square, Milton Park, Abingdon, Oxon OX14 4RN

and by Routledge
711 Third Avenue, New York, NY 10017

Routledge is an imprint of the Taylor & Francis Group, an informa business

British Library Cataloguing-in-Publication Data
A catalogue record for this book is available from the British Library

Library of Congress Cataloging-in-Publication Data
A catalog record for this book has been requested

ISBN: 978-1-138-69815-4 (hbk)
ISBN: 978-1-315-51973-9 (ebk)

Typeset in Bembo
by Apex CoVantage, LLC

Πόλις ἄνδρα διδάσκει

Σιμωνίδης

Contents

Acknowledgements

The research presented here was conducted under the EU's Marie Curie Programme of Intra-European Fellowships (FP7-People-2011-IEF, CETH, 298656). I thankfully acknowledge this programme and express the wish that it is retained and expanded, as it is one of the few initiatives that support independent research. I would like to thank the officers who undertook the formal details of the fellowship, Astrid Cermak from the DPU (Danish School of Education, Aarhus University), Nancy Bolain from the European Commission and Renate Ubachs from Humboldt University. From the DPU, in Copenhagen, I am very thankful to professors Thyge Winter Jensen and Susan Wright for their support in the formal process that led to this Marie Curie fellowship. From the Institut für Erziehungswissenschaften in Berlin, I am grateful to Professor Jürgen Schriewer, original host of the fellowship, as well as to his students and colleagues, particularly then MA student Matti Steinitz and Lecturer Patrick Ressler. I thank especially Bettina Eweleit, Secretary of the Institute, who undertook all the necessary organisational tasks, including the delivery of the piles of books that accompanied this intellectual journey for almost two years. During my stay in Berlin, I took part in various self-organised debate groups, mainly in sociology, philosophy, history and psychoanalysis, where I presented parts of my work and shared ideas with many interesting interlocutors. I would like to thank in particular Leila Gordon for her cooperation and the debates we had during the activities that she organised. I would also like to acknowledge the permission to use material from my articles published by the journals *Thesis Eleven, Academic Journal of Interdisciplinary Studies, Globalisation, Societies and Education* and *Compare*. Details of these papers are given in the bibliography (Moutsios 2009; 2010; 2013a; 2013b). Finally, many thanks to the anonymous reviewers for their useful comments, as well as to Routledge Editor for Education, Heidi Lee, Editorial Assistant Matthew Bickerton, and Project Manager Chris Mathews for their kind communication and their work on the publication of the book.

Stavros Moutsios
Copenhagen, spring 2017

Prologue

This book explores the social-historical institution of education and comparative studies in Europe. It is an inquiry into the relation of society to education and the purpose of cross-cultural comparison.

The embeddedness of education in society has often been of theoretical interest for sociology of education and comparative education. However, society is usually separated from its own past, thus hindering our understanding of education as a social institution, its origins and alterations. To examine education as an institution in Europe, I am drawing and elaborating on the ontology of Cornelius Castoriadis with regard to social imaginary as a force of social-historical creation, and particularly with regard to the Western European social imaginary. I explicate these concepts by discussing imagination at the level of the singular human being and at the level of society and its culture. Accessing a culture is tantamount to accessing the web of meanings constitutive of a society in the course of its history. Social meanings or significations are incarnated in institutions, including education which takes place officially, but also across social institutions. The analysis, therefore, of the social-historical field and its alterations allows us to understand what it means to be educated in a particular society and a particular historical era.

The social-historical institution of European education is traced back to Ancient Greece, where we find the first form of what we call today an 'education system'. The task here is to access the web of significations that gave rise to the creation of the school and higher education. We observe that education was instituted in contrast to mere training and independent of any practical goals. The emergence of education was an incarnation of meanings and values associated with reasoned knowledge and democratic citizenship, and, in general, with the culture of autonomy that characterised the Greek polis. Active quest for knowledge and the truth, logical argumentation and critique, political participation and the belief in everybody's potential for self-development throughout one's life are some of the main attributes of Ancient Greek education which were to be bequeathed to European Modernity.

Indeed, as in Ancient Greece, education in Europe emerged as an institution that should be promoting reasoning, scientific inquiry and critical aptitude, and it was related with the democratic movements that spread in the continent from the 18th century on. The Modern Era drew on the Greek legacy to call into question the medieval status quo and to establish knowledge and learning free from religious dogmas. Childhood was recognised, for the first time after Antiquity, as a distinct phase of life, and attention was paid to the developmental traits of the child, on the basis of which schools and teaching were to be organised. Coercive pedagogic methods were rejected in favour of teaching in the vernacular, with the intention to bring the child in contact with their social and natural environment. Autonomous learning through discovery of knowledge within a democratic school community became the main aim of pedagogic movements in Modernity. Academic autonomy arose as a sine qua non characteristic of the university, drawing on the Ancient Greek tradition established by Plato's Academy, where ideas could be freely debated and disputed, and on the early Renaissance tradition of *universitas*, as a community of scholars. However, after the weakening of Church authority, the undertaking of autonomy in education confronted a new social imaginary that foregrounded the perpetual enhancement of mastery and instrumental control of society and nature. The education system was to be regulated by bureaucratic and industrial methods, constructed in accordance to the new social class structure, to worship the nation and serve capitalist development. Accordingly, the university was established mainly as a bureaucratic mechanism and placed in the service of social and economic reproduction, nation-state building and official policymaking. Thus, European education systems have been instituted under two opposing projects and significations, one dating back to the Ancient Greek polis, and the other being a novel creation of Modernity. The conflict between them marks the social-historical institution of European (and Western) education and constitutes its very particularity.

A historical moment in which the project of autonomy in education made major breakthroughs was the student movements of the 1960s that led to a profound transformation of education systems, pedagogic relations and, overall, the way people learn. However, in the following decades, the capitalist imaginary has dominated education as much as other social institutions. The era of Postmodernity and globalisation is the era of massive access to information and knowledge and to formal education. Yet, at the same time, it is the era of general conformity induced by the extensive penetration of economic and bureaucratic norms in the organisation and contents of education systems, the proliferation of spectacle and surveillance technologies and the making of education policies by transnational agencies aiming to enhance 'human capital' production. The idea of academic autonomy in the university is dilapidated under widespread reforms that have subdued research to business strategies, vocationalised and technicised knowledge organisation and communication and placed scholars under intensive productivity controls. Education in Postmodernity is permeated overwhelmingly by significations associated with the expansion of capitalism and the drive towards mastery and instrumental control generated in Modernity.

The social-historical field is presentified not only in education but also in comparative studies, which are an institution too, as are all branches of knowledge. Comparative education has often been concerned with methodology, theory and epistemology, but it has hardly raised questions with regard to the cultural underpinnings of comparison. Isn't the comparative perspective of a society related to the way it 'sees' or imagines itself? Isn't this perspective subject to social-historical change? And shouldn't it be manifested in the theories and methods by which cross-cultural comparisons are performed? If the answer to these questions is positive, then the exploration of the cultural and, even more, the ontological roots of a society's gaze towards the 'other' should be of crucial importance to understand the institution of comparative studies. Illuminating the cultural and the ontological that lie behind the epistemological elucidates the very meaning and purpose of performing cross-cultural comparisons. One of the main aims of this study is to explore how the 'other' has been seen in those eras of European history which gave rise to comparative studies.

In Ancient Greece, we find not only the beginnings of education, but also of cross-cultural comparison, and this is hardly accidental. The appreciation of free inquiry and reasoned knowledge as well as the acknowledgement of multiple viewpoints in the democratic process are reflected in the Greeks' effort to know and understand other cultures. Ancient Greece appears as the first society which, contrary to current stereotypes and unsubstantiated claims, conceived of itself as equal and, simply, as different amongst the other societies of the time. The Greeks recognised the common traits of human nature, but they did not expect other peoples to be sharing their own worldviews and institutions. This is manifested in the impartial attitude by which foreign lands were approached in Greek cultural creations and the historical and ethnographic studies which involved comparison. Foreign education was inquired, as all other institutions, from the perspective of the values it expressed and the purposes it served. For the Greeks, cross-cultural inquiry illuminated the premises of their own values and institutions, and it was an opportunity for self-examination.

Drawing on the Ancient Greek precedent, Western Europe ruptured, during the Modern Era, its hitherto cognitive and representational closure with respect to other peoples and recognised the universality of the human condition but also the multiplicity and particularity of cultures. This gave rise again to an impartial and self-reflective gaze towards the cultural 'other', which was expressed in the institution of comparative studies as field of study in many disciplines (education, law, political science, linguistics, religion, literature, sociology etc.). However, this has not been the prevalent comparative viewpoint. The technological and scientific advancements of the Europeans became the criterion by which they gauged other cultures. Overseas societies were to be judged and compared in terms of their capacity to adopt or serve European models of 'development', something that legitimised colonialism and imperialism, shaped knowledge production in the West and defined its education policies internationally.

The globalisation of capitalism has entailed the globalisation of this comparative viewpoint. International organisations and supranational entities play now a key role in defining the agendas of education comparison, as well as the agendas of education reform worldwide. Education is principally defined in economic terms, and learners are considered to constitute 'human resources' required by the global markets. As a result, entire education systems and the societies to which they belong are studied and compared as instruments of the globalised economy and its agents. If this is the case, then, historically, we are witnessing a new cognitive and representational closure with regard to cultural and education comparison, something which any rethinking of comparative education, as an academic knowledge branch, needs to address.

Capitalist globalisation, notwithstanding its isomorphic effects across countries, does not abolish the multiplicity of societies. Societies have their own history and their own fundamental singularity, expressed in their power structures, in their creations and in the particular complex of ideas that is rooted in their history. Comparative research should therefore break with any hierarchisation of societies and any assumption that they should follow historical pathways conceived or designed by other civilisations. Acknowledging though the particularity of societies does not entail that one should abstain either from cross-investigation or from critical reflection on one's educational institutions and practices. Critical reflection through comparison is precisely that part of the European tradition that we most need to maintain and advance. Hence, the subtitle of the book: it outlines a comparison of what education and cross-cultural studies have meant in pivotal eras of the European social-historical field and what they can mean for us today.

1 Social imaginary, culture and education as an institution

Human imagination and society

To access culture, one should access the web of meanings constitutive of society. Meaning is realised through imagination. The etymology of the word indicates the presence of images, which is also the case in the Greek language (*phantasia* from *phantasma*) as well as in German (*Einbildungskraft* from *Bild*). In Kant's definition, 'imagination is the faculty for representing an object even without its presence in intuition'.[1] However, amongst other philosophers, ancient and modern, and in psychoanalytic theory, imagination is perceived as a faculty whose activity does not depend on the prior presence of an external object or incitement. Most notably, Aristotle, who essentially discovered imagination and elaborated on its properties, in his treatise *Περί Ψυχής* (*On the Soul*), went beyond understanding imagination as merely a faculty of reproduction of sensual/perceptional experience. For the Greek philosopher, the psyche (or soul) is a substance qua form of a natural body that has life potentiality.[2] Imagination is a movement in the psyche that takes place as a result of actual sense or perception.[3] What makes imagination produce movement is desire.[4] Moreover, Aristotle notes, as sight (or vision) is a sense par excellence, the term imagination derives from light (*φάος*), since without light, we cannot see.[5]

The Aristotelian thesis emphasises two very important characteristics of human imagination. First, it stresses that imagination consists in an incessant flux of images that takes place beyond visual perception or intention. Sights appear to us even with the eyes closed.[6] Secondly, it posits that imagination in humans, in contrast to animals that possess this faculty, is the condition of thinking. Although imagination cannot be identified with perception or thought, without imagination, there can be neither perception nor belief.[7] Animals have imagination, too, but they do not have beliefs, because their own imagination is capable of perception but not of inference.[8] Human imagination allows for thought and decisions about the future in relation to the present.[9] That which can think, therefore, as Aristotle writes, thinks forms in images.[10] Through this point Aristotle arrives at a fundamental conclusion in his understanding of human imagination: although it can represent or recall something at will, believing is not up to us, for we must be either in trueness or in falseness.[11] In other words, there is always image, we always imagine and, thus, we formulate unavoidably a view because it is necessary to be either in trueness or in falseness.

Aristotle's insight that the soul never thinks without an image[12] would be supported today by neuroscience, with a notable example being that of Nobel laureate Gerald Edelman's and Giulio Tononi's research. In their book *A Universe of Consciousness: How Matter becomes Imagination*, the two biologists underline that the brain, contrary to conventional claims, does not work like a computer.[13] Their review of the anatomy and dynamic of neurons shows that the brain has special features of organisation and function that are incompatible with the conviction that it performs calculations or follows instructions. The billions of connections of a brain are not characterised by accuracy, nor are they identical with other brains, even on the smallest scale – and this applies to monozygotic twins, too. Although one can identify patterns of connections in a given area of the brain, the variability existing in the more refined ramifications of the neurons on a microscopic level is enormous and testifies to the uniqueness of every brain. Every brain is 'printed' by the development and experience of the individual, which constitute his/her subjective history. Individuals' thoughts, inner deliberation and mental representations indicate the presence of images that can be created, as the authors note, even in the absence of external stimuli. Dreams testify to this: although they have their peculiar characteristics (e.g., loss of thinking capacity or absolute concentration on one thing), the states of dreaming and waking consciousness are very similar. As Edelman and Tononi point out:

> We are truly imagining, and short of schizophrenic hallucinations and dreams, we know it. Given the close relationship between perception and memory in a complex brain whose functional connectivity matches the statistics of the environment, it is perhaps no surprise that what we perceive or image in the waking state and what we imagine in dreams is remarkably similar.[14]

In their study of consciousness, the two researchers clarify that their concern is the material arrangements in the brain that allow for conscious thinking, but as thinking has to do with meaning, it cannot be limited to energy or matter, though it includes both. This is an important qualification to be made in the context of nowadays' biologistic accounts of human behaviour spurred by neuroscience. Indeed, most of contemporary brain research regards essentially all individual experience and conduct as outcomes of electrochemical processes in specific regions of the brain. Heavily sponsored research projects employ various techniques of brain scanning and measurement, claiming that thoughts, feelings and ethics have a physical locus, thus reducing human personality to molecular functions in the cerebral cortex. This trend – an earlier version of which was to attribute everything that people do to their genes – has not left uninfluenced social sciences. Manuel Castells, for example, identifies now the mind with the brain and conceives the latter as a processor of internal and external stimuli aiming to ensure the survival and increase the well-being of the 'brain's owner'[15] – something that, of course, would hardly apply to an anorexia sufferer or to a suicide bomber.

The reduction of the human being to its biological functions is not new, nor is the critique to biologism. William James, regarded as the father of American psychology, disputed the claim, widespread also in the 19 century, that thought is a function of the brain. He pointed out that this would amount to the false statement that steam is a function of the kettle or light is a function of the electric circuit. Thought, as he observed, is generated spontaneously and created out of nothing.[16] The fact that brain damage disrupts mental functions does not entail, as James remarked, that consciousness and mind (or the psyche, in our terms) are generated by the brain. In the metaphor used by Beauregard, a present-day neuroscientist and psychologist, this would be the same as to conclude that the loss of music, after one demolises a radio's receiver, proves that the radio creates the music.[17]

In other words, neuroscience contributes to the study of the biological substrate of mental phenomena but it has nothing to say about the psychic life of the individual. Neuroscience places emphasis on biology, which does away with value and meaning. Neuroscience can tell us, for example, as Blass and Carmeli point out, of the biology of the mind while dreaming or having an affective experience, but not of the meaningfulness of that biological substrate.[18] The same thoughts or ideas have different meaning depending on time, context, personal biography or psychic state. Thus, biological explanation cannot advance our understanding of the influence of latent meanings or psychic truths. As they write characteristically, neuroscience as a domain of knowledge gives prominence to 'the sensory, the physical, the visual, at the expense of psychological meaning, truth, and ideas that cannot be captured in the images of a PET scan, no matter how technologically advanced'.[19]

Indeed, psyche and therefore imagination fall into the domain of psychoanalysis but also of philosophy, starting with the pioneering work of Aristotle. However, according to Castoriadis, imagination has essentially never had its proper place in either of the two knowledge areas. As he observes, the importance of imagination in Freud appears through his reference to the significance that the phantasm (or image) has for the soul and the relative independence of phantasmisation, though Freud never refers explicitly to imagination. In philosophy, after Aristotle, imagination was re-discovered by Kant, whose reference to it, however, was reduced in his later writings, then it was taken up again by Heidegger, to be eventually abandoned and, finally, touched upon hesitantly by Merleau-Ponty.[20] The same applies to Marx, who acknowledges imagination as the distinctive capacity of humans in his illustrious comparison between a spider or a bee and an architect (who raises a structure first in their imagination before they erect it in reality), as well as his references to commodity fetishism, but never develops these ideas further.[21] In most philosophical traditions, as Castoriadis notes, imagination was understood as a reproductive, imitative and combinatory capacity, but not in its radical sense, i.e. as a faculty of invention and creation.

In agreement with Aristotle, Castoriadis maintains that there is no thinking without images, either in the visual sense or in the general sense of representations or forms. With the exception of dreamless sleep, human psyche is always characterised by a flux of representations (visual, acoustic, verbal etc.), which arise, congest, leak, refer to other images, reappear and disappear without necessarily external stimuli.[22] There is psychic life precisely because of this incessant flux of representations. Human psyche differs fundamentally from animal psyche in that whereas in the latter representation happens as figuration of a real object (e.g., a lion imagines its prey), in the former representations do not necessarily have a particular referent. This is why human imagination is radical according to Castoriadis: because it is capable of creating *ex nihilo*, from nowhere (but not *in nihilo*, out of context, nor *cum nihilo*, with no means), representations and forms or *eidē* (εἴδη), in the Platonic sense. Psyche exists through what it forms and how it forms it. Thus, radical imagination is an a-causal *vis formandi*, whose seat is the psyche of the singular human being.[23] In this regard, meaning is realised in the domain of imagination. However, whereas in the animal soul, meaning exists as exclusively organ pleasure, in the case of the human soul, it is realised predominantly as representational pleasure. Namely, for the human being, pleasure ceases to be a sign indicating what is to be sought and what is to be avoided, but it becomes an end in itself, even when it is against the preservation and existence of the human being itself. In other words, representation and pleasure in humans are defunctionalised.[24]

The defunctionalisation of imagination takes place following the socialisation of the human psyche, a process starting right after birth. However, in Castoriadis's account of psychogenesis and sociogenesis, the newborn psyche is not a *tabula rasa*, but a homogeneous, undifferentiated flux of representations; it forms, while at the same time, it is subject to formation. Representations are at this stage undifferentiated and homogeneous because the newborn infant is incapable of distinguishing between itself and the other and between itself and the world. The infantile psyche realises itself as omnipotent, omnipresent and self-sufficient. Castoriadis distinguishes this state from the Freudian 'primary narcissism', which means that the psyche is absorbed by itself to the exclusion of others. This is rather a state of 'totalitarian inclusion', as he argues, as the newborn psyche does not yet have the capacity to make distinctions.[25]

The omnipotence of the singular psyche is challenged when it realises that the world is not subject to its command: the other is the master of pleasure and unpleasure and thus the source of 'must' and 'must not', namely of social norms. The infantile psychic monad moves on then to the 'triadic phase', where it is now capable of distinguishing between itself, the other and the object, though its original 'monadic closure' never ceases to be a driving force. Thus, the psyche is altered and opened up to the social-historical world and its institutions – the mother and the father, as parents, initially, and, through them, language, which is also socially instituted. Thereby, society destroys what until then was meaningful for the psyche (its 'solipsistic' pleasure and self-closure), and it 'compensates' by furnishing it with the meanings incarnated in its institutions. This is how the socialisation process takes place: the psyche sublimates meanings available in the social-historical world and forms its flux in accordance with them. The product is the social individual, deeply immersed in a world of meaning, which, however, can never absorb the psyche as radical imagination. As Castoriadis writes, 'society and psyche are inseparable and irreducible one to the other'.[26]

In summary, human imagination consists in an incessant flux of images that condition thinking and thus belief. Without imagination, according to Aristotle, there can be neither thinking nor meaning. Contemporary research in neuroscience supports the association of imagination with thinking and therefore with meaning making, but neuroscience has nothing to say either about meaning as such or about psychic life – both falling in the domains of philosophy and psychoanalysis. Meaning is realised through imagination, but, as Castoriadis remarks, whereas in animal psyche, meaning exists as exclusively organ pleasure, in human psyche, imagination is defunctionalised, namely meaning is realised predominantly as representational pleasure. This has very important repercussions for the understanding of socialisation and the function of social institutions. Human psyche comes into the world not as a *tabula rasa*, according to the Castoriadian theory of psychogenesis, but as an undifferentiated and homogeneous flux of representations, which later on are destroyed by socialisation but never eradicated completely. Socialisation of the human soul means immersion in the meanings incarnated in social institutions.

Social imaginary significations and culture

The meanings available in the society are what Castoriadis calls *social imaginary significations*. There is need to elaborate on this concept, as, notwithstanding the common talk in social sciences today about imaginaries, we rarely come across precise accounts that can help sociological and cross-cultural research. For example, amongst the well-known works that look at social imaginaries are those of Benedict Anderson, Charles Taylor and, to some extent, Edgar Morin.[27] Morin recognises the importance of imagination and psychic life throughout his major work, *La Méthode*. He regards the psyche (*anima*) as complementary to the mind (*animus*), but the former is largely missing (or is limited to the affective domain), in contrast to the latter, from his theory of culture.[28] Anderson is concerned with the nation as an 'imagined community', constructed through shared frames of interpretation by the use of means such as print languages and media. Anderson points out that this imaginary aspect, the 'new consciousness', is what matters in understanding nation formation, rather than looking for factors such as economic interests. Nevertheless, he does not explore this aspect theoretically beyond the area of nationalism, which is his focus. Taylor, in his effort to identify its key forms in Western Modernity, gives a broad definition of the social imaginary, which he differentiates from social theory: whereas the latter is made by a small minority, the former is the way that people in general imagine their social existence and surroundings as well as their expectations and underlying notions and images. In other words, social imaginary is 'that common understanding that makes possible common practices and a widely shared sense of legitimacy'.[29] This is a useful definition that needs, however, to be refined through the Castoriadian ontology, from which, after all, Taylor borrows the concept.[30]

Social imaginary significations do not constitute simply meanings in which the newborn is immersed, but they constitute for a society its very world. Societies should be seen in both their functional and instrumental dimension as well as their imaginary dimension, the latter being indissociable from the former. A functional-instrumental dimension exists because there is a natural stratum on which the society leans and that is subject to this kind of organisation. There are animals, stones, sun, moon, rivers and mountains, men, women and children. There is day and night, humans give birth to humans and horses to horses. There is, in other words, a biological and physical reality, the first natural stratum, which the institution of a society cannot ignore. In this natural stratum there are properties and classes that can be discerned, identified, categorised or ensembled. The world is ensemblisable and thus subject to what Castoriadis calls *ensemblistic-identitary* logic, which expresses the functional-instrumental dimension of society: we can distinguish, choose, posit, count and speak in certain terms instead of others. Mathematics depicts fully this logic, which the author exemplifies with reference to Cantor's definition of sets ('A set is a collection into a whole of definite and distinct objects of our intuition or of our thought. These objects are called the elements of the set').[31] The ensemblistic-identitary logic is present in language, the *legein* (*λέγειν*) of the society. Language is itself organised in accordance with this logic, but also it conveys it through the *social representing/saying*. Moreover, the ensemblistic-identitary dimension is expressed in the *teukhein* (*τεύχειν*) of the society, its technique, through its function to assemble, adjust, fabricate, construct. *Teukhein* is manifested in *social doing*. Both social representing/saying and social doing have ineffaceably an ensemblistic-identitary dimension, manifested in *legein* and *teukhein*. In other words, no society can be instituted without a functional-instrumental dimension.[32]

But at the same time, no society can be instituted without an imaginary dimension – otherwise, society would be a functional-instrumental automaton. It is a natural fact that there are male and female human beings but the way they are related and reproduced is subject to how a society 'sees' and institutes the two genders and their relations, as we know, at least, from Margaret Mead.[33] It is a natural fact that there are children, but how they are raised in different societies and different periods touches upon the given imaginary significations with regard to childhood. Similarly, social relations (man-woman, adult-child, lord-serf, employer-employee etc.) are instituted in particular, and complementary, ways in different social-historical contexts. Objects are also immersed into the social-historical context. Tools are tools, but they are never only manifestations of *teukhein*. A bow with arrows does not have the same importance today as in Antiquity; a sword in medieval times could well have been thought to have magical powers; and today, a car may well be considered, with the help of the advertisement industry, an expression of masculinity or social status rather than simply a means of transportation. Even if tools or machines are simply seen as 'nothing more' than efficient devices in the production line, as Castoriadis remarks, they are 'loaded' with the significations of efficiency and productivity, characteristic of modern industrial societies. Equally, time, part of the natural stratum, is not merely a matter of identification, demarcation or counting, but penetrated by social significations. The Christian calendar (BC and AD), national holidays and the duration of a working day are indicative examples that time is punctuated and, thus experienced, always with an imaginary signification. The same applies to economy, which is commonly considered to obey the functional-instrumental logic. However, we know, as the anthropological study of Karl Polanyi has shown, that the placement of the economy at the epicentre of societies is a historically recent phenomenon, connected with the rise of industrialism in the West, and cannot be found earlier in Europe or elsewhere.[34] Likewise, the rise of the calculative *homo economicus* and the penetration nowadays of practically all aspects of social life by the 'economic' has to do with a web of significations associated with the emergence and expansion of capitalism. In short, in society, the ensemblistic-identitary element is inseparable from the imaginary element. Social imaginary significations permeate objects and individuals and are presentified and figured by them, directly or indirectly. Or, in another sense, social significations create objects as well as individuals and organise their world.

Thus, after it has removed from the newborn psyche what was meaning for it (i.e. its limitless egoism and omnipotence), as Castoriadis writes, society offers to its members another meaning: the organisation of the world in accordance with its imaginary significations. The latter lean on the radical imagination of the individual psyche, but on the other hand, without a pre-existing society that makes available these significations, the newborn would not survive, or it would remain in its solipsistic phase, unable to create meaning.[35] It is because of the social significations that the newborn child becomes a subject. This does not mean that they exist for the individual as phantasms or representations. It would be impossible for an individual to represent the totality of significations permeating a society and its institutions. Nor does it mean that they have a particular referent. There is no referent, for example, for the imaginary significations of God, citizen, capital or nation – or, in a sense, they are their own referent. Imaginary significations are what formulates human beings as social individuals, categorising and reproducing them and organising their social relations; they are also what makes individuals capable of thinking and acting in a coherent way and taking part in the social representing/saying and in the social doing.[36]

Each society, then, is instituted by creating its own world of significations, which hold it together: they bring a sense of co-belonging to objects, acts, functions and individuals, and they condition and orient what is doable and what is representable in this society. The society exists through its world of significations, which itself has brought to existence, and immerses whatever new appears immediately into this world.

In other words, according to Castoriadian ontology, each society constructs a representation of itself and, consequently, of other societies, in the past and in the present. Human beings become social individuals by internalising the imaginary significations incarnated in social institutions; ways of thinking, rules, values and their very identities as individuals depend on this internalisation. Social imaginary significations have a triple role: they structure the general representations of the world; they set the types of affects characteristic for each society – its emotional relation to life; and they indicate the aims of social doing – i.e. where a society should be heading – and the hierarchy it posits on its aims. It is this representational, affective and intentional complex conveyed by imaginary significations that defines how a society 'sees' its present and its past, but also the future that it is pursuing. Social imaginary significations are social because, and only if, they are shared by the anonymous collectivity, and they are imaginary because they do not derive from natural laws or rational syllogisms, but they are created by societies. However, they are real, as they indicate what is valued and what is not valued, what has worth and what does not have worth for a particular society; they point to what a society regards as information, and the weight, value or importance granted to this information; and they are presentified in the institutions, projects and, ultimately, the history of a society. To understand, therefore, the particularity of a period, one has to understand its characteristic imaginary significations.[37]

However, this understanding is not possible through mathematical, physical or biological notions of social organisation – a typical approach in social sciences. This is because accessing the imaginary significations of a society is something that does not follow the analytical process pertaining to its ensemblistic-identitary dimension. Imaginary significations are related in such a complex and inter-referential manner, which makes it impossible to reconstitute the whole set of its elements. It is only the ensemblistic-identitary dimension that follows the schemata present in the logico-mathematic theory of sets, i.e. elements, classes, properties and relations, which can be distinguished, ordered, counted, arranged, rearranged etc. This is the functional-instrumental aspect of social institutions, which follows the operative schema of determinacy: something exists because it can be defined and determined. In the case of the imaginary, though, something exists as signification. Imaginary significations can be identified but not determined, nor can they be reassembled or reproduced. The way they are related with each other is that of *referral*. For example, the signification of 'priest' refers to 'church', 'church' to 'religion', 'religion' to 'God', 'God' to 'sin' etc. Imaginary significations cannot be clearly distinct nor can they be reconstructed or recombined and thus reconstitute a particular society or epoch.[38]

To describe the complex way in which imaginary significations are associated, Castoriadis uses the concept of magma. In geology, magma is a flow of molten rock, volatiles and solids, a material in a constant state of transition from flux to structure, formed and formless at the same time. The term indicates the fluid and dynamic character of significations, their cross-flows and interminglings, and helps us understand their non-reducibility to sets and subsets: any ensemble separated from the whole is a dynamic flux, and extracting a part from magma is to extract another magma.[39] More specifically, in Castoriadis's definition: 'a magma is that from which one can extract (or which one can construct) an indefinite number of ensemblist organisations but which can never be reconstituted (ideally) by a (finite or infinite) ensemblist composition of these organisations'.[40] In other words, magma cannot be reduced to the sum of its parts, nor can it be reproduced by assembling these parts. In this regard, because of the magmatic mode in which significations are intermingled, a given society cannot be seen as a system of distinct objects.

This does not mean, as Castoriadis underlines, that magma is chaos: it is organised by the central imaginary significations characterising each society, which define its primary sources of meaning and which permeate all peripheral significations; it is also organised by the earlier central and peripheral imaginary significations (or traces of them) existing in the history of the society in question; and it can be distinguished through the institutions that incarnate peripheral significations. Moreover, they can be discerned by their three 'vectors': intentions, namely where the society is heading, as this is expressed in its major activities and hierarchisation of values; representations, how the society conceives of its world and what makes meaning for it; and the effects induced by social institutions. Imaginary significations, in this regard, should not be confounded with ideologies. Ideologies are related to the domination of specific social groups and they offer 'rational' arguments to sustain this domination. Thus, ideology, in its most specific sense, indicates the attempt of a social group (e.g., social class) to justify its goals to retain or to change the existing status quo.[41] Nor are imaginary significations 'ideal types'. Imaginary significations are immanent to the society in question, while ideal types are products of reflection on the society by the theoretician, which, despite their illuminating potential, neglect context specificity. To think of a society in its specificity, or its haecceity, one should think of it as the institution of this particular magma of significations, not any other, in its particular history, organised in this particular mode, not otherwise, and presentified in the acts, senses and dispositions of individuals through their socialisation.[42]

Approaching the haecceity of a society is tantamount to approaching its culture. In other words, culture can be traced, as it will be maintained throughout this study, by accessing the particular magma of imaginary significations prevailing in a given society. Culture has been traditionally one of the most elusive concepts in social sciences, despite the numerous definitions available in the literature. Kroeber and Kluckhohn, for example, in their classic compilation *Culture: A Critical Review of Concepts and Definitions*, published in 1952, collected 164 definitions.[43] Notwithstanding, though, the numerous definitions and the centrality of the term in social sciences in general and comparative education in particular, culture remains a concept that is subject to debate and clarification.

The term *cultura*, as Cuche writes in his overview of culture as a concept in social sciences, appeared around the end of the 13th century to indicate a cultivated piece of land, and by the beginning of the 16th century, it was taken to mean the very act of cultivation.[44] The term's metaphorical sense was formed by the middle of the 16th century to connote the cultivation or development of a capacity. In the 18th century, culture was still used in the singular, to indicate, in full accord with the idea of progress that was celebrated by European Modernity. This applies also to the term 'civilisation', which was already used, in the singular, too, during the same period, with reference though to societal advancements in education, law and governance, whereas culture referred more to an individual state achieved mainly through education and arts. In Germany, during the 18th century, the word *Kultur* was essentially a transfer of the French notion, while *Zivilisation* was identified largely with economic and technological advancements. However, from the 19th century, culture was framed by a national understanding: on the one hand, culture was redefined under the post-1806 current of nationalism that sought the 'German character' and the uniqueness of the German culture; and on the other, this new understanding resulted from the pioneering work of Johann Gottfried Herder (i.e. *Ideen zur Philosophie der Geschichte der Menschheit*), which identified culture with nationality, though at the same time opposed nationalism and foregrounded instead the idea of mankind as a common species organised in different nationalities and cultural forms, thus relativising the concept of culture.[45] Apparently, this perception, as well as the fact that education from the 18th and especially the 19th century came under the auspices of the nation-state, had an impact on comparative education studies, as is testified by the preoccupation of some of its early authors with the 'national character': Issac Kandel, Nicholas Hans, and Vernon Mallinson looked at 'national character' as the generator but also the outcome of an education system.[46]

Notwithstanding the framing of culture by the nation or by nationalism, it is important to note that from the late 19th century, and especially in the early 20th century, culture, now used in plural, became the object of Anglo-American anthropology, which gave to the term a largely descriptive definition. For example, the British anthropologist Edward Tylor defined, in 1871, 'culture or civilisation' as 'that complex whole which includes knowledge, belief, art, law, morals, customs, and any other capabilities and habits acquired by man as a member of society'.[47] The new perception was also present in the works of other anthropologists since then, with notable examples: Franz Boas, who opposed culture to the notion of 'race'; Bronislaw Malinowski, a proponent of a functionalist approach to culture; and Ruth Benedict and Margaret Mead, who emphasised the pedagogic role of 'cultural transmission'.[48] Drawing on more or less known works from anthropology, Kroeber and Kluckhohn (1952) cite various definitions of culture, characteristic of which are the following:

- A culture is any given people's way of life, as distinct from the life-ways of other peoples.
- The culture of a people may be defined as the sum total of the material and intellectual equipment whereby they satisfy their biological and social needs and adapt themselves to their environment.

- Culture . . . may be defined as all behaviour learned by the individual in conformity with a group . . .
- Culture is the rationalisation of habit.
- Culture consists of patterned and functionally interrelated customs common to specifiable human beings composing specifiable social groups or categories.
- . . . a culture is a definite association complex of ideas.
- Culture is all behaviour mediated by symbols.[49]

Castoriadis's definition of culture combines the traditional French/German definition (culture as the works of the human spirit and the access of individuals to them) with the more relative and descriptive understanding of culture offered by the Anglo-American anthropology, which, as the above examples indicate, intends the entire institution of society: culture is 'everything, in the institution of society, that goes beyond its ensemblistic-identitary (functional-instrumental) dimension and that the individuals of this society positively cathect as 'value' in the largest sense of the term'.[50] In these terms, there is no society without culture, since there is no society reduced to its functional-instrumental dimension. Apart from this dimension, or apart from the natural stratum on which a society leans for its institution, there is a-meaning and chaos (in the sense of void, not disorder). But this chaos is also subject to creation, to a power of formation or *vis formandi*, which imposes on the chaos a *cosmos*, a more or less ordered world. The singular psyche is a-meaning and chaos, too. As the individual is a being of imagination (at the level of the singular psyche) and of imaginary (at the level of the social), it is also him/herself a *vis formandi*, but also a *libido formandi* (a desire and passion for formation and creation). The creative potential and the desire for formation constitute the *poietic* element of humanity – which in turn constitutes a culture. Culture is precisely this giving of form to the chaos, namely giving meaning and signification to a groundless world.[51]

Who or what grants the world meaning and what meaning is given has to do with the institution of society. The most characteristic case is that of religion, which gives to the chaos a single meaning, a single image, a single form or a single name – the name of God – thus covering up the chaos and 'closing' meaning by granting for it a transcendent guarantee. In such a case, both *vis formandi* and *libido formandi* are curtailed and channelled to repetition and the enjoyment of the existing creations, which are attributed to a transcendental being. In this case, there is *heteronomy* (from *heteros* = other, and *nomos* = rule, institution). To speak of *autonomy* (from *autos* = self), meaning should not be directed by a transcendental guarantee or from any kind of extra-social source. In the case of autonomy, societies and individuals should be aware that it is they themselves who give meaning and form to the chaos, with their own thinking and works.[52]

In extending this distinction to education, we can infer that under the conditions of heteronomy, education promotes knowledge and structures pedagogic relations in a way that radical imagination is constrained and meaning is 'externally' imposed. In contrast, whenever and wherever autonomy is pursued, there should be the least possible curtailment of the radical imagination of the learner and the greatest possible development of his/her reflectiveness.[53] Learners are thus enabled to utilise both their *vis formandi* and *libido formandi* and, consequently, to give form or image to the chaos, i.e. to create meaning. This is possible when education as an institution has embodied as significations the perpetual questioning of its cognitive and pedagogic practices and the development of learners' self-initiative – namely, when we have *paideia* or *Bildung*.[54]

In short, societies in Castoriadian ontology (which is also Ancient Greek – see next chapter), have a functional-instrumental dimension because there is a natural stratum (i.e. the physical and biological reality) on which they lean and which is subject to this dimension. But they also have an imaginary dimension that expresses their culture, that is, the meanings that societies give to a groundless world. In order to approach the culture of a society, we should access these meanings or social imaginary significations. Imaginary significations constitute the world of each society in which its members are socialised. They are organised as a magma, as a fluid and dynamic complex, rather than as a set whose elements can be distinctly arranged and rearranged. To approach the magma of imaginary significations in any given society, one has to approach its other most important creation, i.e. its institutions.

Education as an institution

The socialisation of individuals takes place in institutions. An institution is a *sine qua non* condition for a society to exist. There can be no society without institution, or, in other terms, without law. As Montesquieu writes in opening *The Spirit of Laws*: '[the world's] motion must certainly be directed by invariable laws; and could we imagine another world, it must also have constant rules, or it would inevitably perish'.[55] For the Ancient Greeks, the law, or *nomos*, as the institution and convention of a particular society, is distinguished from *physis*, i.e. from natural conditions. Without nomos, or institution, human beings cannot exist. Hence Aristotle's famous phrase in *Politics*: '. . . he who is unable to live in society, or who has no need because he is sufficient for himself, must be either a beast or a god'.[56]

But what exactly is an institution? Drawing on the so-called neoinstitutionalist theory, an '*institution* represents a social order or pattern that has attained a certain state or property; *institutionalisation* is the process of such attainment'.[57] Meyer and Rowan, two of the main authors of the 'Stanford School', define institutions as rules institutionalised as cognitive and normative principles.[58] In their cognitive aspect, these rules provide classifications or reality that enter social life as taken-for-granted facts and shape the interpretations of social actors. In their normative aspect, these rules set the obligation to act according to prescribed structures and patterns of activity. Institutionalisation, in this respect, as Meyer et al. write in another paper, is the 'process by which a given set of units and a pattern of activities come to be normatively and cognitively held in place, and practically taken for granted as lawful [. . .]'.[59] The cognitive or learning function in institutionalisation is quite central in the Stanford School's theory.

However, it is inadequate as it neglects the very history of institutions as societal creations: if institutionalisation is chiefly a matter of cognition, and therefore of knowledge accumulated over time and diffused across space, why do institutions vanish in the course of history? Nevertheless, in the above-mentioned paper, the authors offer an improved definition of institutions, taking into consideration this time culture, which, as they point out, involves the values of actors and their actions: 'We see institutions as cultural rules giving collective meaning and value to particular entities and activities, integrating them into larger schemes'.[60] More specifically:

> . . . *institutions* can be described as *cultural accounts* under whose authority action occurs and social units claim their standing. The term *account* here takes on a double meaning. Institutions are descriptions of reality, explanations of what is and what is not, what can be and what cannot. They are accounts of how the social world works, and they make it possible to find order in a world that is disorderly.[61]

This is a quite illuminating formulation, but still it lacks an elaboration of what these 'large schemes' (or 'culture structures', or 'frameworks of society', or 'forces', or 'ideologies' etc.) are, and, more importantly, how they act upon, create or change institutions and under what power dynamics.[62] We do find this elaboration in Castoriadian formulation, which accentuates the imaginary component of institutions, and therefore, it allows for the understanding of their formation, transformation or waning. More specifically, Castoriadis defines an institution as 'a socially sanctioned symbolic network, in which a functional component and an imaginary component are combined in variable proportions and relations'.[63] The symbolic is important in institutions, but they cannot be reduced to it. To understand symbols, one needs to identify the imaginary significations they convey and, by extension, institutions themselves. To put it simply, an institution is unthinkable without signification. Social imaginary significations are incarnated in institutions, and first and foremost in the two major social institutions, manifestations of the functional-instrumental (or ensemblistic-identitary) dimension of society, as also noted above: that of *teukhein* (i.e. techniques, technologies, tools etc. – the functional-instrumental aspect of *social doing*); and that of *legein* (i.e. language – the functional-instrumental aspect of *social representing/saying*). Indeed, language is not merely a 'tool of communication', but one of the most important institutions that a society creates, in which the individual is immersed from the start of his/her life. Notwithstanding universal and invariant structures across languages, the latter also convey the imaginary world of particular societies. In Castoriadis's terms, language embodies a *code*, an identitary or univocal dimension, which is constituted by a system of ensemblisable relations (e.g., grammatical classes or syntactical types), but it is also *langue* (*φάτις*), namely, it includes a signitive dimension that refers to the magma of imaginary significations available in the society.[64] Institutions are also, for example, economy, political organisation, family or the individual itself, as societies fabricate, in different periods, different types of individuals.

The latter are what the author calls second-order institutions. The *first* or *primal institution* of society is the very fact that society itself creates itself as society by creating institutions incarnating imaginary significations specific to it. This first institution is articulated through *second-order institutions*. Second-order does not mean secondary; it means that these institutions are held together by the primal institution of the society that embodies its central significations. It is not a relation of priority, but of reliance, in the sense that one cannot exist without the other. Castoriadis divides them into two categories: transhistorical institutions, and those that are specific to particular societies. Transhistorical institutions are, for example, language, the individual and the family – institutions that exist across history and societies, no matter what content they give to them. In other words, there is no society without language; all societies institute some type of individual (i.e. what a man, a woman or a child means for them), and all societies have in place some form of family, whatever this may be, to assure reproduction and socialisation of new generations. Second-order institutions specific to given societies are absolutely essential for them as they convey their particular imaginary significations. For example, Ancient Greek society is inconceivable without the polis, and capitalism is unthinkable without the business enterprise. Moreover, one has to take into account the interaction of institutions. To access the concrete texture of a society one has to consider the way the transhistorical and society-specific institutions are interwoven. In addition, institutions are connected to each other in numerous ways, so that changes in one of them have repercussions for other institutions (e.g., the dislocation of the traditional roles and relations between men and women have effects on education and labour markets).[65]

Education is also, of course, an institution, which should not be identified only with the state education system, established since European Modernity. This identification is in fact typical amongst the writings of neoinstitutionalist authors[66] but also in most comparative education tradition. The study of education within and across cultures should take into account that education is a lifelong and life-wide process, to use today's terminology. Namely, education is embedded in the very institution of society; i.e. it takes place not only in designated institutions but throughout social life. This was common knowledge already in Ancient Greece (see the next chapter) but also in modern sociology and cultural anthropology. Margaret Mead's influential studies, for example, in New Guinea tribes in the 1930s, demonstrated the pedagogic role of social institutions in sexuality and gender formation,[67] while today, many anthropologists investigate widely children's learning in various contexts (i.e. family, play, work, neighbourhood, streets etc.), including the impact of the old as well as the new media.[68] In sociology, Durkheim has also defined education from a broad perspective: education 'is the influence exercised by adult generations on those that are not yet ready for social life . . .', and it develops the states demanded 'by both the political society as a whole and the special milieu for which [the child] is specifically destined'.[69] Contemporary scholars of lifelong learning, with the exception perhaps of those who promote the skills-updating policy of official agencies, understand also the relation of education to socialisation.[70]

Thus, education is a second-order institution, both transhistorical (as there can be no society without some form of knowledge impartation to its young generations) and specific to particular societies. Moreover, in each society, education may take place in designated institutions (e.g., by sophists' classes in Ancient Athens, by monasteries, by private mentors, in the army, by an enterprise, by a community, or by the state schools and universities), but it is also *transinstitutional*, as it takes place through and across institutions (e.g. language, family, state, nation, church, medical system, workplace, media, the market etc.) by which a given society socialises its members. The state education system, which has been the main object of comparison, and whose emergence is explored in this book, has been the typical form of a designated institution for education in Europe during the last two centuries.

In short, a society cannot be conceived without institutions, but also without imaginary significations that are incarnated in institutions. For Castoriadis, these two forms constitute the *social-historical* field, which expresses the symbiosis but also the tension between the *instituting society* and the *instituted society*, what structures and what is structured, or history in the making and history made. The instituting society is the social imaginary, which creates significations and institutions. It is, at the social level, what radical imagination is at the level of body/soul. Whereas radical imagination leans on the living being and receives/alters what has already been represented by the psyche, the social imaginary leans on the first natural stratum and receives/alters what has already been instituted. Thus, there is tension between the instituting and instituted society, which expresses its perpetual state of self-alteration, and the very fact that society cannot be separated from its history:

> As instituting as well as instituted, society is intrinsically history – namely, self-alteration. Instituted society is not opposed to instituting as a lifeless product to an activity which brought it into being; it represents the relative and transitory fixity/stability of the instituted forms-figures in and through which the radical imaginary can alone exist and make itself exist as social-historical. The perpetual self-alteration of society is its very being, which is manifested by the positing of relatively fixed and stable forms-figures and through the shattering of these forms-figures which can never be anything other than the positing-creating of other forms-figures.[71]

Society thus is the self-institution of the social-historical, but this self-institution, in Castoriadian ontology, is concealed by societies themselves which live in a state of self-alienation or heteronomy. Heteronomy, at the collective level, means, as pointed out above, that societies are not aware of the fact that they are the creators of their institutions, and they consider them a creation of an extra-social source (e.g., God). Autonomous societies, on the other hand, are those societies that are conscious that they themselves, in the past and the present, are those that create their institutions and thus can change them. This consciousness arose, according to the Castoriadian thesis, on which the following chapters will elaborate, in two moments of European history: in Classical Greece and in Modernity.

The creation and alteration of institutions brings us unavoidably to the questions of power and politics – both neglected by neoinstitutionalism – which need to be specified. A plausible definition of power is given by Castells: 'Power is the relational capacity that enables a social actor to influence asymmetrically the decisions of other social actor(s) in ways that favour the empowered actor's will, interests and values.'[72] For Castoriadis, this would be *explicit power*. But both these and a number of other social theorists have sought to define power beyond the established relational terms (i.e. the capacity of a person or an authority to make someone do or not do something) by looking at its sources of legitimation.

Talcott Parsons, for instance, proposed, from the point of view of his structural-functional theory, that: '. . . political power is above all the problem of integration, of building the power of individuals and sub-collectivities into a coherent system of legitimised authority where power is fused into collective responsibility.'[73] Hannah Arendt also argued that power relies on social consensus. Arendt disputed all traditional definitions that identified power with force or violence: Weber's argument that the state's power over people is based on the means of legitimate violence; Marx's thesis that the state is an instrument of repression in the hands of the bourgeoisie; Wright Mills's perception of politics as a struggle for power whose supreme form, to his understanding, is violence; and Mao Zedong's popular dictum that power grows out of the barrel of a gun. Arendt notes that power should be distinguished from strength (an individual property), authority (recognition of one's view or decision as correct), force (energy stemming from physical or social moves) or violence. She agrees that power and violence usually appear together, but, as she indicates, in reality, they are separate phenomena. Power, as Arendt remarks, is the ability of humans to act and to act with others and in this respect it does not belong to a single person but to a group. Power arises wherever people act concertedly, and their concerted actions take place in the political arena. The perception of power as collective action entails political institutions expressing and materialising the power granted to them by the people; in other words, expressions such as 'he holds the power' and 'they are in power', as Arendt notes, indicate acceptance and support by a number of people.[74]

Collective action in the public arena constitutes *politics*, an activity which is capable of transforming the instituted society. Castoriadis distinguishes politics from *the political*, which exists everywhere, wherever a person or an authority has the capacity to posit sanctionable injunctions. Politics appears only whenever and wherever there is explicit, rational questioning of the instituted society. This definition draws on the Ancient Greek understanding of politics (see the next chapter) and refers to the participation of citizens in public activities aimed at dialogue, critique and deliberation on existing or new policies. Similar is also the way that Hannah Arendt, in her classical essay *Was ist Politik?*, understands the meaning of politics, which, as with the concept of power, she differentiates from violence. Violence and war are anti-political in the sense that they collapse the space of debate and deliberation, since they are waged with command and obedience.[75] Politics requires a space of unconstrained, argumentative speech or, in Habermas's terms, a space of *communicative rationality*, based on the mutual recognition of criticisable validity claims.[76] Or, again in Castoriadis's terms, politics refers to the conscious, critical, self-critical and rational activity that is concerned with the institution of society.[77] In other words, politics is the activity that calls into question the directions, projects, laws and institutions of a society and alters them or creates new institutions.

In this sense, politics is a project of autonomy; it is premised on the fact that institutions are human creations, and they do not stem from natural laws or some divine will. In contrast, under conditions of heteronomy, this fact is covered up. In the heteronomous institution, any questioning of the established laws and the existing explicit power is set aside or is regarded as meaningless or, at most, any question capable of being posited is answered with the terms of the established meanings. Namely, in the heteronomous institution, there is closure of meaning. Autonomy, on the other hand, consists in the potential for endless questioning of the very dominant imaginary significations and the ushering in of another form or *eidos* of society and institutions. For this potential to exist, social institutions should embody questioning and self-examination as imaginary significations in which individuals are socialised and therefore enabled to reflect on the instituted power.[78]

If this is the case, then power lies fundamentally in social imaginary significations, rather than merely in legitimised political authority. A similar point is made in much of discourse theorisation. Foucault, for instance, underlined that power cannot be established without the production, accumulation, circulation and operation of a discourse. Thus, he sought to 'cut off the head of the king', that is, to move the analytical light away from the political realm, and throw it instead on the multiple forms of subjection existing in the social organism – the final destinations of power and its discursive practices in constituting individuals.[79] Similarly, for Castells, power is exercised by coercion and/or by 'the construction of meaning on the basis of the discourses through which social actors guide their action'.[80] In education studies, Ball raised the importance of education policy discourses in constructing truth claims, possibilities of thought and meaning.[81] Likewise, the emergence, classification and distribution of educational discourses on the basis of power relations are core elements in Bernstein's theory. In his conceptualisation of 'pedagogic discourse', Bernstein distinguishes an 'instructional discourse' and a 'regulative discourse'; the former, a discourse of skills, is embedded in the regulative discourse, which is the dominant discourse, as it defines the criteria and rules of social order.[82]

Nevertheless, despite the recognition that discourses derive from broader social, economic and political power relations and discourses, and in spite of the acknowledgement that discourses embody meaning, much of discourse theorisation pays inadequate attention to the link between meaning and power. Discourses are discourses precisely because they convey meaning. Power is established not simply because individuals and institutions 'speak' the dominant ('regulative') discourse, but because they internalise the meaning it embodies – i.e. what has worth and what does not have worth, what is valued and what is not valued. Parsons was apparently aware of that when he remarked that power 'is based on the existence and use of institutionalised opportunities to exert influence . . . [and through these opportunities] the system of power is furnished with consensus in the context of social values'.[83] In Castoriadis's terms, values are conveyed by social imaginary significations. Namely, power lies in the adherence by societies or large segments of their population to the dominant social significations. He calls this power *radical ground-power*: it is a manifestation of the social historical, which, in contrast to explicit power, cannot be located. Radical ground-power is exercised by the instituted society, but also, in the background, by the instituting society, which, no matter how profound an alteration it can bring about, works always with what is already there. Thus, radical ground-power is the power of the instituted society, the instituting society and the preceding history. It is the non-locatable power of the social-historical, and thus, essentially, the power of nobody.[84]

This is how society forms individuals and how they reproduce it. Nevertheless, notwithstanding established social reproduction theories, this power is not absolute; otherwise, there would be no history. The fact that there is history – even in primitive or traditional societies that live under perpetual repetitions for long periods – indicates precisely that the ground-power of the instituted society cannot be absolute. Castoriadis attributes this first to the fact that, as noted above, each society creates its own world of imaginary significations essentially out of chaos and a-meaning, leaning only on natural regularities; this a-meaning may always intrude in society and lacerate the established magma of social significations, thus challenging the power of the instituted society. Secondly, power can be challenged by the fact that human beings possess radical imagination, whose manifestations are informed by socialisation but not destroyed. Human psyche is malleable by the institution of society but it does not lose its radical imagination, which can be manifested at any moment (for example, as a dream, psychic illness, conflict, personal intervention or contribution etc.). Thirdly, a society's world of significations can be challenged by those of another society, since there is a plurality of societies, and there is contact between them. Contacts between societies may endanger seriously each other's significations and institutions. Lastly, beneath the instituted society there is always the undercurrent of the instituting society, i.e. the social imaginary. It is because of the social imaginary that there is a plurality of societies, synchronically and diachronically.[85]

In summary, imaginary significations and institutions are sine qua non creations of human societies. In Castoriadis's terms, they both constitute the social-historical, which expresses the coexistence and simultaneously the tension between the instituting and instituted society. It is the instituting society – or the social imaginary – that creates significations and institutions. And it is the instituted society under which they are crystallised. The tension between the two, what structures and what is structured, is an expression of the perpetual state of self-alteration that societies live in and the very fact that they cannot be detatched from their history. There is always power in society, both in terms of decision making by those in authority and, at a deeper level, in terms of the adherence of societies to their dominant imaginary significations. The very fact that there is history and that institutions change means that this power cannot be absolute. Change or alteration of institutions can come over time because of the action of the instituting society or – something that is of particular relevance to the present study – because of the contacts between societies. But change can also happen explicitly under politics, i.e. the activity through which societies put into question their directions, projects, laws and their very own significations. Significations are embodied in both the primal institution of society and in a host of second-order institutions, education being one of them. Education in a society is provided not only formally through its designated institutions (e.g., the state system) but also across institutions, i.e. it is transinstitutional. Thus, by accessing the magma of imaginary significations of the society under consideration, we are enabled to approach education as a second-order institution in both these terms.

A research outline

It should be clear, then, that to explore effectively the institution of education and its comparative study in Europe, we need to place them in its social-historical field. Pivotal moments in this field are Ancient Greece and Modernity, during which education in Europe was instituted, as well as the systematic comparative interest in the institutions of other societies, as the following two chapters will show. The research will delve into the imaginary dimension of these historical periods, as well as our own. It will be looking at the magma of central and peripheral social imaginary singnifications in these eras, within the limits, of course, that the nature and scope of this study pose. Although focus will be placed on the institution of designated or official education, the depiction of the social-historical field will indicate what it means to be socialised and educated in those eras. However, the prime purpose is to understand how the social imaginary significations characteristic of each historical period are presentified, in symbiotic or conflictual ways, in the institution of education. I will be also looking at how these significations shape the way Europeans have been comparing their institutions with those of other cultures. The comparative gaze of a society is an institution itself and thus subject to understanding that can enable us to see more clearly the relation between theory and method, epistemology, and, ultimately, ontology.

The next chapter will explore the Ancient Greek social imaginary during the classical times and its association with the emergence of education and the begginings of cross-cultural studies. Education incarnated a web of significations associated with the creation of the polis, the most prominent of which were the distinction between nature and culture, philosophical and scientific inquiry, democratic politics, love for knowledge, arts and the truth, and critique of existing beliefs and representations. These significations are also at the root of cross-cultural examination, which also emerged first in Greece. The rise of self-reflectiveness and self-questioning in the Greek polis gave also rise to the genuine interest in the institutions of other societies which the Greeks saw both as particular creations, like their own, but also as sharing the common features of the human condition. The Greeks' curiosity to know about other societies was driven by intellectual interest and the desire to know better their own society through comparison. Cross-cultural inquiry was an activity associated with the ethos of philosophical and political critique that characterised democratic life in Greece. Precisely because of this ethos, comparative inquiry in Greece arose as impartial and self-critical examination, as it will be suggested through illustrations from the literature of the time.

The following chapter moves to Modernity. European Modernity revived and expanded what Castoriadis calls the central social imaginary signification of collective and personal autonomy that first emerged in Ancient Greece, but it also created a new central signification that he calls rational mastery and control, similar to Max Weber's *Zweckrationalität*, i.e. purposive or instrumental rationality. I will elaborate on the significations that mark the social-historical field of Modernity, and I will examine their interaction in the institution of education systems, with emphasis on the establishment of the university. The European university is distinguished from similar institutions existing around the world in the same era, as I will argue, from the signification of academic autonomy, which, however, arose in conflict with the appropriation of higher education by nation-state building and the industrial economy. I will also examine the presentification of the central imaginary significations of Modernity in the emergence of comparative studies. Already from the Renaissance, but especially in the Enlightenment period, we witness the emergence of a self-reflective attitude in the way the cultural 'other' was seen and studied, similar to that of Ancient Greece. Going further than Greece, the Enlightenment regarded overseas societies as being not only culturally singular but also that their members are entitled to universal rights. However, as it will be argued, the viewpoint that dominated and was internalised by social sciences and comparative education was that of technological, scientific and economic progress, that emerged during the same era, and became the main criterion by which the 'other' was to be gauged.

In Postmodernity, the capitalist imaginary and rationalistic mastery and control prevail in society and education, as well as in the way countries and their education systems are reformed and compared, as it will be pointed out in Chapter 4. Although collective and personal autonomy is embedded in the social-historical institution of European societies, or broadly, of the West, our era is witnessing the absorption of this signification by neoliberal capitalism. Here, I will examine the alteration of institutions created in Modernity, and I will focus on how capitalism is appropriating or collapsing opposed meanings and values across institutions, including education. Despite the fact that digital technologies have allowed for independent access to and diffusion of information and knowledge, the project of autonomy in education has retreated, as I will suggest, with the emphasis again on higher education. The idea of academic autonomy is displaced since universities no longer function as corporations according to Modernity's project, i.e. as communities of scholars, but according to the later meaning of the term, i.e. as business organisations controlled by managerial bureaucracies. Education overall is understood in economic terms, and education systems are studied and compared as means to ends defined by the global production system. This state of affairs and the predominance of reductionist methodology necessitate a reconsideration of what educational comparison means today. This is attempted in the final chapter, which draws theoretical lessons from the preceding social-historical analysis.

Notes

1 Kant ([1787] 1998: 256).
2 Aristotle (2003: B412a, 19–21, *«ἀναγκαῖον ἄρα τὴν ψυχὴν οὐσίαν εἶναι ὡς εἶδος σώματος φυσικοῦ δυνάμει ζωὴν ἔχοντος»*).
3 Aristotle (2003: Γ429a, 2–5, *«ἡ φαντασία ἂν εἴη κίνησις ὑπὸ τῆς αἰσθήσεως τῆς κατ' ἐνέργειαν γιγνομένη»*).
4 Aristotle (2003: Γ433a, 23–24 *«ἓν δή τι τὸ κινοῦν, τὸ ὀρεκτόν»*).
5 Aristotle (2003: Γ429a, 2–5, *«ἐπεὶ δ' ἡ ὄψις μάλιστα αἴσθησίς ἐστι, καὶ τὸ ὄνομα ἀπὸ τοῦ φάους εἴληφεν, ὅτι ἄνευ φωτὸς οὐκ ἔστιν ἰδεῖν»*).
6 Aristotle (2003: Γ428a, 15, "*«φαίνεται καὶ μύουσιν ὁράματα»*).
7 Aristotle (2003: Γ427b, 15–17, *«"φαντασία γὰρ ἕτερον καὶ αἰσθήσεως καὶ διανοίας, αὕτη τε οὐ γίγνεται ἄνευ αἰσθήσεως, καὶ ἄνευ ταύτης οὐκ ἔστιν ὑπόληψις»*).
8 Aristotle (2003: Γ428a, 22–23, *«τῶν δὲ θηρίων οὐθενὶ ὑπάρχει πίστις, φαντασία δὲ πολλοῖς»*).
9 Aristotle (2003: Γ431b, 6–7, *«ὁτὲ δὲ τοῖς ἐν τῇ ψυχῇ φαντάσμασιν ἢ νοήμασιν, ὥσπερ ὁρῶν, λογίζεται καὶ βουλεύεται τὰ μέλλοντα πρὸς τὰ παρόντα»*).
10 Aristotle (2003: Γ431b, 1, *«τὰ μὲν οὖν εἴδη τὸ νοητικὸν ἐν τοῖς φαντάσμασι νοεῖ»*).
11 Aristotle (2003: Γ427b, 21–22, *«δοξάζειν δ' οὐκ ἐφ' ἡμῖν· ἀνάγκη γὰρ ἢ ψεύδεσθαι ἢ ἀληθεύειν»*).
12 Aristotle (2003: Γ431a, 17–18, *«. . .οὐδέποτε νοεῖ ἄνευ φαντάσματος ἡ ψυχή»*).
13 Edelman and Tononi (2001).
14 Edelman and Tononi (2001: 203).
15 Castells (2009: 138).
16 James ([1898] 1956).
17 Beauregard (2012: 10).
18 Blass and Carmeli (2007).
19 Blass and Carmeli (2007: 37). PET ('Positron Emission Tomography') is the imaging technique used today widely in medical examinations.
20 Castoriadis (1997: 319–337).
21 Marx (1887).
22 Castoriadis (1987: 323).
23 Castoriadis (1997: 321–322).
24 Castoriadis (1997).
25 Castoriadis (1997).
26 Castoriadis (1987: 320).
27 Anderson (1983); Taylor (2004).
28 See Morin (1986; 2001).
29 Taylor (2004: 23).

30 See Smith (2010: 3, footnote 2).
31 Castoriadis (1987: 223).
32 See Castoriadis (1987: chapter 5).
33 See Mead ([1949] 2001b).
34 Polanyi ([1944] 2001).
35 See Theodoridis (2007).
36 Castoriadis (1987: 366).
37 Castoriadis (2000: 63–94).
38 Castoriadis (2010).
39 See Smith (2010: 12–15).
40 Castoriadis (1987: 343).
41 See Eagleton (1991).
42 Castoriadis (1987: 334). Theodoridis (2007).
43 Kroeber and Kluckhohn (1952).
44 Cuche (1996).
45 Cuche (1996: 26).
46 See Jones (1971).
47 Kroeber and Kluckhohn (1952: 43).
48 Cuche (1996).
49 Kroeber and Kluckhohn (1952: 51, 56, 58, 60, 61, 66 and 69).
50 Castoriadis (1993: 301–302).
51 Castoriadis (1993).
52 Castoriadis (1993).
53 Castoriadis (2007).
54 Castoriadis (2000: 93–96). Not accidentally, the term *Bildung* comes from the noun *Bild* (= image, picture) and the verb *bilden* (= to form, to shape, to develop, to educate). Bildung in this sense means to educate according to an image, but also the potential of the learner to create their own images, through a pedagogy which gives them access to their own *vis formandi*. See for the definition of Bildung, Wulf (2002: 103).
55 Montesquieu ([1750] 1911: 1).
56 Aristotle (1996: 1253 and a28–29).
57 Jepperson (1991: 145). Emphases in the original.
58 Meyer and Rowan (1991).
59 Meyer, Boli and Thomas (1987: 13).
60 Meyer, Boli and Thomas (1987).
61 Meyer, Boli and Thomas (1987: 29). Emphases in the original.
62 See Hasselbladh and Theodoridis (1998: 68).
63 Castoriadis (1987: 132).
64 Castoriadis (1987: 237–244).
65 Castoriadis (2007).
66 See, for example, Meyer (1977: 55–77).
67 Mead ([1935] 2001a).
68 See for example Lancy, Bock and Gaskins (2010).
69 Durkheim (1956: 71).
70 See for example Jarvis (1983).
71 Castoriadis (1987: 371–372).
72 Castells (2009: 10).
73 Parsons ([1951] 1991: 86).
74 Arendt (1969).
75 Arendt (2005).
76 Habermas (1986).
77 Castoriadis (1991).
78 Castoriadis (1991).

79 Foucault (1986).
80 Castells (2009: 10).
81 Ball (1994).
82 Bernstein (2000).
83 Quoted in Beck (2005: 58).
84 Castoriadis (1991: 150).
85 Castoriadis (1991: 151–153).

2 Self-reflectiveness, education and cross-cultural inquiry in Ancient Greece

Ancient Greece was the place where the school, as we would know it thereafter, was born, but it was also there that the systematic interest and exploration of other societies emerged. It is highly relevant, then, to access the magma of social imaginary significations that gave rise to education as an official institution as well as to the comparative study of other societies. Castoriadis's own argument, which could well be supported by the work of other prominent thinkers and Hellenists to be cited here, is that Ancient Greece marks the first rift with heteronomy and the emergence of the central imaginary signification of social and personal autonomy, presentified in novel institutions, forms and activities. Heteronomous societies are not aware of the fact that they are the creators of their institutions, which they usually attribute to transcendental or extra-social sources (God, prophets, heroes etc.). In autonomous societies, there is a consciousness that it is they themselves that have created their institutions, and it is their activity that can alter them. This activity is politics, as democratic citizenship, which allows for the explicit questioning of the instituted society and appeared first in Greece. The Greek *πόλις* (*polis*), and especially Athens, which will be the locus of this inquiry, moved towards autonomy, as it was the first society which questioned its own laws, traditions, representations and taken-for-granted knowledge – something that happened not only through politics, but also through philosophical, artistic and educational activities. The cognitive closure, and in general, the closure of meaning, a characteristic of heteronomous societies, was ruptured for the first time there, allowing for the socialisation of individuals who were capable of directing their *vis formandi* and *libido formandi* to new creations – which marked European, but also world, history.

The rise of reflective self-examination and self-questioning in the Greek polis also gave rise to a genuine interest in the institutions of the cultural 'others'. The Greeks understood that if they create their institutions according to their own worldview, so do other peoples. The other society was therefore neither inferior nor superior; it was simply another society, and its study was a matter of curiosity, of interest in knowing, but also a matter of getting to know their own society better. Cross-cultural and comparative examination, in this regard, informed self-reflection. To substantiate this argument, the chapter will start by exploring the Ancient Greek social imaginary and the significations and institutions that it gave rise, from, roughly, the 8th to the 4th centuries BCE. The second section will examine the institution of education, while the third and the fourth sections will trace the Greek comparative gaze through illustrations from the function of democracy, the literary works of the time and the first cross-cultural studies.

Greek society and the creation of the democratic polis

At the core of the Greek social imaginary lay an ontological view according to which the world derived from the chaos, i.e. from void. For the Greeks, there was neither a transcendental source of meaning nor a divine or apocalyptic truth which they should follow and whose terms they should fulfil. Religion was, of course, a significant part of their lives, but their gods did not make any apocalypses, dictate any commandments or provide any dogma. The Greek gods had human qualities: they could be dishonest, vicious, unfaithful, jealous or liars, just like every human being. They were conceived as ruthless in claiming or preserving their authority and even as capable of turning against humanity. Prometheus, for example, tells us in Aeschylus's *Prometheus Bound* that Zeus, once he assumed his throne, did not care about humans, and, in fact, he wanted to destroy them.[1] As Moses Finley, the renowned Classical scholar, observed, the Greek gods did not make the world, and thus, they bear no responsibility for it.[2] In contrast to monotheistic traditions, in the Greek religion, there is no divine anthropogenesis, namely, a special act of creation of the human being by a supreme entity or force. The human being, notwithstanding its distinct place in the world, has no particular advantage over the other beings in nature. Jean-Pierre Vernant's account of the Greek mythology points to a perception of the natural world by the Greeks in three levels: the non-human (i.e. natural objects and the non-'humanised' plants and animals), the human (which also includes plants and animals raised by humans) and the level of gods.[3] All three levels emerge simultaneously and independently from the chaos, and they are all subject to *Moira* (*Μοῖρα*), namely, to their lot and destiny in life. Hence, the Greek gods had no decisive role in public matters; even if people turned to the Delphic oracle to ask what to do in particular cases, they would not ask them about what laws should be adopted or how the polis should be organised.[4] Gods did not have any say about the political affairs of human societies, nor about their prospects. The Greek religion gave no promise or hope to human societies, not even the promise of life-after-death or reincarnation of other religions. The Greeks did believe in a realm for the dead, the underworld, which was governed by Hades, but that was a worse, not a better, place to be. As an illustrious dialogue in Homer's *Odyssey* indicates, when Odysseus visits Achilles in the underworld, the latter says that he would prefer being alive again, even as the poorest and most subordinate labourer, than being lord over all the dead.[5]

In contrast to monotheism, in the Greek religion, hope – ontological hope, in the sense that the world order has answers to the expectations of human beings – is missing. This is apparently the meaning of the Hesiodic myth of Pandora in *Works and Days*: Pandora opens the jar (*πίθος*) given to her by the gods and releases all evils and harms to humanity, except Hope. Hope remained in the jar, which can never be opened again.[6] This is, therefore, a world with no hope, according to the Greek social imaginary, at the core of which lies, as Castoriadis notes, a tragic perception of the world.[7] There is neither a transcendental guarantee for human acts nor a divine source of meaning. The origin of the world, as Hesiod, the major poet of Antiquity writes in his *Theogony*, is *Chaos* (*Χάος*). '*In truth at first Chaos came to be . . .*' («*ἤ τοι μὲν πρώτιστα Χάος γένετ. . .*»).[8] Chaos, along with *Γαῖα* (*Gaia* – earth) and *Ἔρως* (*Eros* – love), were the elements which made the world rise. Chaos is where all beings, including supernatural beings, originate. This conception in Hesiod's poetry is similar to the idea of *ἄπειρον* (*apeiron*), which is found in the writings of the Milesian philosopher Anaximander.[9] *Ἄπειρον* is the opposite of *πέρας* (*peras* – end, limit, or completion); it means that which has no end – the indeterminate. For Anaximander, everything comes from *ἄπειρον* and returns to *ἄπειρον*. Castoriadis finds the same idea in Anaxagoras and Xenophanes, but also in Aristotle and even in Plato, the major advocate of ontological determinacy: for Aristotle, the matter contains the *ἄπειρον*, the element that lacks form and determination, and Plato, in his dialogue *Timaeus*, indicates that there is something in the natural world that makes it resist domination by the power of the creator, and, thus, he cannot impose a complete order upon it.[10] The Ancient Greek ontological view is that the world originates from the chaos, an abyss which is the source of non-being and non-meaning and which is subject to the creation of a *cosmos*.[11] This is the world-order that humans make by creating their institutions – language, laws, arts, political organisation etc. – or their *nomoi*. In other words, there is no pre-existing meaning, and there is no social law given 'from the start'; it is humans who undertake to establish their own *nomos* against the chaos and against the absence of hope and the promise of an afterlife.

It is this idea which liberated thinking and acting in Ancient Greece and made nomos, as social institution and as law, the other major Greek signification, the actual ruler of their social and political life.[12] The Greek world distinguished *physis* (*φύσις*) from *nomos* (*νόμος*), namely, natural conditions from human and social creation; «. . .*τὸ δίκαιον εἶναι καὶ τὸ αἰσχρὸν οὐ φύσει, ἀλλὰ νόμῳ*» is the phrase attributed by Diogenis Laertius[13] to the 5th-century BCE philosopher Archelaus, who was allegedly a teacher of Socrates. The phrase means that that which is just (*δίκαιον*) and that which is unjust (*αἰσχρὸν*) is not a matter defined by nature, but by convention or, in broader terms, by the institution of society (*νόμῳ*). Laertius attributes a similar phrase to Democritus, who is regarded as the father of science: «*νόμῳ θερμόν, νόμῳ ψυχρόν*», meaning that which is warm (*θερμόν*) and that which is cold (*ψυχρόν*) and, broadly speaking, our sensual perception of taste is a matter of convention, i.e. of social institution (*νόμῳ*).[14] It is human beings, through their institutions, who establish these conventions as a necessary condition for social and political life.

This perception is also present throughout the major works of poetry and drama in Ancient Greece, as well as, as it will be argued below, in the sophist movement and in the creation of historiography. The Greeks believed that the capacity to establish *nomos* is what distinguishes human societies from the animals, but also from the gods, as well as from those living in a pre-human or pre-social condition. Zeus, as Hesiod tells us in *Works and Days*, gave justice to humans (*«ἀνθρώποισι δ' ἔδωκε δίκην»*) but not to the fish and the animals, which thus devour each other.[15] Similarly, Aeschylus in *Prometheus Bound* describes the pre-human condition of humankind, during which people lived in dark cages: they had no rules, they could not distinguish seasons and time, they were not aware of death and they acted without thinking (*«ἄτερ γνώμης τὸ πᾶν ἔπρασσον»*). Prometheus going, according to the myth, against Zeus, gave humans all of the necessary techniques (*«πᾶσαι τέχναι βροτοῖσιν ἐκ Προμηθέως»*) for them to constitute societies. He gave people techniques, rules, reason, art and knowledge, and the awareness of death.[16] Indeed, the Greeks were quite aware of death, as they used the word mortal (*θνητός*) to mean human (*ἄνθρωπος*). Likewise, in Euripides's *Suppliants*, the mythical Theseus (a name apparently deriving from *thesmos* [*θεσμός*] – meaning institution) is thankful to whichever god brought humans to 'live by rule from chaos and from brutishness, first by implanting reason, and next by giving us a tongue to declare our thoughts . . .' as well as technical knowledge.[17] Much earlier than these tragedies, Homer's *Odyssey* makes the existence of institutions and laws a distinctive characteristic of what a political society is. The epic presents various cultures that Odysseus encounters on his long journey home (including the Lotus-eaters, who also eat human flesh), but the one which is regarded as monstrous is that of the Cyclopes, who lead lawless lives. The Cyclopes do not have *θέμιστας*, institutions and laws, nor do they have *βουληφόρους ἀγοράς*, that is, public assemblies. They do not organise their communal life; rather, they only mind about their families and not about others (*«παίδων ἠδ' ἀλόχων, οὐδ' ἀλλήλων ἀλέγουσιν»*), and, for their affairs, they rely only on gods (*«οἵ ῥα θεοῖσι πεποιθότες ἀθανάτοισιν»*).[18] In other words, the *Odyssey* indicates that, even in the 8th century BCE, the Greeks considered the lack of nomos and political community as commensurate to a non-human or asocial condition.[19]

In the Athenian tragic poetry of the 5th century BCE, this perception is present in an even more eloquent way. Again, Euripides's *Suppliants* makes clear reference to the importance of laws in securing equality and democracy in Athens. Theseus says emphatically that, when the city is governed by a tyrant, it is his will which is the law. But when there are written laws, the rich and the poor are equal before them (*«γεγραμμένων δὲ τῶν νόμων ὅ τ' ἀσθενὴς ὁ πλούσιός τε τὴν δίκην ἴσην ἔχει»*).[20] The tragedy identifies the existence of laws with justice, equality and especially *ἰσονομία* (*isonomia*), equality in law making, another main signification that is closely connected with the Athenian democracy. Sophocles's tragedy *Antigone* gives a good illustration of this idea. The tragedy is centred on the controversy between King Creon and his niece Antigone. Antigone asks for the burial of her brother Polynices, while Creon denies it, following the law which forbids the burial of those who attack the city. The controversy is usually discussed for the opposition between private and public rules or human compassion and the harshness of authority. However, the tragedy also raises the issue of nomos and the capacity and the activity of humans in instituting and sustaining political societies.[21] The tragedy's chorus expresses admiration for human creativity through the well-known line: «*Πολλά τα δεινά κουδέν ανθρώπου δεινότερον πέλει*» – 'Wonders are many, and none is more wonderful than man'.[22] Humans create and teach themselves their institutions – language, thinking and the disposition to give laws to their cities («*καὶ φθέγμα καὶ ἀνεμόεν φρόνημα καὶ ἀστυνόμους ὀργὰς ἐδιδάξατο. . .*»).

In short, nomos or law is a distinctive imaginary signification of the Greek world. Citizens must fight for their laws as if they were the walls of the city («*Μάχεσθαι χρὴ τὸν δῆμον ὑπὲρ τοῦ νόμου ὅκωσπερ τείχεος*»), Heraclitus writes.[23] Similarly, Herodotus in his *History* underlines this importance through a dialogue between Xerxes, the Persian emperor who invaded the Greek mainland, and Demaratus, an exile magistrate from Sparta who resorted to Xerxes's court. When Xerxes asked Demaratus what the Spartans would fear most, he replied: 'law is their master, whom they fear much more than your men fear you'.[24] The same high regard for law is witnessed in Athens too, as it is testified by Pericles' *Funeral Oration*: 'We give our obedience to those whom we put in positions of authority, and we obey the laws themselves, especially those which are for the protection of the oppressed, and those unwritten laws which it is an acknowledged shame to break'.[25]

Neither law nor justice would be possible without the emergence of another signification that marked the creation of the Greek polis and especially the creation of democracy: the signification of *λόγος* (*logos*), as speech, dialogue, rational communication, accounting for and critique. The verb *λέγω* and the associated noun *λόγος* already appeared in Homer's *Iliad* and in the writings of Heraclitus. The etymological analysis of the verb by Nikoloudis identifies a variety of uses before it takes its current meaning: *λέγειν* (*legein*) meant to lay, lie down, collect, aggregate, choose, select, count, calculate and, later on, to express, say, speak, state, articulate a thought in an organised way through language.[26] The author agrees with Heidegger's similar analysis, who maintains that in German the verb evolved from *legen* (to spread, extend or place) and *lessen* (to gather, collect, concentrate or read) to *sagen* (to say, speak or express) – in the sense of 'I spread words (that I have previously gathered)'. Interestingly, though, *λέγω*, deriving in Homer from *διαλέγομαι* (to engage in dialogue), takes precedence over other verbs with similar meanings, such as *φημί* (to convey a holy word), *μυθεύομαι* (to narrate) or *ἀγορεύω* (to speak in the agora). In this regard, *λέγω* indicates, first, the secularisation of speaking: it is not the announcement of the sacred or royal discourse, but the expression of one's own opinion. Second, it indicates a dialogic intent: the speaker communicates their views, discusses them and submits them to critical testing in dialogue with others. The person who *λέγει* does not simply interpret, describe or present, but communicates their thoughts, explains, engages in dialogue and tries to convince their interlocutors. Besides, *λόγος*, as Heraclitus wrote, is *ξυνός*, that is, common; everyone is capable of conveying logos, as everyone is capable of thinking (*φρονεῖν*), but also thinking well (*σωφρονεῖν*).[27] Logos, as a common property, also indicates that knowledge is no longer esoteric, the privilege of a social class or a holy figure, but belongs to everyone.

The rise of logos is associated with the creation of politics by the Greeks. As Christian Meier writes characteristically, in his seminal study on the emergence of politics in Antiquity, there were no Greeks before the Greeks, in the sense that they knew nothing about politics until they created it.[28] Indeed, politics in the Greek sense does not refer to the actions of monarchs or statesmen, or to the imposition of a ruler's decisions on individuals by force. Coercion and violence have nothing to do with politics; politics presupposes a space of logos – of dialogue, deliberation, rational argumentation and questioning – which allows citizens to act and to change or establish new laws and institutions. Thus, politics is born in Greece as democratic politics, associated with the rise of logos and the creation of the polis, which was already in the historical process of formation when Homer was writing his epics and the pre-Socratic philosophers appeared in Ionia. Jean-Pierre Vernant, in his classic treatise *The Origins of the Greek Thought*, writes that logos was the child of the polis, underlining the close relation between rational discourse and politics.[29] On the other hand, as Castoriadis points out, the creation of the polis, not simply as a geographical location, but as a democratic community, was possible precisely because of the emergence of logos as a Greek signification. Citizens were able, through logos, i.e. through public debate and contestation of views, to question the established laws and the very institution of their society and to create new laws and new institutions. Thus, Greece emerged as the first society ever which questioned itself.[30]

This questioning extended to existing knowledge structures and representations, thus giving rise to *ἐπιστήμη* (*epistēmē*) as reasoned knowledge. The emergence of logos, and the beginnings of Western rational thinking, is located in the Greek colony of Miletus in Asia Minor, where the first steps to philosophy and science were made. With the Milesian School (i.e. Thales, Anaximander and Anaximenes), we see the establishment of a space of thinking which breaks with religion. Natural phenomena were no longer to be explained as the outcomes of the adventures and achievements of supernatural forces. The theogonies of the past ceased to be sources of explanation; the study of nature, the origins and constitution of the world and the meteorological phenomena were to become objects of systematic and independent research. The Milesian School broke with the myth, desacralised knowledge and ushered in a new kind of thinking that was external to religion.[31]

As Geoffrey Lloyd writes, the Ionian philosophers established a distinction between the natural and the supernatural, namely, the acceptance that natural phenomena are not the outcomes of arbitrary impacts, but they are characterised by regularities and cause-effect sequences. Moreover, their research was about categories of physical phenomena – a characteristic of scientific thinking, which looks for general patterns, rather than for isolated occurrences. In addition, the overall value that the Greeks placed on the critique and contestation of views is expressed in the natural philosophers' concern to pursue the best explanation by checking the validity of their propositions, their evidence and their arguments, and the weak points of their opponents' theories.[32]

Lloyd identified the extension of this mode of thinking to medical doctors in Ancient Greece as well, who showed that disease is itself a natural occurrence, rather than the outcome of divine intervention. The author mentions, as an example, epilepsy, which was considered, due to its particular symptoms, a divine condition, but the *corpus hippocraticum* rejected this conception as superstition and based on ignorance. Similarly, the scientific spirit that was born in Ionia found its way to astronomy, to which the Greek contribution was not in the areas of observation techniques or data collection, but in the application of mathematical methods in the study of complex natural phenomena – as mathematical thinking was also developed in Greece. Although the Egyptians, and especially the Babylonians, were more advanced in mathematics, their knowledge was based on first-hand calculations and empirical practice. The Greeks' innovation was the transformation of empirical observations to a set of rigorous logical sequences and properties. For example, as Lloyd writes, what came to be established as the Pythagorean Theorem (the square of the hypotenuse is equal to the sum of the squares of the other two sides) was already known to the Babylonians. What the Greeks did was to prove it. The development of methods of mathematical proof took place at the end of the 5th century, and it also concerned other mathematicians, besides Pythagoras. The use of mathematical methods in understanding natural phenomena and the conduct of empirical inquiry mark, according to the author, the role of the Greeks in establishing scientific thinking. However, as Lloyd observes, for the Greeks, science was useful in order to understand nature, not in order to control or exploit it. The view that scientific knowledge was to fulfil practical aims was foreign to the ancient world.[33]

It is also important to note that the rise of philosophical and scientific thinking in Ancient Greece is inextricable linked with the rise of the polis, following the collapse of the Mycenaean palatial civilisation and the end of the Greek 'Dark Ages' (around 800 BCE). The power of the king and his officials, who controlled social and economic life, was to be replaced by a political community of equal citizens debating openly in the ἀγορά (*agora* – the marketplace) and the decision-making institutions of the polis. The polis, as pointed out above, was characterised by the dominance of oral logos, not as stereotypical talk, but as conversation, as dialogue and as contestation of arguments. Indeed, the advent of the polis did not entail only economic and social changes, but a move to an entirely new mentality and the establishment of a political space marked by publicity, free debate, deliberation and questioning of existing traditions and power relations. The written discourse, conveyed by the Greek alphabet (which appeared between the 9th and 8th centuries BCE, based on the Phoenician alphabet), also followed the same principle of making views, artistic creation, laws and knowledge a public property open to discussion and critique, again breaking away from the specialised and occult discourse of the royal officials.

As there was no longer a mystical or transcendental source of truth or dogma, nor any special transmitters and interpreters of the divine or the royal discourse, knowledge, as politics, became a matter of activity in the field of logos: examining, debating, speaking and persuading, through what the Greeks called *κρείττων λόγος*, i.e. the strongest argument. It is in this context that philosophy was born, not as the isolated intellectual activity of wise individuals or tenants of the king's court, but as a public questioning of the established beliefs and representations of the community. In other words, the advent of logos and of philosophical questioning went hand in hand with the Greek democratic movement.

The locus of this movement was the polis, which appeared in mainland Greece and across the Mediterranean around the 8th century. When Homer wrote his epics, the polis was there, although it was not yet democratic. Many *poleis* would become democratic through time, roughly from the 8th to the 4th century BCE. A landmark for the ending of democracy is considered to be the Macedonian invasion in 338 BCE of Athens, on which this chapter is mainly focusing.

Geographically speaking, the polis included both the agricultural and the urban space, the actual city or *ἄστυ (asty)*. The polis was understood by the Greeks as a political community and, as such, was not identified with its territory – no matter how important the territory was for its inhabitants. Not accidentally, Aristotle named his book *Ἀθηναίων Πολιτεία*, *The Constitution of the Athenians*, not of Athens, as it is usually translated in English.[34] Thucydides says this clearly through the words of Nicias, the Athenian general: 'Men make the city and not walls or ships without men in them'.[35] The same perception is reflected in another known extract from Herodotus's *History*: Themistocles, the Athenian general, says that if Attica is conquered by the Persians, then the Athenians will take their families and will transfer their polis to Italy.[36]

A common misunderstanding in the modern literature is to regard the polis as a state, if ones considers the established translation of the polis in English and German as 'the state' and 'der Staat'. The Greek polis was not an administrative mechanism separated from the citizens that exercised its power on them. The polis was the citizens. There was certainly administration, but it executed the decisions made by the citizens. Executive/administrative tasks were carried out by the slaves (e.g., treasurers and accountants, guards and policemen, archive-keepers etc.).[37] Ancient Greek poleis were not states, and, although the Greeks shared a common language and tradition, they did not institute a nation, which is a modern creation.

The polis was democratic when power was distributed equally amongst citizens, who constituted a *δῆμος* (*dēmos*). Democracy was the rule of the *dēmos*, as opposed to the monarchy (the rule of a single person) or oligarchy (the rule of the few). The dēmos, which was composed by all adult males, was the sovereign in the Greek polis. This is stated in the very preamble of the laws, which famously always started with the phrase *«ἔδοξε τῇ βουλῇ καί τῷ δήμω»*, meaning this is what the *boulē* (the executive body in charge of the general assembly) and the dēmos thought.

Following the terminology of Thucydides, the democratic polis was *autonomous (αὐτόνομος), autodicus* (*αὐτόδικος*) and *autotelic* (*αὐτοτελής*).[38] *Autonomous* meant that it was the dēmos that gave laws to itself, rather than a ruler or any divine authority above the polis. In Athens, by the end of the 5th century BCE, following successive reforms (i.e. of Solon in 594, of Cleisthenes in 508–6 and Ephialtes in 462 BCE), everything was decided by the *ἐκκλησία* (*ekklēsia*), the general assembly of the Athenians, which was held at least once a month. As Aristotle writes in *The Athenians' Politeia*: 'They have made themselves supreme in all fields; they run everything by decrees of the Ekklesia and by decisions of the dikasteria in which the people are supreme'.[39] The public participation in the *Ἡλιαία* (*Hēliaia*), the Athenians' court, is what is indicated by Thucydides's term *autodicus*. This meant that there were no professional judges, but the court was constituted by a subset of the dēmos; every year, 6000 citizens were selected by lot to constitute the *Hēliaia*, which, by the 4th century, increased its powers, as again testified by Aristotle, who praised this institution as largely incorruptible: '. . . the judicial powers of the Boule have passed to the people, which seems a correct development, for a small number are more open to corruption by bribery or favours than a large'.[40] The democratic polis was, finally, *autotelic* in the sense that it was self-governed. There was no executive authority external to the dēmos to make decisions. In other words, the polis did not follow the contemporary distinction between the legislative, judicial and executive powers. Apart from laws, the *ekklēsia* of the dēmos also made decisions on current matters (e.g., warfare, peacemaking, public buildings etc.); namely, it was the actual government.

Besides nomos and logos, democracy in Athens incarnated other social imaginary significations, essential for its function. There was a strong belief in *isonomia*, which meant not merely equality before the law, as we conceive it today, but primarily equality in making the law through the democratic process. Associated with this were the significations of: *ἰσοψηφία* (*isopsēphia* – equality of vote for every single citizen); *ἰσηγορία* (*isēgoria* – the equal right and the value of everybody's speech); *πειθώ* (*peithō* – one's capacity to persuade the assembly); *παρρησία* (*parrhēsia* – the citizen's moral obligation, not merely right, to speak up in the assembly with absolute sincerity). All citizens were invited to offer their opinions to the assembly with the phrase: «*Τίς ἀγορεύει βούλεται;*»– 'Who wants to speak?'

But offering a view in the general assembly was not 'just' speaking. As Hanna Arendt points out, speech in the ancient democracy was a form of action: it was highly possible that it leads to a decision made by the dēmos, but also indicated the willingness of the speaker to take the initiative and to actualise what he proposed. Not accidentally, then, the Greeks used the verb *ἄρχειν* (*archein*) to mean both to initiate and to rule.[41] The capacity to rule (*ἄρχειν*) and to be ruled (*ἄρχεσθαι*) is what characterises a democratic people, according to Aristotle. Aristotle defines the citizen (*πολίτης*) as the person who has the power to take part in the deliberative or judicial administration of the polis («*ᾧ γὰρ ἐξουσία κοινωνεῖν ἀρχῆς βουλευτικῆς ἢ κριτικῆς, πολίτην ἤδη λέγομεν εἶναι ταύτης τῆς πόλεως*») and to hold some office («*ὁ δὲ πολίτης ἀρχῇ τινὶ διωρισμένος ἐστίν*»).[42]

In this, Aristotle expressed well the Athenian reality according to which most offices were distributed amongst the citizens through allotment or rotation. An *ἐπιστάτης* (*epistatēs*), for example, the equivalent, perhaps, for us today, of prime minister, was selected by lot for a single day, from the *πρυτανεία* (*prytaneia*), the delegation which presided by rotation for a month in the *boulē*. Hundreds of other offices were allotted amongst the citizens, the highest ones usually taken once in a citizen's life. Only a few offices were distributed through elections. Elections, for the Greeks, was an *aristocratic* institution, because they were seeking to choose, through this process, the *ἄριστοι*, meaning the excellent – such as army generals or architects of public buildings. All officeholders, including the elected ones, who could be elected recurrently, were revocable; the *ekklēsia* could replace them at any time, following deliberation and voting upon any citizen's negative reporting. In general, over time, the Athenian democracy developed numerous mechanisms and procedures which protected democracy from power abuse, personal antagonisms or interest group formation and secured the equal participation of all citizens.[43]

The fact that the Athenians made the vast majority of offices available to all through allotment or rotation was not accidental; it was based on a fundamental distinction between *δόξα* (*doxa*) and *ἐπιστήμη* (*epistēmē*), opinion and expertise, which was embedded in the function of democracy. The distinction is discussed in the famous Platonic dialogue *Protagoras.*[44] In the dialogue, Protagoras and Socrates agree that when decisions are to be made about the affairs of the polis, everybody can express their opinion. Technical or specialised knowledge is needed when it comes to specific tasks, and it is then that experts are summoned to give advice or materialise the decisions made in the political process. Expertise, therefore, must be distinguished from political opinion, which is essential for politics to take place. Plato himself was, of course, against this perception, as he was against democracy overall. In his *Republic*, but particularly, in *Statesman* he proclaimed politics as epistēmē and considered the political regime in which the rulers are wise men who possess the 'right' knowledge, and therefore, the 'right' way to govern, to be supreme.[45] If politics is epistēmē, then it cannot be available to the many, but only to those few who possess the knowledge and the skill to suggest the appropriate solution to a specific problem – as a doctor knows the right medicine for every illness. This fundamental perception gave rise to the Western tradition of political science, and consequently, to policymaking, as an activity based on specialisation and expertise, as it will be pointed out in the next chapter. For the Athenian democracy, however, political opinion was a universal capacity, and thus, politics was an affair of the dēmos, not of the experts.

All democratic institutions structured the space of the polis accordingly, as a space of freedom. This includes the *agora*, the main square, whose placement in the *asty* associated with the life and the activities of the polis as a political community. The agora was a space of logos, of free discussion based on the exchange of arguments, and therefore, a space of freedom. In her classic essay *Was ist Politik?*,

Hanna Arendt underlines that freedom is spatially delimited, and it is found wherever politics is present.[46] In fact, Arendt, drawing on the Athenian democracy, identifies freedom and politics, because, as she writes, politics in Athens was concerned with everything that ensures the existence of freedom, and freedom could exist only in the space of politics.

Freedom (*ἐλευθερία*) and equality (*ἰσονομία*) were indeed possible within the space of politics which, however, did not include the slaves, the women and the *μέτοικοι* (*metics* – the foreign residents), who were *ἄνευ λόγου* (they had no say). Women and slaves were part of *οἶκος*, the household, where inequality was clearly the rule, whereas equality was the rule for citizens in the context of the polis. Slavery (which was quite widespread in the ancient world and survived as institution in some countries as late as the end of the 19th century) never became a matter of politics in Greece, despite the fact that it was questioned by the sophists. But, at the same time, it was never justified on racial or ethnic grounds, because it was common knowledge that potentially anybody (even aristocrats and royals) could be enslaved as a result of defeat in warfare, piracy, etc. This is what is indicated in one of the most quoted fragments of Heraclitus: 'War is the father of all and the king of all . . . some he makes slaves, others free'.[47] Similarly, women never acquired a place in political life, notwithstanding their wide presence as goddesses in the Greek Pantheon and as heroines in the theatre, including the 'feminist' satires of Aristophanes (e.g., *Ekklēsiazusae* and *Lysistrata*). Remarkably, in Europe, women were granted suffrage mainly during the 20th century (in Switzerland not until 1971).

The exclusion of the above categories of people from the dēmos in Classical Greece should also be seen in conjunction with two other interrelated significations: a strong separation between political and private life, and a disregard for material necessities and forced labour. Private life in Athens was fully respected, not from the perspective of private property, but because home was considered necessary for a man to take part in public life.[48] Moreover, economic affairs were considered to be private affairs, hence the etymology of the term *οἰκονομία*. For the Greeks, as Arendt suggests, the expression 'political economy' would be a contradiction in terms: whatever was 'economic', namely, whatever was related to the life and the survival of the individual, was, by definition, a home affair, not a political affair.[49] This does not mean that labour for subsistence was discredited. As Pericles underlines, in his *Funeral Oration*, it was considered shame not to act in order to overcome poverty.[50] Moreover, the rich were required to sponsor many of the public works and performances of the polis through the so-called *λειτουργίαι*.[51] However, as Finley writes, no labour ideology ever appeared in Ancient Greece, nor did any other concept which signified work as a general social function.[52] In fact, many types of labour, and especially forced labour, were disappreciated as something inappropriate for free men, or as *βάναυσον* (*banauson* – vulgar). For the Greeks, *banauson* was, as Egon Friedell also writes in his seminal cultural history of Ancient Greece, whatever was aimed at making a profit, whatever one was forced to do or whatever demanded excessive physical effort.[53] This was expressed by Aristotle, too, who castigated such labour, especially technical labour, as deforming the mind and the body: 'Hence we entitle vulgar all such arts as deteriorate the condition of the body, and also the industries that earn wages; for they make the mind preoccupied and degraded'.[54] It is in line with this perception that slavery in Classical Greece was seen: not as means to maximise wealth, as in capitalist exploitation, but as a means to release the masters from labour in order for them to be free in the space of politics. This is what Arendt observes about the function of slavery (but also about the metics, who undertook many production and trade activities) in Athens, in connection to the prevalent understanding of freedom in the polis: 'Man must first be liberated or liberate himself in order to enjoy freedom, and being liberated from domination by life's necessities was the true meaning of the Greek word scholē . . .'.[55] Not accidentally, the same word would be used to mean the act and place of education.

In summary, within a general state of heteronomy that characterised historical societies, Ancient Greece foregrounded autonomy as a central imaginary signification which was presentified in the institutions of the polis. It was a society which, notwithstanding the presence of religion, did not believe in a divine anthropogenesis or in any transcendental meaning. The Greeks believed in humans' capacity to establish their nomoi, which were distinguished from natural conditions. There was physis, but it was they themselves who made their nomos. Nomos could be just if it was made through logos, as rational dialogue, deliberation, critique, account giving and truth seeking – the signification which made and was made possible by the institution of the polis. Logos was associated with democratic politics – as direct citizen participation and not as 'representation', which the Greeks did not regard as democratic – and a web of other significations and institutions (such as justice, freedom, isonomia, isopsēphia, isēgoria and parrhēsia). Logos also gave rise to epistēmē, as knowledge seeking the truth, through observation, examination, and logical argumentation. Logos was expressed as reasoned opinion by which political decisions could be made and as reasoned knowledge based on scientific thinking. But scientific thinking was not understood as a tool to control nature or to maximise economic profit. Subjecting knowledge to economic ends was considered by the Greeks to be vulgarity. It is this complex of imaginary significations, which valued social self-institution, collective and personal autonomy and fervour for politics and freedom, that gave rise to *παιδεία* (*paideia*), the Greek perception of education.

Democracy and paideia

Individuals are educated, in a broad sense, in accordance with the social imaginary significations characterising a given society and incarnated in its second-order institutions. Thus, education, besides its formal provision, has lifelong and life-wide dimension, i.e. it is transinstitutional. The Ancient Greeks, as the historical record and the writings of numerous authors of the time testify, were fully aware of the transinstitutional dimension of education. '*The polis teaches the man*' («*πόλις ἄνδρα διδάσκει*») famously wrote the poet Simonides.[56] What the

Classical Athenians were taught on a daily basis in their polis was not only to be ruled, but also to rule, through the potential that every citizen had to undertake some office and to exercise power. That was, in other words, lifelong learning in a democratic citizenship whose effects on the overall educational level of citizens have also been underlined by modern political philosophy. As, for instance, John Stuart Mill writes '. . . the practice of the dicastery and the ecclesia raised the intellectual standard of an average Athenian citizen far beyond anything of which there is yet an example in any other mass of men, ancient or modern'.[57]

Interestingly, contemporary Athenians seemed to be aware of this achievement. Pericles, in his *Funeral Oration* to the Athenians during the Peloponnesian war, was quite straightforward about the pedagogic function of their polis: 'our polis is an education to Greece' (*«τήν τε πᾶσαν πόλιν τῆς Ἑλλάδος παίδευσιν εἶναι»*).[58] Pericles explicates this statement – which, notwithstanding its apparent boastfulness, proved to be valid, not only for Greece, but for the world in general – with reference to the autonomy and self-fulfillment that citizens enjoyed in Athens. And in another famous statement, he expressed succinctly the way of living in democratic Athens: *«φιλοκαλοῦμέν τε γὰρ μετ' εὐτελείας καὶ φιλοσοφοῦμεν ἄνευ μαλακίας»*[59] – 'We love beauty without exaggeration and we philosophise without effeminacy'. Arendt, as well as Castoriadis, has pointed out that the two verbs (*φιλοκαλοῦμεν* and *φιλοσοφοῦμεν*) indicate an active experience, as well as an articulated unity, of the individual and the collective within the context of the polis.[60] Castoriadis, in his etymological analysis of the phrase, and considering the whole Oration, proposed the translations: 'We live within the love of the beautiful and through it and we are active in seeking knowledge', or 'we exist within and through the practice of beauty and wisdom'.[61]

This phrase could epitomise the Athenian *paideia*, given that one includes its inextricable political dimension, the citizens' participation in the democratic institutions of the polis, which is also underlined by Pericles. The term *paideia*, because of its broad meaning, defies easy translation. It indicates primarily the Greek perception that it is the society as a whole that forms the individual – and, therefore, all of its institutions play an educational role. Perhaps for this reason, the most frequent translation is that of 'culture', which is also adopted by one of the most prominent scholars in this field, Werner Jaeger, in his classic trilogy *Paideia: The Ideals of Greek Culture.*[62] In the case of Athens, because its democratic institutions allowed for collective participation and individual self-fulfilment, paideia indicated, to borrow the book title of another German Hellenist, Christian Meier, a 'culture of freedom'[63] or, more precisely, a culture of autonomy: the awareness of the Athenian citizens, as individuals and as a polis, that it was they themselves who gave laws and meaning to their lives.

This culture of autonomy marked the institution of Greek education. Behind the rise of education, we discern the democratic signification and the distinction physis/nomos which entailed the potential of everybody to pursue knowledge and to form themselves as citizens and personalities, as well as the appreciation by the Greeks of *eros* and *logos*. *Eros* should be understood as both physical love, which was common in the early phases of Greek education, but primarily, as the passion to inquire, to discover, to learn and to know the truth, as well as the emotional energy cathected by the learner and the teacher in each other, in the knowledge and in the very investigative activity.

We find traces of this web of values and meanings even before the actual institution of the school and the spread of literacy, namely, in the 5th, but especially, in the 4th century BCE, when Ancient Greece was still an 'oral society'. Education took place through the public recitation of poetry and the interpersonal relations between adolescents and elders who acted as teachers, philosophers and guides. The Greeks used to enjoy listening to the verses of great poets such as Pindar, Hesiod and Homer. Especially, the epics of Homer prevailed in Greek paideia for centuries. This is what Plato also famously writes in his *Republic*, in which he notes that Homer 'educated Greece' (*«τὴν Ἑλλάδα πεπαίδευκεν»*).[64] His poems were sung by Rhapsodists who wandered across Greece with some musical instrument (mainly string) and improvised on selected themes. The Homeric epics were read frequently in Athens during the *Panathenaea*, the city's annual festival, which was open to the entire population, including women, children and slaves. When the epics became available in written form, they were also taught in schools, and through them, pupils learned reading and writing. In other words, the epics were not literature that was addressed to a certain social group, but to all Greeks, numerous generations of whom were raised learning Homer's verses by heart, quoting them and using them in their everyday lives as sayings and proverbs.

Indeed, for centuries, Homer's poems were at the heart of the ethical socialisation of children and adults in Ancient Greece, and, thus, they matter in the study of Greek education. But they also matter because they express the Greek social imaginary significations related to the institution of the polis: *μοῖρα*, as destiny and acceptance of mortality; *ἀρετή* and *ἀριστεία*, as the pursuit and accomplishment of excellence; *κλέος*, as recognition and glory; *δίκη*, as justice; *καλοκαγαθία*, as beauty and goodness; *ὕβρις*, as exaggeration and arrogance, and *νέμεσις*, as retribution; questioning of established values; freedom and individualisation; and impartiality.

Yet, the world of Homer is a world of aristocracy and warriors, and much of this web of significations was in an early form, while others would be transformed following the advent of democracy in the 5th century. Education, until then, was a privilege of the aristocratic classes that was closely attached to the military, and later, to athletic training, and it included the memorisation and recitation of poetry and the moral formation of character. This education took place in the form of *συνουσία* (*synousia*), a pedagogic relation between an elder and an adolescent, which could also involve sexual bonding.[65] Although *synousia* faded away as education was formalised and opened up to citizens in general, the erotic signification that it embodied marked the understanding of education throughout Greek Antiquity, and it was celebrated by philosophy, too, as we know from Plato's *Symposium*, for the humane and spiritual aspect of eros over its merely physical aspect.[66] The fact, of course, that eros had to do mainly with male love was because women were excluded from public activities and men's circles, where *παιδεραστία* (*pederasty*) developed. Nevertheless, eros would also be a part of female learning environments, such as that of the 6th-century music and poetry school on the island of Lesbos, which Sappho extoled in her poetry.[67]

Παιδεραστία was recognised and appreciated in Ancient Greece as a dimension of knowledge impartation, before learning took its organised form in the schools. The historiography of the time testifies to the pedagogic role of affection between mentor and learner. Xenophon, for example, writes in his *Constitution of the Lacedaimonians*: 'I think I ought to say something also about intimacy with boys, since this matter also has a bearing on education'.[68] The love relation was thought to grant acknowledgement and distinction to the senior (*ἐραστής*) and to prove the worth of the junior (*ἐρωμένος*), while it amplified the pursuit of *καλοκαγαθία* and of *κλέος* for both. In fact, in Sparta, this tradition was so firmly accepted that the *ἐραστής* was considered by law to be morally responsible for the development of the *ἐρωμένος*.[69]

The presence of eros in education and the pursuit of knowledge was widely acknowledged in Greece. The very term *φιλοσοφία*, from *φιλῶ* (to love) and *σοφία* (wisdom), signifies the Greek appreciation of the emotional energy lying behind the genuine pursuit of knowledge. Interestingly, according to the etymological analysis of logos in Homeric epics made by Nikoloudis, there is an association between logos and eros, in the sense that one presupposes the other, or even that one is identified with the other – as Pascal would also put it many centuries later ('We have unaptly taken away the name of reason from love and have opposed them to each other without good foundation, for love and reason are but the same thing').[70] Nikoloudis traces in the *Iliad* derivatives of *λέγω* to mean lying in bed with someone. For example, Zeus slept («*παρελέξατο*») with Laodameia; Zeus made love («*τῷ ἔνι λεξάσθην*») with Ira; or Hermes slept in secret («*παρελέξατο λάθρῃ*») with Polimili.[71] Eros is, after all, ever-present in the *Iliad* and the *Odyssey*. Eros is also associated etymologically with *εἴρω* (to say), *ἐρωτῶ* (to inquire, investigate) and *ἔρομαι* (to seek to learn). Eros, in this regard, grants verbal and logical wealth to the individual, as well as liberation energy – which constitute important elements of personal autonomy; it constitutes the biological, anthropological and ontological condition of talk, communication, dialogue and learning.[72]

In the 5th century, training, as a preparation for war, was retained in the institution of *ἐφηβεία* (*ephēbeia*), which spanned from the eighteenth to the twentieth year of all males, who, on its completion, acquired the status of full citizen.[73] But, overall, the advent of democracy marked the decline of the military and the exclusively athletic content of education and a move towards the development of personality and active citizenship. Formal education was democratised in the sense that it was no longer a privilege of aristocracy, but it became widely accessible and organised in groups, although it was still a private matter. As Jaeger writes: 'It is true that nowhere else had even the simplest citizen so many opportunities of acquiring the foundations of elementary education as he had in Athens – even without a state-directed educational system'.[74] In the Classical period, education was addressed, potentially, to all citizens through the creation of the *school*, which developed later on, in the Hellenistic period, into an 'education system'.

Indeed, the school is a Greek creation, etymologically deriving from *scholē*, which originally meant free time or vacation from physical employment and, later, disputation, learned discussion and disposal of one's free time to intellectual cultivation. Certainly, the school is not a Greek invention in the sense of having a group of learners and an instructor placed in a classroom. Schools, in these terms, existed already in Egypt, Mesopotamia and Syria, as Marrou testifies in his classic *History of Education in Antiquity*.[75] But these were merely classes of scribes attached to royal authorities and their courts – privileged amongst the illiterate masses occupied in manual labour. Prospective scribes were taught copying, calligraphy and text reproduction and a code of conduct appropriate for the royal court. There were also classes for scribes in the Mediterranean during the Mycenaean period (1400–1200 BCE) attached to administration or classes for technical training. But as Philip Nemo remarks, only when there was epistēmē, independent of any practical intent, and an intellectual activity that was free from military, athletic or technical applications was there a ground to create an institution devoted specifically to this epistēmē and its impartation to the young generation.[76] This ground, as noted above, was created first in Ionia in the form of scientific thinking and philosophical questioning and led to the establishment of knowledge areas, which were then turned, especially by the sophists, into curriculum areas intended for teaching.

However, one should also consider the invention of the Greek alphabet, with its characteristic precision and simplicity, as opposed to earlier scripts, which were more accessible and thus allowed for the development of a literate society. As Robb writes in '*Literacy and Paideia in Ancient Greece*', the Greek alphabet, with a relatively limited number of symbols that does not burden the memory, allowed for the understanding of any text by a reader familiar with the underlying language. This is something that, as he notes, no earlier script, the Old Phoenician and Hebrew included, had achieved until then. And he adds: 'Taken together, these two features, economy and ready recognition, are what made widespread popular literacy – as opposed to the always restricted and largely scribal literacy of the Near East – possible for the Greeks and ultimately ourselves'.[77]

Yet, the learning of literacy from an early age would not be possible without the recognition of its particularity or, in other words, without the emergence of the signification of childhood. As Postman remarks, 'wherever there are schools, there is consciousness, in some degree, of the specialness of the young'.[78] This specialness was first acknowledged in Greek Antiquity, before we see it again established in European Modernity. As representations on vessels and sculptures (but also the recommendations of Plato and Aristotle) indicate, the Greeks understood childhood as a stage of human growth which is subject to special care and instruction, part of which, gradually, from the 5th century, was literacy.[79]

Literacy was certainly what was taught in the schools of the 5th century during childhood and early adolescence, but there was also an emphasis on art education and the cultivation of spirit. The school 'curriculum' had three main components that were undertaken respectively by three different instructors. First, there was the *παιδοτρίβης*, who was in charge of children's physical education. It took place in *παλαίστρα* (wrestling place) and included sports such as running and jumping, wrestling and throwing the javelin and the discus. The emphasis was on the formation of a strong body with an agonistic spirit. Then, there was the music teacher or *κιθαριστής*. The main instrument taught was the cithara, a string instrument, but there were also a number of other music-related competences that were developed, such as singing and dancing. Singing and dancing would develop self-discipline and a sense of harmony, as well as sensibility, which were qualities that had been enjoyed, up until then, by the aristocracy. However, *μουσική* (*music*) could refer to any of the arts represented by the nine Muses, including literature and especially poetry.[80] The cognitive or intellectual part of the curriculum was the task of the *γραμματιστής* or *διδάσκαλος*, the teacher in charge of reading and writing. Reading and writing included the study of Homeric poems, from which, as mentioned above, extracts had to be copied or memorised. In the second half of the 5th century, this part of the school programme would include tragedies, too. In fact, Aristophanes mentions, in his comedies *Clouds* and *The Frogs*, that the learning of the cithara, as well as of gymnastics, was overtaken by the reading of Euripides.[81] By studying Greek literature, the pupils were immersed in the complex of meanings delineated above, which now, during the 5th century, was directed towards the development of autonomous personalities and active citizens in the democratic polis. As Protagoras would put it in the homonymous Platonic dialogue, elementary education in Athens was *«οὐκ ἐπὶ τέχνῃ»*, not for technical skill, but *«ἐπὶ παιδείᾳ»*, for paideia, as this befits, Protagoras remarked, the private and the free man (*«ὡς τὸν ἰδιώτην καὶ τὸν ἐλεύθερον πρέπει»*).[82]

Protagoras, as the sophists in general, strongly advocated paideia and the cultivation of the soul, despite the emphasis that their teaching gave to oratory skills – the usual accusation towards them, especially by Plato.[83] The sophist movement played a major role in the blossoming of democracy in Athens and the advancement of the idea of personal and collective autonomy. The sophists, most of them metics in an Athens that was hospitable and open to new knowledge, ushered in further or higher education as a learning institution that was linked with the development of democracy. In broader terms, they initiated lifelong learning by encouraging the idea that education can encompass the entire life of the individual. The sophist movement was basically an educational movement, which turned the literature and knowledge of the time to educational content. However, it would be inadequate to limit its contribution only to this. The sophists also wrote treatises and reflected on the major ideas and concepts of their time. As Romilly writes, 'they were not just teachers of rhetoric but philosophers too, in the strongest sense of the term . . . [who] liberated and stimulated people's minds, opening up new avenues of explorations'.[84]

The sophist movement would not be possible, of course, outside of the space of philosophical and political questioning that characterised democratic Athens, something that Jaeger expressed very well in his classic study:

> [. . .] the great educational movement, which distinguished the fifth and fourth centuries and which is the origin of the European idea of culture, necessarily started from and in the city-state of the fifth century. It aimed, as the Greeks understood it, entirely at political education, training to serve the polis . . . At any rate, unless the whole population had been given an active part in government (and that is the basis and one of the distinguishing marks of democracy), it would have been impossible for the Greeks to ask and answer the eternal questions which exercised them so deeply at that period of their history and which they left for posterity to answer in its own way . . . Only at this stage of spiritual development are such problems as those of freedom and authority, or education for citizenship and education for leadership, conceived and answered, and only at this stage do they acquire their full urgency as moulders of men's destiny. They do not arise in primitive societies, in herd-communities or family-communities where there is no conception of the powers of the individual mind.[85]

In other words, the democratic and the sophist movement incarnated the central imaginary signification of personal and collective autonomy that emerged in the Greek society, transforming earlier or developing new significations. *Aretē* (*ἀρετή*) is a good example of a transformed signification. Aretē (usually, but inaccurately, translated in English as 'virtue') denotes the accomplishment by the individual of their highest potential, or those qualities which attract the admiration of one's fellow citizens. Before the advent of democracy, aretē was supposed to be inherited from noble ancestors and expressed through military and, later, through athletic, achievements. In the 5th century, the meaning of aretē changed; now, it was associated with distinction in the domains of politics, knowledge and the arts. As a consequence, aretē was considered something that can be developed by any person through education. This idea was endorsed by the sophist movement, which devoted much of its pedagogic activity to exploring what kind of education was required for one to acquire aretē. Personal development, then, became one of the movement's main aims, but, given that aretē referred now primarily to political life, this development was understood as inseparable from citizenship. To quote again Jaeger:'. . . despite the new emphasis on individual personality, it would then have been unthinkable that education should be founded on anything but membership of the political community'.[86] In fact, the emphasis on individual autonomy was not 'despite', but due to the political community, as this community not only allowed but encouraged personal development. For the Greeks, as Jaeger correctly points out elsewhere, a purely private ethical code, without reference to the polis, was inconceivable.[87] The sophists were aware of this interrelation and explicated it through their philosophical discourse and educational practice. Protagoras, for example, underlined that education does not end after school, as the whole polis is an educational force. The perception of justice (*δίκη*) that characterised the polis, and more broadly, its laws, was what educated citizens. In other words, as Protagoras put it, the nomos of the polis is the ultimate teacher of everybody.[88]

This, and many of the main ideas of the sophists, conveyed the core significations embedded in the tradition of Greek poetry and the Ionian philosophy and in the institution of the democratic polis. First, logos, in its various forms, was at the heart of sophist education: logos, as talk in citizens' assemblies, on which the function of democracy was based, and logos as philosophy and epistēmē. In Athenian democracy, as noted above, speech was itself a form of action. *Ἰσηγορία* (speech equality), *παρρησία* (speaking with sincerity) and *πειθώ* (the capacity to persuade) were highly valued. Therefore, learning to 'speak well' (*εὖ λέγειν*) was of crucial importance for one to effectively take part in politics. The sophists taught *εὖ λέγειν* in various forms: to speak fluently; to speak briefly; to lecture on a topic; to establish the truth by reasoned argumentation (dialectic); to see the same issue from different standpoints (antilogic); and to contest on a matter in order to prevail in a debate (eristic). They also organised public debates between competing speakers and contests of argumentation. The 'Socratic method', which was based on meticulous questioning to stimulate self-reflection and the elucidation of ideas, was part of the sophist movement, as was Socrates himself.[89]

In short, the sophist movement gave emphasis on the persuasive presentation of a *doxa* as the foundation for citizen participation in politics, as opposed to epistēmē, which seeks to establish the truth. But epistēmē was also a main part of the sophist movement. As Marrou points out, the Ionian initiators of scientific thinking did not undertake any educational activity to disseminate it; the sophists did. They recognised the value of pure theoretical knowledge in seeking the truth and in cultivating the intellect, and, for this purpose, they also taught astronomy and mathematics. Mathematics was considered important in strengthening the learners' analytical power. Overall, they prioritised scientific thinking and logical argumentation, and they also taught grammar, poetry and music, but they opposed extreme specialisation. In other words, they promoted paideia, as a condition for one – *anyone* – to cultivate their soul and to accomplish aretē.

Thus, universality constitutes another major breakthrough of sophist education, which, however, drew on an existing Greek signification: the distinction between physis and nomos, 'translated' by the sophist movement as the 'nature/nurture' distinction, which thereafter was to mark European educational philosophy. There is physis, the biological nature, whose medical study was also initiated in that period, and there is the soul, the spiritual nature – together constituting 'human nature'. Human nature, then, is the ground that *διδασκαλία* (teaching), *μάθησις* (learning), *ἄσκησις* (exercise), and, ultimately, *παιδεία* can cultivate. A few centuries later, Plutarch would create, out of this perception, the metaphor which became thereafter traditional in education: human nature is the land to be cultivated, the teacher is the farmer and logos is the seed that is planted.[90] But it was the sophists, in the framework of democratic Athens, who first foregrounded the universal potential of humans to develop themselves through education. Protagoras, who was amongst the main advocates of this perception, expressed it with the well-known phrase 'Man is the measure of all things . . .' (*«πάντων χρημάτων μέτρον ἐστὶν ἄνθρωπος»*).[91] For Jaeger, this phrase, as well as the entire sophist movement, signifies a 'rift between culture and religion',[92] (which, in fact, Plato successfully tried to undo by replacing 'man' with 'god').[93] As Romilly adds: 'If man was the measure of all things, the only justice was his justice, that is to say, his particular idea of justice, as expressed in his laws'.[94] Here, in other words, we see once more the Greek signification, present also in Homer, Hesiod and the Athenian tragedy, that social institutions are human creations, and thus, each society has its own nomos.

Yet, the most important contribution of the sophists to the democratic life of Athens was that they put into question the major representations and beliefs of the Greek society. Religion, myths, traditions and established ideas came under the scrutiny of philosophical questioning, which became an integral part of the sophists' educational practice. As Romilly points out, although there were differences in the sophists' work, 'all were innovative as teachers and all were harshly critical of all kinds of transcendentalism, making a more or less sweep of the values of the past and replacing them, also more or less uncompromisingly, with new values founded on the needs of human life and city life'.[95]

The critical intellectual practice that the sophists established through their educational activity, as well as the entire democratic atmosphere of philosophical and political questioning set in the Athenian agora, is the background of another signification, which was to mark the European tradition of higher education: academic autonomy. Academic autonomy was initiated, paradoxically, by Plato, the major enemy of the Athenian democracy, and the founding of his Academy in 387 BCE. The establishment of the Academy was the actual expression of Plato's opposition to the Athenian polis. As he manifested in some of his major dialogues (e.g., *The Republic* and *Statesman*), political decisions should be made by a limited number of individuals, philosophers or designated statesmen who possess the knowledge to do so. This knowledge, and therefore, the political criteria and standards on which decisions are to be based, should be developed by philosophers in a space that allows for free dialogue and the contestation of ideas. In other words, Plato transplanted the spirit of political freedom that existed in the Athenian polis into the Academy, thus creating a space of intellectual freedom. Or, as Hanna Arendt put it: 'the free space of the Academy was intended as a fully valid substitute of the marketplace, the agora, the central space for freedom in the polis'.[96] Thus, the Academy, and, by extension, the Athenian polis, that allowed its establishment, despite Plato's opposition to democracy, became the birthplace of academic autonomy.

Besides higher education, democracy gave rise to another major institution, both educational and political, which incarnated the Ancient Greek imaginary: the tragedy. The tragedy, which was specifically Athenian, rather than Greek in general, was inextricably linked with the life course of the Athenian democracy.

We know today the 7 tragedies of Aeschylus, the 7 of Sophocles and the 18 of Euripides, but each one of them wrote more than 90. Overall, the tragedies which were written throughout the Classical period exceed 1,000 and may even be around 1,500.[97] The tragedies were not plays made to be addressed only to a specific audience. They constituted a collective activity, embedded in the public life of the polis, and addressed its entire population. Beyond citizens, women and children, as well as the slaves who escorted them, were allowed to attend a tragedy. There was even a compensation provided by the polis to the poor in order for them to attend tragedies.

The 'raw material' of tragedy was usually the Greek myths with universal themes which referred to human character and passions – e.g., weakness, ambition, envy, love or suffering – and most often, they were elaborated to address the challenges of political life in Athens: justice, democracy, opinion, decision dilemmas, war and peace. Above all, the tragedy expressed the ontological foundations of Greek society: that Being is chaos, that humans cannot have full control over the meaning of their actions, that they are prone to *hubris* (*ὕβρις*) and that nothing but their self-limitation can protect them from it.[98] Self-limitation was also what the democratic polis as a whole should do to protect itself from hubris.

The political dimension of tragedy is acknowledged by contemporary Hellenists.[99] The tragedy was an institution of paideia, in the sense that it educated the Athenian population in democratic thinking and practice, as well as in the exploration and understanding of the human condition. As Cartledge writes in *The Cambridge Companion to Greek Tragedy*:

> [. . .] participation in the democratic process . . . was conceived primarily as an education for Athenian citizens, most of whom had received no formal schooling during childhood beyond the inculcation (perhaps) of basic literacy, numeracy and musical appreciation. For such average citizens, tragic theatre was an important part of their learning to be active participants in self-government by mass meeting and open debate between peers.[100]

Indeed, the tragedies are full of references to politics and the challenges that citizens encounter in participating and living in democracy. In echoing, for example, the public call in the assemblies of the dēmos (*«Τίς ἀγορεύει βούλεται;»* – 'who wants to speak?'), Euripides, in the *Suppliants*, celebrates this invitation and the beneficial role that a citizen's view may have for the polis: 'who has an opinion that benefits the polis and wants to make it known to all?' (*«Τίς θέλει πόλει χρηστόν τι βούλευμ' ἐς μέσον φέρειν ἔχων;»*). And he adds: 'What greater equality can there be in a polis? (*«τί τούτων ἔστ' ἰσαίτερον πόλει;»*).[101] *Antigone*, by Sophocles, also provides another major example of democratic thinking. Humans may be good or evil, but in Sophocles this has a political, rather than a moral dimension: when one forms and observes the laws, they honour the polis – one is *ὑψίπολις*, that is, highly regarded; but when one is rash (*«τόλμας χάριν»*), due to excessive boldness or insolence, one is *ἄπολις*, that is, they exclude themselves from the political community.[102] *Antigone*'s main theme (the dispute between King Cleon and Antigone about whether her brother Polynices, who attacked Thebes, should be left unburied or not) is also itself a reference to arrogance or hubris in connection to democratic deliberation and resolution: Creon's insistence on applying the law and leaving Polynices unburied leads to Antigone's suicide, but also to the suicide of his own son Haemon, to whom Antigone was betrothed. This tragic end is caused by Creon's perseverance; he was right, but as his son tells him, he wanted to be the only one who was right («*φρονεῖν μόνος δοκεί*»); namely, he did not weave his opinion with that of Antigone (who also acted on her own as she attempted to secretly bury Polynices). In other words, Sophocles, through this tragedy, elaborates on aspects of political disputation, and foregrounds the consequences of hubris, thus advancing democratic thinking.[103]

In fact, this can be argued for the tragedy in general. As Hall observes, the mode of democratic thinking in the plays was far more advanced than the reality of the society which produced the tragedy.[104] It granted equality of participation to all of the social groups appearing on the stage, thus providing a hint of a vision of absolute isonomia. In the world of the tragedy, all people, regardless of ethnicity, gender or social status, have the right and the ability to express their opinions; the tragedy recognises isēgoria and parrhēsia for them, rights and the qualities that only the men-citizens enjoyed in real Athens. In this respect, through the tragedy, the Athenians were educated in a more inclusive reality than what they experienced in their everyday lives.

In short, the Ancient Greek society regarded education as a matter of the political organisation of the community, that it takes place within and across institutions and that it is not limited to formal learning, i.e. it is lifelong and lifewide. The central imaginary signification of autonomy that arose in Ancient Greece was presentified in the educational institutions of the polis, whose democratic function was reinforced by them. Love for knowledge and truth, free self-expression, dialogue, critique and self-critique, political participation, logical reasoning and the belief in everybody's potential for self-development are some of the main attributes which marked Greek education, but also an educational legacy to Europe. Part of this legacy was the foundation of cross and comparative studies.

The emergence of cross-cultural comparison

The discussion about the way that the Greeks looked at other cultures is usually centred on the distinction between the 'Greeks and the barbarians', which is supposed to imply a derogatory viewpoint by the former to the latter. However, language carries the imaginary significations of a particular society in a particular time, and, thus, words should be understood in that specific context. For the Ancient Greeks, the word 'barbarians' meant those who spoke another language, and it had no disparaging sense. In Homeric epics, as Thucydides writes, there was not even a distinction between Greeks and Barbarians.[105] Two to three centuries after Homer, Herodotus treats them with the same impartiality already from the foreword of his *History*: 'This is the display of the inquiry of Herodotus of Halicarnassus, so that things done by man not be forgotten in time, and that great and marvellous deeds, some displayed by the Hellenes, some by the barbarians, not lose their glory, including among others what was the cause of their waging war on each other'.[106] It is indeed, remarkable that a historian (but also, a geographer and an ethnographer) of the time, belonging to a certain nation, considered the achievements of other nations equally glorious and worthy of being commemorated. As Jacob Burckhardt remarked, 'such an idea would not have occurred to an Egyptian or a Hebrew'.[107]

Nevertheless, the word 'barbarian' was not free of value judgement, but it seems to have had a political content. This is already indicated in Homer's *Odyssey*, in the way it presents the Cyclopes, who lacked political institutions. This is also what Thucydides would indicate in his history of the Peloponnesian War: in earlier times, for the Greeks to wear arms to protect themselves and their habitations 'was as much a part of everyday life with them as with the barbarians', as he writes, and this custom was still present in his time, amongst some Greek populations which did not live under the rule of law.[108] According to some modern authors, the political content of the distinction between Greeks and barbarians also had to do with the presence or lack of democratic institutions; namely, the term distinguished those who lived in self-governance and those who never managed to live without a king or a despot. The latter were for the Greeks, as Arendt notes, *ἄνευ λόγου* (they had no say – as the slaves).[109] And as Hartog writes: 'The Greek is 'political', in other words free, while the Barbarian is 'royal' meaning submissive to a master (*δεσπότης*)'.[110]

The political dimension in the Greeks' viewpoint towards other nations was present in their literature and historiography, but this did not prevent Greek authors from expressing their admiration for these nations' achievements. In fact, the Greeks' political (i.e. democratic) standpoint was indissolubly associated with their impartiality when they referred to or compared their beliefs and deeds with those of other peoples. Arendt attributes this to the political realm created by the polis which established the idea that there can be more than one view to an issue under consideration. A public political space is the realm which recognises the existence of various perspectives. Arendt identifies this recognition already in the Homeric epics, especially in the *Iliad*, where the Trojan War is seen 'no less through the eyes of the Trojans than through those of the Greeks'.[111] Indeed, there are parts in the *Iliad* which give the sense that the poet is on the side of the Trojans, such as the emotive scene in which Hector leaves his baby-son and his weeping wife for his last battle.[112] The epics cultivate the listeners'/readers' capacity to see the universality of the human condition across cultures, as well as the different sides that a situation or an issue might have, an attitude which characterised the democratic life of the polis. In the words of Arendt:

> Since for the Greeks the public political space is common to all (koinon), the space where the citizens assemble, it is the realm in which all things

> can first be recognised in their many-sidedness. This ability to see the same thing first from two opposing sides and then from all sides – an ability ultimately based in Homeric impartiality, unique in antiquity, and whose passionate intensity is unexcelled even in our own time – also underlines certain tricks of the Sophists, whose importance in liberating human thought from the constrictions of dogma we underestimate if, in following Plato, we condemn them on moral grounds.[113]

The author apparently refers to the pedagogic technique of speaking 'from both sides', namely, defending and standing against the same view, which was common in sophist education and which is presented in *Δισσοί λόγοι* (*Double Speeches*), which was written by an unknown sophist.[114] Nevertheless, as it was pointed out above, the sophist movement also foregrounded the distinction between physis and nomos, which was present in Classical poetry and natural philosophy, not only in terms of its 'nature/nurture' dimension, by which they promoted the idea of the educability and personal development of all; the sophists also elaborated on this distinction in its sense that every society establishes its own institutions (i.e. conventions), while human beings share the same nature. Thus, we witness in Classical Athens the rise of a conception of cultural relativity along with a truly universal perception of humanity. Except for the words of Protagoras, mentioned above, there are fragments by other sophists, such as Antiphon, who expresses, in his treatise *On Truth*, this universal understanding of human nature:

> We have only to think of things which are natural and necessary to all mankind; these are available to all in the same way, and in all of these there is no distinction between barbarian or Greek. For we all breath out into the air by the mouth and the nostrils, and we laugh when we are pleased in our mind, or we weep when we are grieved, and we receive sounds with our hearings, and see by the light of our vision, and we work with our hands, and we walk with our feet . . .[115]

This remarkable perception of human nature as universal was already present in Greek mythology and literature, especially in the Athenian tragedy, which highlights the emotional and ethical world of the individual and the tragic situation in which he/she can be found, regardless, again, of their nation or status. One of the early examples of the universal and impartial gaze towards the cultural 'other' is Aeschylus's tragedy *Persians*, which was presented first in 472 BCE at the major Athenian festival, *City Dionysia*. The tragedy deals with the defeat of the Persian emperor Xerxes and his massive army after their 480/79 BCE expedition against Greece. What is impressive in the tragedy is that it is not about the hardships and the sufferings of the Greeks in fighting back the gigantic enemy – despite the fact that Aeschylus himself, as well as much of his audience, fought in that war. The tragedy is about the sufferings and the devastation of the enemy, which thus faced the *nemesis* (*νέμεσις*) that the *hubris* of

Xerxes caused, who mobilised his entire army for his overambitious endeavour to conquer Greece but finally destroyed his own people. The dialogues between his mother Atossa and the ghost of his father Darius, as well as between Atossa, Xerxes and the chorus, are remarkable for the way that Aeschylus puts himself and the Greek audience in the place of the 'other'.[116]

Another example from the Athenian tragedy, which is indicative of this empathic attitude toward the cultural 'other', is the play *Trojan Women* presented in 415 BCE by Euripides. The tragedy is about the devastation and conquest of Troy by the Greeks, who killed most of the men and were to take the women and their families back to Greece as slaves. The Trojan women are lamenting the loss of their home country and the death of their husbands, sons and brothers and are mourning about their future life in Greece as slaves. The tragedy presents the brutality of the Greek assault on Troy and makes the viewer identify with the victims of the assault. But that was the plot of the tragedy; the real issue to which the play indirectly referred was the Athenian invasion, the year before, of the island of Melos, because of its descent to Sparta, where they executed the men and sold the women and the children as slaves. The tragedy was a condemnation of the Athenians' ruthlessness, written by an Athenian poet and presented to the Athenian audience – an audience open to self-reflection and ready to face its own *hubris* – which also granted him a prize.[117]

But the Athenian audience was also open to self-reflection through another poetic creation of the time: comedy. Although ludicrous episodes, farces and burlesques existed much earlier, comedy arose mainly in the 5th century BCE in competition with tragedy, both addressing the whole polis and both being expressions of its democratic life. The staging of comic poetry had similarities with that of dramatic plays but it had its own specialness, e.g., the choruses personified freely animals and objects (birds, goats, wasps, clouds etc.), and faced at times the spectators. Comic plays satirised institutions of the polis, the political life of the time, public figures, social classes, and even gods, by making up grotesque situations. Aristophanes was the prominent comic poet (amongst several others – such as Cratinus, Eupolis, Telecleides, Hermippus and Prynichus, to mention only few from the 'Old Comedy' – whose work though survived only in fragments). In *Lysistrata*, *Ekklēsiazusae* and *Thesmophoriazusae*, Aristophanes parodies established gendered roles and envisages a society in which women come to political power to bring about peace and full economic and gender equality; in *The Wasps* and *The Knights*, he challenges demagoguery and abuse of political and judicial powers; in *Plutus*, he castigates the unjust distribution of wealth; and with *Peace* and *The Acharnians*, he mocks warmongering and appeals for peace amidst the Peloponnesian War. As Burckhardt writes: 'Other periods of history have left satiric self-portraits but none so grandiose and concrete as that of Aristophane's comedy'.[118] In addition, the author emphasises the remarkable fact that this self-parody was acceptable even in the middle of a fierce war:

> [. . .] there was an Athens that enjoyed placing its eyes at the focus of this mirror. Whereas the French Revolution would have lopped off the head of

> anyone who cast the slightest doubt on the value of its passionate enthusiasms or dared to portray them as grotesque, Athens lived her mad life, desiring to know how she appeared in the eyes of her great poets and allowing them a high degree of independence in their views, often no doubt minority views. At the same time, these comic poets were also balanced against the tragedians and spurred on competition with them.[119]

Indeed, the Greeks looked in the mirror through the theatre plays, the practice of democracy, sophist education but, also through the comparison with other societies, induced by the emergence of historiography.

Comparative inquiry: *historein* and *sēmainein*

Written accounts of the past did not appear first in Greece. The Egyptians, for example, wrote annals which recorded the acts of their kings for centuries before the Greeks. Yet, what is characteristic of those records, as Hartog notes, is that 'the Egyptians didn't see anybody but themselves and the gods'.[120] Their gaze to the past exhibited not a curiosity, but a desire for eternity. Similarly, in Mesopotamia, history was the history of the kings, written by royal scribes and inscribed on monuments. For the ancient Hebrews, history was what the sacred books said, which reproduced the sayings and experiences of their great ancestors, with no curiosity to investigate the past as such. For the Indians, finally, history was their 'Veda', their holy books, which included, basically, the 'visions' of extraordinary or sacred persons. Knowledge was supposed to be revealed to these persons, and they transmitted it to humanity through a text, so that it is learned and repeated in the future by Brahmans.

For the Greeks, after the Mycenaean kingdoms, history was neither a memorisation of royal deeds, nor a holy revelation nor a preserve of a caste of scribes. As Hartog writes, 'epistemologically, the Greeks always privileged seeing (over hearing) as the mode of knowledge. To see, to see for oneself, and to know were one and the same thing'.[121] *History* (*ιστορίη* – the Ionic form used by Herodotus) is derived from the verb *historein* (*ιστορεῖν*), which means to inquire. It indicates the act of going and seeing first, thus expressing an approach, rather than a knowledge field. But it also indicates the readiness to question taken-for-granted traditions and knowledge – a readiness which could only arise in the context of the self-reflectiveness that emerged in Ancient Greece. 'I write what I deem true; for the stories of the Greeks are manifold and seem to me ridiculous',[122] wrote the first known historian, Hecataeus of Miletus, a phrase that could not be written by an annals-scribe of an Eastern monarchy or in any culture which did not allow the direct questioning, let alone rejection, of their traditional knowledge structures.

But the real rupture in historiography comes during the 5th century with Herodotus. Herodotus wrote his History (or *Histories*) investigating the Greco-Persian wars, but at the same time, he explored neighbouring civilisations, also creating the disciplines of geography and ethnography and, in a sense, comparative studies. Especially in the first books (*Clio*, *Euterpe*, *Thalia* and *Melpomene*), he makes long references to the customs and institutions of the countries he visited, and especially to Egypt and Persia. Throughout his nine books, Herodotus *ἱστορεῖ*, investigates, but also, as Hartog notes, he shows, reveals and signifies, or in Greek, *σημαίνει*. The verb *σημαίνειν* (*sēmainein*) is used for someone who sees and reports.[123] By *sēmainein*, Herodotus also looks for significations, in the sense that he investigates what certain customs, traditions or institutions mean for the peoples under consideration. Both the approaches of *historein* and *sēmainein* are, as Hartog writes, 'two intellectual tools by which to 'see clearly' further, beyond the visible, in space or time'.[124] And in doing so, Herodotus recurrently questions the established knowledge of his own people, through a remarkably impartial research attitude. It is worth quoting a few examples:

> The Greeks say among many foolish things that Psammetichus had the children reared by women whose tongues he had cut out . . .[125]
>
> These customs, then, and others besides, which I shall indicate, were taken by the Greeks from the Egyptians.[126]
>
> I have indeed a lot of other evidence that the name of Heracles did not come from Greece to Egypt, but from Egypt to Greece . . .[127]
>
> In fact, the names of nearly all the gods came to Hellas from Egypt. For I am convinced by inquiry that they have come from foreign parts, and I believe that they came chiefly from Egypt.[128]
>
> It would seem, too, that the Egyptians were the first people to establish solemn assemblies, and processions, and services; the Greeks learned all that from them.[129]
>
> It would seem that the robe and aegis of the images of Athena were copied by the Greeks from the Libyan women.[130]
>
> These Phoenicians who came with Cadmus and of whom the Gephyraeans were a part brought with them to Hellas, among many other kinds of learning, the alphabet, which had been unknown before this, I think, to the Greeks. As time went on the sound and the form of the letters were changed.[131]
>
> As to the customs of the Persians, I know them to be these. It is not their custom to make and set up statues and temples and altars, but those who do such things they think foolish, because, I suppose, they have never believed the gods to be like men, as the Greeks do.[132]

Herodotus's historical, ethnographic and comparative inquiry should be seen as part of the political, philosophical and educational movements taking place at that time in Athens, which called into question established traditions and representations. Through examining the institutions of the others, this inquiry instigated self-examination and self-reflection by breaking the cognitive and representational closure with respect to other cultures and taking the critical approach that was initiated by these movements further. The incredible impartiality of Herodotus – who even reaches the point of considering his own people's customs of god representation foolish in comparison to those of their traditional enemy (the Persians) – is characteristic and not at all negligible, especially given the fact that his *Histories* were presented in public performances in various Greek poleis (e.g., in Athens, Thebes, Corinth and Olympia).[133]

We find the same impartial attitude in his description of the Persians' educational institutions. Boys, Herodotus says, lived amongst the women and were not allowed into the presence of their fathers until the age of five, so that their fathers would suffer no grief in case their sons died at this young age. Moreover, he tells us that the education of the boys spanned from their fifth to their twentieth year and that they were taught only three things: riding, archery and telling the truth (*ἀληθίζεσθαι*).[134] Impartiality in Herodotean history and ethnography also reflects the Greek distinction between physis and nomos, which makes him aware that each culture sets its own conventions over natural reality. He expresses this very well through a short story which he attributes to Darius, the Persian emperor, who comes across the customs that different cultures establish with regard to the way they treat their dead:

> When Darius was king, he summoned the Greeks who were with him and asked them for what price they would eat their fathers' dead bodies. They answered that there was no price for which they would do it. Then Darius summoned those Indians who are called Callatiae who eat their parents, and asked them (the Greeks being present and understanding through interpreters what was said) what would make them willing to burn their fathers at death. The Indians cried aloud, that he should not speak of so horrid an act. So firmly rooted are these beliefs; and it is, I think, rightly said in Pindar's poem that custom is lord of all.[135]

Because the custom or the institution is the lord in all societies, what looks normal to one society may look despicable to another, and vice versa. It is this awareness that drives the comparative gaze of Herodotus to other cultures. This gaze is not Hellenocentric. Although 'them' and 'us' runs through the text, there is no explicit or implicit viewpoint, as Hartog remarks in his study *The Mirror of Herodotus*, that 'us' represents the truth, a model or the progress that should be achieved by 'them'. Nor do the barbarians represent the truth or a natural way of living that should be imitated by 'us'. Further, as the same author notes, what is particularly remarkable in the Herodotean narrative is that 'them' and 'us' becomes 'them' and 'they', namely, the barbarians and the Greeks, or the 'others' and the Greeks.[136]

However, Herodotus's impartiality does not entail resignation from his judgement nor endorsement of despotism and its political or educational practices. As well as the tragedies, the Herodotean history sees universality in human conduct which he judges accordingly – e.g., identifying *hubris* in the excessive manifestation of power and force. Moreover, his appreciation of democracy appears in parts of his work, because, after all, it was democracy which allowed him to write and publicise the history that he did. For example, he appreciates, as also mentioned above in the dialogue that he quotes between Xerxes and Demaratus, the Greek freedom under the law, and the empowerment that it bestows to men: the Athenians, he writes in the fifth book, proved that equality is a good thing, and their achievements show that 'while they were oppressed, they were, as men working for a master, cowardly, but when they were freed, each one was eager to achieve for himself'.[137]

If Herodotus tried to present facts, customs, institutions and the meaning they had to the peoples under consideration, Thucydides, who wrote not a cultural history, but about the Peloponnesian War, tried to understand social and political phenomena by looking for deeper causes and associations of events. With Thucydides, who lived in the second half of the 5th century BCE and experienced this major war first-hand, inquiry, as well as critical thinking, became more systematic. Here, we have another major work which is not to serve any personal or political interest, but to communicate an accurate account of the time to future generations, as Thucydides put it emphatically in his first book:

> The absence of romance in my history will, I fear, detract somewhat from its interest; but if it be judged useful by those inquirers who desire an exact knowledge of the past as an aid to the interpretation of the future, which in the course of human things must resemble if it does not reflect it, I shall be content. In fine, I have written my work, not as an essay which is to win the applause of the moment, but as a possession for all time.[138]

The last phrase, that the history of the Peloponnesian War should remain a possession for all time («*κτῆμά τε ἐς αἰεὶ*»), should be seen as an indication of the universality in which Thucydides also believes, with regard to fundamental human characteristics, especially the struggle for power, across history and societies. This is because Thucydides identifies progress in the material, technical and force domains, but not in the domain of ethics.[139] Societies, in other words, become more advanced in technological or military terms over time and perhaps in comparison to other societies in the same historical time, but not necessarily ethically.

Thucydides's aim, to write his history as *κτῆμά τε ἐς αἰεὶ*, was served through his seeking the truth («*ζήτησις της ἀληθείας*») and, in accordance to the scientific inquiry of nature and the human body, that emerged in the same era, through the exclusion of metaphysical explanations from his research of historical events.[140] Thucydides should be considered the initiator of human or social sciences, as his work includes elements of what would later be accommodated under the knowledge branches of war studies, political philosophy, strategic planning and sociology, as well as psychology. Indeed, looking at the emotional layer of human behaviour, both personal and collective (fear, range, boastfulness, ambition etc.), is a constant characteristic of his inquiry. For example, the deeper cause of the Peloponnesian War was, for him, the fear of the Spartans towards Athenian supremacy. However, an ethical judgement is present here too: human actions are subject to hubris, but hubris, in the Thucydidean history, is committed not only through the excessive demonstration of power. It is also manifested through politically wrong decisions which result in failure.[141] Moreover, Thucydides endorses the physis/nomos distinction, as well as the sophist technique of presenting two views about the same issue (*Δισσοί λόγοι*) in orations and dialogues. The dialogue between the Athenians and the Melians, which demonstrates that justice can exist only where there is equality, but not between competing powers, is a well-known example of Thucydidean writing, but also an example of raw truth or *parrhēsia*, which the Athenians highly valued.[142]

The history of the Peloponnesian War was continued by another well-known Greek historian, Xenophon, in his *Hellenica*. Xenophon wrote many other books, including *Anabasis* (about the expedition of the Persian king, Cyrus the Younger, in which Xenophon took part as a mercenary), the *Constitution of the Lacedaimonians*, mentioned above, as well as *Cyropaedia*, the Education of Cyrus (the Great or the Elder, who founded the Achaemenid Empire in the 6th century BCE). The latter is usually mentioned in comparative education textbooks as one of the first descriptions of a foreign educational institution. Nevertheless, it is not exactly a historical book or an ethnographic study. It was, rather, a treatise with many elements of a fiction-story or novel. For this reason, Romilly would consider Xenophon to be an innovator in literary writing but not in historiography.[143]

Xenophon, after all, tried, with his *Cyropaedia*, to present a major example of a monarchy which he personally admired, as he was a supporter of oligarchic and aristocratic ideas. Although a student of Socrates, Xenophon was a man of the 4th century, in the sense that he lived and acted during the decline of the Athenian democracy, which he, as Plato, opposed. Xenophon expressed this opposition through his writings, but also by fighting with the Spartans and in support of the Persians. As Due remarks, in a content analysis of *Cyropaedia*, although Plato would envisage in his *Republic* a polis governed by philosopher-kings, Xenophon's preference was a gigantic state governed by a charismatic monarch who concentrates all kinds of power under his command.[144] This ideal ruler would govern his subjects in the way a father leads his family, by instilling in its members respect and fear and by punishing or rewarding them accordingly. Xenophon's model of this ruler was Cyrus.

It was the formation of this ruler which was of interest to Xenophon in writing this book, rather than a detailed presentation of Persian education. The few pages he devotes to the description of Persian education serve as a kind of background knowledge which helps in developing his narrative on the socialisation, personality and achievements of the leader that he admired so much. However, it is worth making reference to this knowledge, not in order to give an additional example of the impartiality which characterised the above-mentioned authors, but as another manifestation of the same cognitive openness of the Athenian democracy which allowed everybody, both its supporters and its adversaries, to inquire about and evaluate 'barbarian' institutions according to their judgement. As the democratic polis permitted Plato, a major adversary of democracy, to oppose it through his writings and the founding of his Academy, so it allowed historians like Xenophon to praise the political institutions of the traditional enemy of his own people.

The description, though, in *Cyropaedia*, of what constituted an educational institution in Achaemenid Persia is an impartial depiction of principles and practices under which children and adolescents were socialised, which was similar – though more extended – to that given by Herodotus: 'The boys go to school and give their time to learning justice and righteousness: they will tell you they come for that purpose, and the phrase is as natural with them as it is for us to speak of lads learning their letters'.[145] Xenophon describes a form of education in which there is learning neither of literacy nor of music nor of poetry. Nor is there actual teaching, but supervision of children's moral conduct and punishment of culprits: 'The masters spend the chief part of the day in deciding cases for their pupils . . . of picking and stealing, of violence, of fraud, of calumny, and so forth. The case is heard and the offender, if shown to be guilty, is punished'.[146] Moral instruction and surveillance include temperance, self-restraint and respect for the elderly and especially submission to political authority; children 'are taught to obey their rulers, and here again nothing is of greater value than the studied obedience to authority manifested by their elders everywhere'.[147]

The other main part of children's education, as also mentioned by Herodotus, is military training ('they are taught to shoot with the bow and to fling the javelin') and continence in food ('They bring from home the staple of their meal, dry bread with nasturtium for a relish'). Personal hardship is enhanced in adolescence, after the sixteenth or seventeenth year, through a form of preliminary military service to the community ('For ten years they are bound to sleep at night round the public buildings . . . to guard the community and to practice self-restraint'). The trainees spend their days basically serving the ruling class ('these young men are also employed by the magistrates if garrison work needs to be done . . .'; 'they present themselves before the governors for service to the state . . .'; 'when the king goes out to hunt . . . he takes half the company with him, and each man must carry bow and arrows'). This latter part of youth training marks thereafter their lives as adults: obedience and service to the state and the rulers.[148] A stark contrast from the values of the Greek paideia.

In summary, cross-cultural inquiry was born by a society which did not expect other cultures to share its own significations and which believed that societies create their own world of meanings and their own institutions, which are neither more nor less valid than those at home. A foreign society thus was seen neither as superior nor as inferior, but simply as other. And this otherness was worth being studied for the sake of knowledge and understanding.

This comparative gaze was an actualisation of the Greek social imaginary which gave rise to the idea of autonomy and a web of significations embodied in the institution of the democratic polis. Amongst those was the distinction between physis and nomos. Physis was the natural, biological and psychic reality which all humans share. Barbarians enjoy and suffer, succeed and fail, act with judgement or in hubris, as the Greeks do. Universality and empathy are present in Homeric epics, in tragedies, in the teachings of the sophists and in the writings of the first historians. But, at the same time, the barbarians are not an undifferentiated 'other'; they have distinct cultures with their own representations and institutions about and from which the Greeks can learn.

The Greeks recognised cultural diversity as they recognised the multiplicity and equality of views in the framework of the democratic polis. As there can be a different doxa about the same issue amongst interlocutors, so can other cultures have different perspectives. This should not be confounded with political equality in the democratic process. For the Greeks, as the illustrious dialogue between the Athenians and the Melians indicates, equality did not apply in 'international relations'. However, their perception that there was diversity of doxai and of nomoi allowed them to acknowledge cultural diversity.

Behind the Greek comparative gaze also was the philosophical and political questioning which characterised the life of the democratic polis. Philosophical inquiry, from the Milesians down to the sophists, questioned the representations and the cognitive traditions of their own people. The inquiry of the traditions of other peoples was, as Herodotus's *Histories* testify, an activity associated with that ethos of philosophical critique. Similarly, questioning of the Greek laws and institutions and its related values and practices (e.g., *isēgoria* and *parrhēsia*), as part of Greek politics, is associated with the effort of the first historians to reflect on home institutions through researching those of others.

Finally, cross-cultural and comparative research should be seen as part of the scientific spirit that arose in Greece in the 6th century and the overall appreciation of knowledge and learning that was characteristic of the 5th century. In other words, it is part of the emergence of epistēmē and philosophia, as a love for knowledge that is independent from material benefits. Epistēmē, as a form and activity in the field of logos, marked the break of cognitive closure and advanced empirical inquiry, logical argumentation and the search for truth. This high esteem for intellectual activity gave rise to a genuine curiosity about other cultures – which has lain thereafter at the heart of comparative inquiry.

Notes

1 Aeschylus, *Prometheus Bound* (lines 230–235).
2 Finley ([1954] 2002).
3 Vernant (1972).
4 Castoriadis (2004).
5 Homer, *The Odyssey* (Book 11: lines 488–491).
6 Hesiod, *Works and Days* (lines 90–105).
7 Castoriadis (2004).
8 Hesiod, *Theogony* (line 115).
9 Castoriadis (2004: 299).
10 Castoriadis (2004: 270–272).

11 Castoriadis (2004).
12 Castoriadis (2008).
13 See Diogenis Laertius, Lives of Eminent Philosophers.
14 Diogenis Laertius, *Lives of Eminent Philosophers*. See also: Castoriadis (2004: 390–391).
15 See Hesiod, *Works and Days* (lines 276–285).
16 See Aeschylus, *Prometheus Bound* (lines 250, 441–506); Castoriadis (1991: 5–38).
17 See Euripides, *The Suppliants* (lines 200–218).
18 Homer, *The Odyssey* (Book 9: lines 105–115). See also Castoriadis (2004).
19 Castoriadis (2004).
20 Euripides, *The Suppliants* (lines 433–434).
21 Castoriadis (1991: 5–38).
22 Sophocles, *Antigone* (line 334). The adjective *δεινός* is conventionally translated as 'wonderful', but it can also mean competent, capable, strong or even fearsome.
23 Heraclitus, *Fragments* (DKB44).
24 Herodotus, *The Histories* (7.104.4).
25 Thucydides, *Pericles' Funeral Oration* (74, lines 1–3).
26 Nikoloudis (1999).
27 See Heraclitus, *Fragments* (DKB2, DK B113, DK B112).
28 Meier (1980).
29 Vernant (1962).
30 Castoriadis (2004).
31 Vernant (1962).
32 Lloyd (1970).
33 Lloyd (1970).
34 See Aristotle (1996).
35 Thucydides, The Peloponnesian War (7.77.7, *«Ἄνδρες γὰρ πόλις, καὶ οὐ τείχη οὐδὲ νῆες ἀνδρῶν κεναί»*).
36 Herodotus, *The Histories* (8. 62).
37 Friedell (1940).
38 Castoriadis (2008).
39 Aristotle (1996: 242, XLI2).
40 Aristotle (1996: 242, XLI2).
41 Arendt (2005: 126).
42 Aristotle, *Politics* (1275b, 20 and 1276a, 5).
43 Mossé (1992).
44 Plato, *Protagoras*.
45 Plato, Statesman.
46 Arendt (2005).
47 Heraclitus' *Fragments* (DK B53).
48 Arendt (1999).
49 Arendt (1999).
50 Thucydides, *Pericles' Funeral Oration* (74, Lines 36–40).
51 Mossé (1995).
52 Finley (1983).
53 Friedell (1940).
54 Aristotle, *Politics* (1337b).
55 Arendt (2005: 116–117).
56 Cartledge (2006: 266).
57 Mill (1861: 67).
58 Thucydides, *The Peloponnesian War* (2.41.1).
59 Thucydides, *The Peloponnesian War* (2.40.1).
60 Arendt (2006: 213); Castoriadis (2008).
61 Castoriadis (2008: 244–247).

62 Jaeger (1939).
63 Meier (2009).
64 Plato, *The Republic* (606e).
65 Robb, K. (1994: 198).
66 Plato, *Symposium*.
67 See Marrou (1982); Reisensberg (1989).
68 Xenophon, Constitution of the Lacedaimonians (2.12, «. . .*λεκτέον δέ μοι δοκεῖ εἶναι καὶ περὶ τῶν παιδικῶν ἐρώτων: ἔστι γάρ τι καὶ τοῦτο πρὸς παιδείαν*»),
69 Marrou (1982).
70 Pascal (1652–1653: para 54).
71 Nikoloudis (1999: 119).
72 Nikoloudis (1999: 92–93).
73 See Vidal-Naquet (1986).
74 Jaeger (1939: 290).
75 Marrou (1982).
76 Nemo (2005).
77 Robb (1994: 279).
78 Postman (1982: 7).
79 Tames (2002); Postman (1982: 8).
80 Morgan (1998: 10).
81 Morgan (1998: 10–11).
82 Plato, *Protagoras* (312b).
83 See: Plato, *Sophist*.
84 Romilly (1992: 9).
85 Jaeger (1939: 288).
86 Jaeger (1939: 287).
87 Jaeger (1939: 326).
88 Jaeger (1939: 310).
89 Kerferd (1981).
90 Plutarch, De liberis educandis (2b).
91 Diogenes Laertius, Lives of Eminent Philosophers (9.8).
92 Jaeger (1939: 302).
93 Plato, *Laws* (4.716).
94 Romilly (1992: 112).
95 Romilly (1992: 10).
96 Arendt (2005: 131).
97 See: Romilly (1970); Castoriadis (2008).
98 Castoriadis (2008).
99 See for example: Meier (1988); Romilly (1970); Castoriadis (2008); Easterling (1997).
100 Cartledge (1997: 19).
101 Euripides, *The Suppliants* (lines 438–441).
102 Sophocles, *Antigone* (lines 355–371); Castoriadis (2007: 12–13).
103 Castoriadis (2007: 13–14).
104 Hall (1997).
105 Thucydides, *The Peloponnesian War* (1.3.3).
106 Herodotus, *The Histories* (1.1.0).
107 Burckhardt ([1958] 2002: 332).
108 Thucydides, *The Peloponnesian War* (1.5.3, 1.6.1 and 1.6.2). See also Castoriadis (2011).
109 Arendt (2005: 118).
110 Hartog (2000: 393).
111 Arendt (2005: 166).
112 Homer, *Iliad* (6.466).
113 Arendt (2005: 167).

114 Jaeger (1939: 315).
115 Dillon and Gergel (2003: 314).
116 Aeschylus, *Persians*. See also Vernart and Vidal-Naquet (1985).
117 See Castoriadis (2004).
118 Burckhardt ([1958] 2002: 261).
119 Burckhardt ([1958] 2002: 262).
120 Hartog (2000: 385).
121 Hartog (2000: 386).
122 Quoted in: Shotwell (1922: 138).
123 Hartog, (2000: 395).
124 Hartog, (2000: 395).
125 Herodotus, *The Histories* (2.2.5).
126 Herodotus, *The Histories* (2.51.1).
127 Herodotus, *The Histories* (2.43.2).
128 Herodotus, *The Histories* (2.50.1).
129 Herodotus, *The Histories* (2.58.1).
130 Herodotus, *The Histories* (4.189.1).
131 Herodotus, *The Histories* (5.58.1).
132 Herodotus, *The Histories* (1.131.1).
133 See: Bichler and Rollinger (2000).
134 Herodotus, *The Histories* (1.136.2).
135 Herodotus, *The Histories* (3.38.3–4).
136 Hartog (1988: 369).
137 Herodotus, *The Histories* (5.78.1).
138 Thucydides, *The Peloponnesian War* (1.22.4).
139 Castoriadis (2008: 404).
140 Regakos (2009).
141 Romilly (1990).
142 Thucydides, The Peloponnesian War (5).
143 Romilly (1992).
144 Due (1989: 210–211).
145 Xenophon, *Cyropaedia* (Book 1: C2).
146 Xenophon, *Cyropaedia* (Book 1: C2).
147 Xenophon, *Cyropaedia* (Book 1: C2).
148 All extracts in the brackets are from: Xenophon, *Cyropaedia*, (Book 1: C2).

3 The institution of education and comparative studies in Modernity

The central social imaginary signification of collective and personal autonomy, created in Ancient Greece, re-emerged after the Middle Ages as a new social-historical project. A project, in Castoriadis's words, 'is the intention of transforming the real, guided by a representation of the meaning of this transformation, taking into consideration the actual conditions and inspiring an activity'.[1] The Renaissance was inspired by Antiquity and questioned the medieval status quo, leading to a variety of transformations, which, in the ensuing centuries, were radicalised through a series of revolutions and social movements. During the European Modern Era, the project of autonomy confronted the *Ancien Régime* and, later on, the drive towards the rationalistic mastery and control of nature and society, a novel central imaginary signification that arose in Modernity. By 'Modern Era', I refer to the historical period that began with the Renaissance, and by 'European Modernity', I mean the last phase of this period, from the 18th to the mid-20th centuries and the cultural changes that took place mainly in Western Europe (but also in its colonies by settlement, especially in the USA). The geography and the extensive time span that this era covers make the task of this chapter challenging. However, as the European world emerged as a 'printed civilisation',[2] its 'spirit' can be traced in the writings of the time, key illustrations of which will constitute, along with current contributions, the main sources of this chapter. Besides, the intent of this study is analytical and interpretive, rather than encyclopaedic. Its aim is to access the magma of imaginary significations of selected eras in order to understand the institution of education and the comparative gaze towards other civilisations. In other words, the aim here is to trace the main complex of significations and institutions, and their clashes and syntheses, that gave rise to the European world, in the context of which educational institutions and comparative inquiry emerged.

The social imaginary of European Modernity

The idea that institutions are social creations, which was generated first in Ancient Greece, returned in post-medieval Europe, and it took a radical political form in the 18th century. Heteronomous societies attribute the establishment of their institutions to transcendental or extra-social sources, something that has characterised Christian Europe as well as societies across the world. However, in Europe, a rupture had started taking place already in the early Renaissance, which, as Jacob Burckhardt writes, in his classic study of the culture of that period, could not happen without Antiquity's appreciation of truth as a driving force.[3] The truth is that it is individuals and societies that give meaning and form to the chaos, with their own creations. The medieval world covered up this fact and gave to the chaos a single meaning, the meaning of God, thus curtailing the creative force and energy (*vis formandi* and *libido formandi*) of individuals.

It took centuries to have political, cultural and intellectual activities liberated from religion, but the rift had appeared already in the early Renaissance, e.g., with the assertion of community rights, the recognition of individuality, the rediscovery of Greek philosophy and its gradual emancipation from theology, the break with the perception that innovation is something blasphemous and, in general, the erosion of sacredness that authority and tradition enjoyed. The following centuries witnessed the development of philosophy and scientific thinking that led to the formation, from the 19th century, of a wide variety of disciplines, including sociology, anthropology and cross-cultural studies. As John Bury in his classic *A History of Freedom of Thought* writes: 'History shows that knowledge grew when speculation was perfectly free in Greece, and that in modern times, since restrictions on inquiry have been entirely removed, it has advanced with a velocity which would seem diabolical to the slaves of the medieval Church'.[4]

The same applies to cultural creations. Art expanded spectacularly in Modernity exploring the human condition and critiquing the status quo – either the age-old power of the Church or the increasing industrialisation of societies. New forms and great creators appeared, particularly in music (e.g., classical, opera and, later on, jazz), painting (e.g., impressionism, cubism, expressionism, futurism and pure abstraction) and literature (e.g., Stendhal, Balzac, Hugo, Austin, Dickens, Dostoyevsky, Tolstoy, Kafka, to name only a few). Hobsbawm's multivolume history of European Modernity underlined the critical and subversive disposition of artists throughout this period: artists, from the 18th century, became sages, teachers and sources of truth, as culture was not for them primarily a matter of individual success but of questioning and reflecting on the social circumstances of their time.[5] As Hobsbawm writes: '. . . the French Revolution inspired [the artist] by its example, the Industrial Revolution by its horror, and the bourgeois society, which emerged from both, transformed his very existence and modes of creation'.[6]

Freedom of thought was inextricably related to the entire historical movement that questioned autocratic rule and strived for the institution of political rights, which appeared first in the early Renaissance. The context was again a self-governing town, the first form of democratic political organisation that appeared since Greek Antiquity. The urban environment of the medieval town provided the conditions for communal movements and for the emerged proto-bourgeoisie to promote their political aspirations for local government against the established forms of authority (emperors, kings or feudal lords). The most remarkable expression of this phenomenon was the Italian 'city-states' (Venice,

Milan, Bologna, Naples, Genoa and others), which managed, from roughly the 10th to the 15th centuries, to acquire independence from their established rulers and introduce institutions of self-government – such as the city councils, headed for short periods by the elected *Podestà*.[7] The city-states were an important development in the history of democracy, as they proved that self-governance was not unthinkable and as they created a host of institutions which marked Europe, such as the university.

Overall, the Italian city-states were part of a social-historical current that put in question and subverted the power structure of European monarchies and promoted the idea of political self-institution. The democratic undertaking was radicalised in the 18th and 19th centuries, having recorded a long series of historical events: the Magna Carta of 1215 and the Great Charter of the Liberties of England, which protected the individual from arbitrary authority, limited royal powers and created a precedent for constitutional law; the adoption of Roman Law, which recognised the individual as a *persona*, who has legal rights and freedoms; the Bill of Rights of 1689 again in England, which limited royal powers while enhancing the role of parliamentary procedures; the American Revolution, the Declaration of Independence in 1776 and the Constitution of 1789; the French Revolution and the Declaration of the Rights of Man and of the Citizen in 1789, which demolished the power of the monarchy and the Church and introduced civil liberties; the European revolutions of 1848, which led to the establishment of constitutional rights in many countries; the Paris Commune of 1871 as an endeavour of self-governance; and the rise of social movements, which proliferated in the 20th century. Over the course of time, the European democratic movement, in comparison to its Ancient Greek precedent, has been universalised by including in its political endeavours for justice, equality and self-determination all human beings and calling into question essentially all established institutions: authority structures, political systems, economy, wealth distribution, social hierarchies, education, family, gender relations, ethnic status and essentially all aspects of social life were placed under critique and became objects of political action.

This century-long democratic movement in Europe was oriented towards collective and individual autonomy, which, almost since its reappearance, has been in conflict, coexistence and mutual contamination with the move towards unlimited rationalistic mastery and control of society and nature. The emergence and conflictual interaction of these two central significations constitute the particularity of Western Europe. To understand the institution of education as well as of the European gaze over the institutions of the 'other', I am exploring below the magma of the new and pre-existing significations and the institutions to which they gave rise. The analysis is inevitably general and condensed, because of the scope and limits of this study, but also because of the fluid and dynamic character of the social-historical field, the detailed investigation of which, in different parts of Europe, would require, of course, specialised accounts.

The most characteristic signification of this era, which re-emerged in Western Europe after Greek Antiquity, was that of *reason*. '. . . Enlightenment requires nothing but freedom . . . freedom to make public use of one's reason in all matters',[8] wrote Kant, expressing the major undertaking of his epoch. With *reason*, societies and individuals would be enabled to set into question tradition, superstitions, and the political status quo. However, although the European reason, like the Greek logos, stimulated questioning and critique, it turned largely into what Max Weber called *Zweckrationalität*, purposive or instrumental rationality.[9] The Greek logos, closely connected with politics, philosophy and epistēmē, questioned the dominant representations of society but also its own premises and limits. Self-limitation was at the heart of the Greek imaginary. The European reason is limitless, in its power and potential, as limitless is God, to whom already the Church Fathers but also modern European philosophers attributed rationality. For Leibnitz, for instance, God, who is perfect and has created the best of all possible worlds, thinks like a mathematician: 'When God calculates and exercises his thought the world is made' ('*Cum Deus calculat et cogitationem exercet, fit mundus*').[10] The European signification of reason drew on the Greek heritage of mathematical and scientific thinking, which were granted, via Christianity, omnipotence, which was to be pursued through technological applications. Moreover, the Greek logos embraced eros, as condition for communication, dialogue and learning. In Europe, the long suppression or subjection of love by religion did not go away with the fading of Christianity. Eros, not merely in its sexual aspect, but as elevation of human existence, had already appeared in the Renaissance, as Octavio Paz recounts, and in Modernity arts saw love as drive for subverting the traditional order and for personal autonomy.[11] However, eros continued to be profane under the industrial (and male-dominated) society, which celebrated, both in its liberal and Marxist versions, productivity and economic efficiency. In this regard, the European rationality is unerotic, as it positions humans in means/ends relations, guided by self-interest and gain maximisation. As David Hume famously expressed it: 'It is not contrary to reason to prefer the destruction of the whole world to the scratching of my finger'.[12] Castoriadis calls this rationality and its drive towards mastery 'pseudo-rationality' and 'pseudo-mastery': it is pseudo-rationality because its ultimate ends are arbitrary and it poses itself as an end, and it is pseudo-mastery because it is detached from any rationally debated ends, thus creating an illusion of omnipotence which can result in enhancing powerlessness instead of power. It is, therefore, more appropriate to speak of the rise of a *rationalistic* doctrine, by which capitalism has legitimised itself as a 'rational' institution, while posing upon societies the exceptionally irrational aim of increasing unlimitedly production and consumption.[13]

Crucial for this development were the scientific and technological advancements of the 17th century. The scientific thinking that arose in Ancient Greece, returned to Europe, fighting superstition and 'sacred truths' and promoting the principles of logical reasoning, supply of evidence, verification or falsification of propositions and quest for validity of scientific arguments. However, a new idea with regard to the purpose of science emerged in Europe, according to which scientific activity was not merely about understanding the natural world but about mastering it. Main advocates of this perception were René Descartes and Francis Bacon. Descartes, with his *Discourse on Method*, published in 1637, advocated the use of mathematics and scientific knowledge to create inventions and instruments that allow humans to dominate nature:

> . . . these scientific notions of mine – showed me that we can get knowledge that would be very useful in life, and that in place of the speculative philosophy taught in the schools we might find a practical philosophy through which knowing the power and the actions of fire, water, air, the stars, the heavens and all the other bodies in our environment as clearly as we know the various crafts of our artisans, we could (like artisans) put these bodies to use in all the appropriate ways, and thus make ourselves the masters and (as it were) owners of nature.[14]

In a similar way, Francis Bacon, a contemporary of Descartes, proposed that the role of scientific knowledge is to exercise command over nature but also over humans. Bacon is the philosopher to whom the dictum 'knowledge is power' is attributed, as he explicitly advocated the utilisation of knowledge for gain and power maximisation ('human knowledge and human power meet in one', as he wrote, and 'truth and utility are here the very same things').[15] His dream was a state that harnesses knowledge through which it governs but also dominates over other states. *The New Atlantis*, a short treatise that he published in 1627, depicts an essentially Platonic polity, ruled by philosopher-kings who send selected citizens to other countries to procure knowledge and inventions.[16] Scientific and technological advancements grant power to a country and justify domination over other peoples, as Bacon wrote in his other treatise, *Novum Organum*:

> If you compare how men live in the most civilised provinces of Europe with how they live in the wildest and most barbarous areas of the American continent, you will think the difference is big enough – the difference in the condition of the people in themselves as well as in what conveniences and comforts they have available to them – to justify the saying that 'man is a god to man'. And this difference doesn't come from the Europeans' having better soil, a better climate, or better physiques, but from the arts [i.e. techniques].[17]

The developments in the scientific field during the 17th and 18th centuries (e.g., the appearance of technological inventions and the founding of scientific associations) were in accord with the visions of Descartes and Bacon, but also driven by another crucial European signification that emerged at the same time, to become prominent from the 19th century on: progress. The imaginary signification of progress appeared as Western Europe broke with the dominance of religion and the representations of the medieval world and as scientific knowledge was pronounced to be the means by which humans can dominate nature. The perception that there is progress in the world did not exist prior to the 17th century. As it was pointed out in the previous chapter, for the Ancient Greeks, Being was chaos, an abyss or apeiron (infinite), but the apeiron did not enter human life – which was subject to institution. Moreover, the Greek society did not imagine itself as placed on some kind of continuum of progress in comparison to other societies. This does not mean that an idea of progress was completely absent in Greece. Progress for the Greeks was something limited only to material and technical forces.

In the medieval world, the idea of progress was unknown: life was a series of events arranged by heavenly interventions and revelations, and innovation was considered something profane. As Bury writes in his other classic book, *The Idea of Progress: An Inquiry into Its Origin and Growth*, for the Christian doctrine, as it was formulated by the Church Fathers, history moved towards securing the happiness of a small number of humans in another world, while there was no further development assumed on earthly life. But the decline of Christianity's power in Modernity did not entail the complete subsidence of its doctrines. Christian significations survived in the new world, but in a different form. Infinity, the main attribute of God, was now translated to progress, a limitless move towards a new land of promise, towards a world for which one needs to sacrifice oneself. As Bury, again, points out, with the idea of progress the centre of interest is transferred to the life of future generations, for which 'our duty is to resign ourselves cheerfully to sacrifice for the sake of unknown descendants'.[18]

Nevertheless, the idea of progress had its variants. According to Arendt, whereas in the 17th century, progress was understood as perpetual accumulation of knowledge, in the 18th century, it was conceived as the 'education of mankind' and from the 19th century took the meaning of an unlimited movement, a course of increasing what 'we have already into something better and higher'.[19] Similarly to Arendt, Castoriadis traces the idea of progress in the Enlightenment philosophy (e.g., Descartes, Leibniz and Condorcet), but he adds that it coincided with the ascendancy of the bourgeoisie and the creation and expansion of capitalist industrialisation.[20] The result of this fusion was the understanding of progress as an unlimited accumulation of knowledge and particularly as an unlimited increase of production and productive forces – an imaginary signification that was shared in the 20th century by both capitalism and communism. In the communist regimes of Europe, the main priorities were to increase economic productivity as well as the state's surveillance and military capacity. In capitalism, where the market economy became the epicentre of social life, the notion of progress would also include the pursuit of economic competitiveness and increasing levels of consumption.

In general terms, progress has been conceived as a move of societies towards expanding knowledge, wealth and domination over nature but also over humans. A society ought to be organised as a nation-state, pursuing economic 'growth' or 'development' by enhancing continuously its scientific and technological capacity – otherwise, it would be considered, 'non-modern', 'backward', 'underdeveloped' etc. Material and technological superiority was equated, from the 19th century, with the transition from barbarism to civilisation, a perception that has shaped the attitudes of the West towards other parts of the world (see the last section of this chapter). Since then, prosperity has been identified with high productivity. '*Tout pour l' industrie, tout par elle*' ('everything for growth, everything through growth') was the dictum of Henri de Saint-Simon, an early socialist theorist and reformer, and his followers. One of them was Auguste Comte, founder of sociology and scientific positivism, who advocated, in concurrence with the social imaginary of his century, the massive application of technological and productive forces for development.[21] Although in its literal sense, development means a course leading to maturation – therefore to the end of a process – in social terms, the concept was established to indicate an infinite process of increases.[22] The direction that societies should take, according to the ideas of progress and development, is essentially a move along a linear axis of descending or, more often, ascending numerical values, with no defined end.

If there is an institution that incarnates most characteristically this move of unlimited increase and more broadly of unlimited rationalistic mastery, this is capitalism. Capitalism and its associated institutions, activities and objects ('self-regulated market', private enterprise, factory, investment bank, stock exchange, machines etc.) are particular European formations that arose in the 18th century, and from the 19th century on, they started expanding, transforming societies. The prime feature of capitalism is its inherent tendency for total domination by infusing its criteria in production, consumption, economy, justice, the political system, education and essentially all spheres of social life. Capitalism drew this tendency from the Christian imaginary. Max Weber analysed, in *The Protestant Ethic and the Spirit of Capitalism*, how religious discipline (i.e. 'save rather than spend') was useful for capital accumulation and especially how the Calvinist perception, that engagement in economic activities is appreciated by God, gave the ethical ground for capitalist enterprise. Nevertheless, there is a more important 'loan' that capitalism has taken from Christianity that does not concern only Protestantism: the sense of omnipotence, and the predisposition to define all life. The Christian God is the creator of all life, an omnipotent, omniscient and omnipresent being. As the Nicene Creed, which is normative for all Christian denominations, starts, '*Credo in unum Deum, Patrem omnipotentem, factorem caeli et terrae, visibilium omnium et invisibilum*' ('We believe in one God, the Father Almighty, Maker of heaven and earth, and of all things visible and invisible'). Almightiness in Modernity was 'bequeathed' to Man, to techno-scientific progress and particularly to capitalism, which pursues unlimited expansion and domination, but with 'rational' means.

Rationality, understood as economic efficiency (i.e. cost reduction – profit increase), is another core feature of capitalism that distinguishes it from any other economic system. As we know from Marx, from Weber but also from Castoriadis, capitalism should not be identified with wealth accumulation – something that existed in all historical societies.[23] Capitalist economic activity has to do primarily with the rationalistic organisation and the recurrent transformation of the process and means production. The main goal in capitalism is profit maximisation, but this cannot be achieved without renewing the methods of production. It is the pursuit of 'forever *renewed* profit, by means of continuous, rational, capitalistic enterprise', as Weber writes, which is the necessary condition for its survival.[24] To organise the capitalist enterprise and restructure its process of production, the role of science, technology and mathematical calculation is crucial. In Weber's words:

> Now the peculiar modern Western form of capitalism has been, as first sight, strongly influenced by the development of technical possibilities. Its rationality is to-day essentially dependent on the calculability of the most important technical factors. But this means fundamentally that it is dependent on the peculiarities of modern science, especially the natural sciences based on mathematics and exact and rational experiment. On the other hand, the development of these sciences and of the technique resting upon them now receives important stimulation from these capitalistic interests in its practical economic application. It is true that the origin of Western science cannot be attributed to such interests . . . Neither was the origin of mathematics and mechanics determined by capitalistic interests. But the *technical* utilization of scientific knowledge, so important for the living conditions of the mass of people, was certainly encouraged by economic considerations, which were extremely favourable to it in the Occident.[25]

Indeed, capitalism utilises mathematics, science and technology to organise production, ensure cost-efficiency and profitability and uses rationality to justify its expansion. The drive of capitalism towards domination is not justified on the grounds of some dogma (e.g., God's will), myth or tradition but on a 'rational' basis: everything must be organised, and everybody must act, calculating costs and benefits, because this is 'rational'. All human activities are (re-)defined according to the principle of economic efficiency, while the very notion of prosperity is identified with profit maximisation.[26] This is why, although all societies in the past had an economy, only under capitalism did it become a main preoccupation, thus inducing the establishment of market societies, as Polanyi called them in *The Great Transformation*.[27] By market society, which, as he writes, was instituted by modern capitalism and the nation-state, he means that the market was placed at the epicentre of social activities, thus creating a profit-maximising mentality amongst people. Polanyi underlines that all societies dealt with their material conditions by establishing some sort of economy and some sort of market in which goods were produced and traded. But placing the pursuit of profit at the heart of social activities is something that we witness only from the 19th century, under the establishment of the so-called 'self-regulating market system' in Western Europe. This system did not presuppose the withdrawal of the state – a typical claim of the proponents of economic liberalism, untrue then as much as today. On the contrary, as Polanyi shows, state institutions and especially their violent apparatuses were crucial in opening up 'self-regulated markets'. The advent of market societies foregrounded the motive of gain as justification of human action in everyday life, for the first time ever, as Polanyi remarks, and the expansion of industrial production induced a 'catastrophic dislocation of the lives of the common people'.[28]

Indeed, the capitalist imaginary dislocated dramatically the time, the space and the lives of people from the 19th century on. Cities became the locus of industrialisation, something that was not possible earlier: the guilds, still existing in the European towns since the medieval times, resisted their treatment as cheap labour under the capitalist enterprise that, up until then, had developed mostly in the countryside.[29] However, in the 19th century, industrialisation took place in the cities, bringing about mass internal migration and transforming dramatically their topography. Industrialisation, as Bayly, in *The Birth of the Modern World, 1780–1914*, writes, did not mean merely building factories: 'It meant establishing systems of management and control of skilled labor, sourcing raw materials, and establishing transport and outlets'.[30] At the beginning of the 20th century, Henry Ford introduced in the USA such a system of management, his well-known assembly line, which was also eagerly adopted by the Soviets.[31]

But capitalist industrialisation was about much more than techniques of productivity control. It changed the city landscape, the family make-up, social relations and, through the economic inequality inherent in the new relations of production and the consequent residential segregation, it instituted two new social classes: the 'working class' and the 'middle class'. The bourgeoisie, the commercial, town-dwelling class that appeared in the later part of the 18th century, was established by the early 19th century following the formation of the new urban-industrial system. The new system gave rise to the 'upper' middle class (e.g., major merchants, bankers and industrialists) and the 'low' middle class (e.g., small traders, manufacturers and managers).[32] The working class was also created in the 19th century through massive industrial expansion (textile manufacturing, coal mining, metal extraction, railway construction, factories etc.). Eric Hobsbawm argues, referring to England, the first industrial nation, that it is only after 1880 that we can speak of the making of the two classes.[33] It was from that time on that industry expanded, but it was also after then that a 'working class culture' appeared (football, food, songs etc.), to the formation and reproduction of which the role of the education system was crucial.

The social inequality brought about by capitalism was accompanied by the political inequality embedded in the new polity that followed the collapse of absolute monarchies, namely 'representative' or 'liberal democracy'. Democracy 'returned' to Europe, this time with a universal scope, in comparison to that of Ancient Greece, but at the same time it was quite restricted, in terms of citizen involvement. In Athenian terms, but also following the classic Aristotelian distinction, the kind of political organisation introduced in European Modernity constituted an oligarchy rather than a democracy.

This seems to have been after all a rather explicit preference amongst statesmen and literati in post-revolutionary France. As Claude Mossé shows in a study on the impact of Antiquity on the French Revolution, the public debates during the Enlightenment with regard to the form of political organisation that should follow the collapse of absolutism sought to draw examples from Rome or Sparta rather than from Athens.[34] The most common argument against the Athenian example was premised on the fact that contemporary nation-states were comprised of large populations, and therefore, direct democracy was not plausible. Political philosophers, who admired the Athenian polis and believed that only full citizen participation is the true democracy, would also adopt this argument. As, for example, John Stuart Mill writes in his *Considerations on Representative Government*: 'But since all cannot, in a community exceeding a single small town, participate personally in any but some very minor portions of the public business, it follows that the ideal type of a perfect government must be representative'.[35] Interestingly, the argument for representative democracy, which became the legitimate political regime in Modernity, was not substantiated on a philosophical basis, but it was either justified on the ground of the large number of citizens of the modern nation-state, or openly rejected. Rousseau, for instance, was quite straightforward in his *Social Contract*:

> Sovereignty cannot be represented, for the same reason that it cannot be transferred; it consists essentially in the general will, and the will cannot be represented; it is itself or it is something else; there is no other possibility. The people's deputies are not its representatives, therefore, nor can they be, but are only its agents; they cannot make definitive decisions. Any law that the people in person has not ratified is void; it is not a law. The people of England believes itself to be free; it is quite wrong: it is free only during the elections of Members of Parliament. Once they are elected, the people is enslaved, it is nothing . . .[36]

Notwithstanding the lack of philosophical substantiation, political representation became the prevalent imaginary signification incarnated in the sort of 'democracy' adopted since Modernity and a host of associated institutions (citizen, government, parliament, elections, political party, left/centre/right-wings, civil rights, interest groups etc.). Representative democracy introduced a division between 'the government' and 'the people' – the latter to be protected from the potential arbitrary action of the former through a set of civil rights or freedoms (freedom of expression, freedom of press, freedom of association, right to assemble, right to fair trial, right to petition, right to vote etc.). Moreover, in Ancient Greece, logos and action were identified because citizens were able through *isigoria* and *isonomia* to both initiate and rule (*archein*).[37] 'Representative democracy' brings about a rift between speech and action, as those pursing an office can use rhetoric in order to get elected, and they are not immediately revocable when their promises are proven false. Moreover, professional politicians are the only ones entitled to initiate/rule, while citizens are confined to free expression and reactions against the rulers' actions. In addition, 'representative democracy' functions with political parties, which are bureaucratic and hierarchical organisations that cluster citizens under fixed ideological and political goals.

Under 'representative democracy', governing is proclaimed to be a matter of epistēmē (following Plato's view, rather than the practice of the Athenian polis), something that obscures or displaces political doxa and legitimises the absence of direct citizen involvement in decision making. In other words, governing becomes a matter of expertise, practised by professionals who have access to specialised knowledge, which supposedly is neutral and objective. Essentially, representative 'democracy' broke with *politics*, in the Greek sense, and instituted *policymaking*, a hierarchical and instrumental process of decisions taken by professional politicians, authorised experts and bureaucratic mechanisms. In fact, the Platonic idea that politics is a matter of expertise is found amongst different ideological currents and thinkers since the 17th century, who advocated that science should be the foundation of governance: for Bacon, Spencer but also Saint-Simon and Engels (who proclaimed Marxism as 'scientific socialism'), to mention some of the most known, scientific knowledge, and those who possess it, can guarantee the efficient running of the political system.

Related to the above characteristics of 'representative democracy' is the European signification of citizen, which differs from that of Greek Antiquity, too. For the Greeks, the individual is formed in/by the society and its political organisation. For Modern Europeans, the individual is self-sufficient, with inalienable rights, and establishes a 'social contract' (e.g., Hobbes, Locke, Hume and Rousseau) with other individuals and the state. Modernity, thus, creates a new perception of the individual, a *liberal* or *possessive individualism*, according to which a person is free by virtue of their sole proprietorship of themselves and the society is essentially nothing more than a set of market relations. Macpherson, in his study on possessive individualism, summarised its basic assumptions, whose roots he locates in the 17th century: a person is considered free when they are not dependent on the wills of others and the relations with them, except those relations that the individual enters voluntarily to serve their own interest; the individual is the proprietor of their own person and capacities, for which they owe nothing to society; society is a series of market relations; one's own freedom can be rightly limited only by rules that are necessary to ensure the same freedom for others; political society is a human contrivance aimed at protecting the individual's property and maintaining orderly relations of exchange.[38] Benjamin Constant, the renowned politician and author of post-revolutionary France, expressed this perception of freedom and citizenship quite clearly, contrasting it to that of Ancient Greece: 'The aim of the ancients was to share social power among the citizens of a single country; that's what they called "liberty". The aim of the moderns is to be secure in their private benefits; and "liberty" is their name for the guarantees accorded by institutions to these benefits'.[39]

This is therefore the role of democratic government in Modernity: to guarantee the private benefits of its citizens. Possessive individualism went hand in hand with the advent of capitalism and the emphasis that contemporary philosophy and especially the newly born political economy would place on self-interest. Already in the 18th century, Helvetius defined a nation as the assemblage of the personal interests of its citizens, an idea that Adam Smith fully shared in his influential *The Wealth of Nations*, published in 1776: 'It is not from the benevolence of the butcher the brewer, or the baker that we expect our dinner', Smith contended, 'but from their regard to their own interest. We address ourselves, not to their humanity, but to their self-love, and never talk to them of our own necessities, but of their advantages'.[40] Part of Enlightenment philosophy and the economic science of the time constructed, in line with the emergence of the market economy, the idea that humans are by definition egoistic and calculative and that social prosperity arises from competition between their private interests, thus displacing social significations deeply rooted in communal life for centuries, such as duty, solidarity, mutual help, gift, friendship or sacrifice.[41]

Overall, the European imaginary accentuated individuality but positioned it out of or against the society and its political organisation. This is related to an ontological notion which drew heavily on Ancient Greece but followed a different course. For the Greeks, individual autonomy was considered inextricably related to collective autonomy, and it was autonomy as long as there was consciousness of limits, in relation to society but also to nature – hence the Greek signification of *hubris*. The advent of the individual in European Modernity was a resurgence of the Protagorean axiom that 'Man is the measure of all things', as the foundation of humanism, but it gave it a different meaning. As humanism broke with Christianity, Man was placed as the hegemon of the world. Man, or more accurately European Man, was to dominate nature, through scientific and technological power, and regarded himself as the only complete being that was meant to bring progress to the 'incomplete' and the 'backward' peoples of the rest of the world.[42]

Progress was related to two other significations instituted during that period, in the framework of which 'representative democracy' was established: the nation and the state. Indeed, 'representative democracy' was associated with the rise of the state, an institution that in Modernity appropriated and was identified with the nation, which became prominent in the European social imaginary from the 19th century on. There is no point in 'explaining' the rise of the nation on the basis of a number of factors (e.g., language, common customs, shared ancestry etc.) as they existed before, but never led to the institution of nations as political entities. The nation, to use Anderson's term, is the 'imagined community' of European Modernity. Before then, a nation indicated the aggregate of the inhabitants of a country or province and homeland was considered one's own place of birth. As such the nation is inseparable from one's culture and identity. George Orwell expressed this eloquently, in his essay *The Lion and the Unicorn*, written during World War II:

> Are there really such things as nations? Are we not forty-six million individuals, all different? And the diversity of it, the chaos! . . . But talk to foreigners, read foreign books or newspapers, and you are brought back to the same thought. Yes, there is something distinctive and recognisable in English civilisation. It is a culture as individual as that of Spain. It is somehow

> bound up with solid breakfasts and gloomy Sundays, smoky towns and winding roads, green fields and red pillar-boxes. It has a flavour of its own. Moreover it is continuous, it stretches into the future and the past, there is something in it that persists, as in a living creature. What can the England of 1940 have in common with the England of 1840? But then, what have you in common with the child of five whose photograph your mother keeps on the mantelpiece? Nothing, except that you happen to be the same person.[43]

But Orwell was also well aware how national culture was abused to justify domination over other peoples. In another essay, *Notes on Nationalism*, written in the 1940s too, he defined nationalism as 'the habit of assuming that human beings can be classified like insects and that whole blocks of millions or tens of millions of people can be confidently labelled "good" or "bad"'. 'The nationalist', he wrote, 'not only does not disapprove of atrocities committed by his own side, but he has a remarkable capacity for not even hearing about them'.[44]

Nationalism should been seen in conjuction with the state, with which it was coupled since in 1648, when the Treaty of Westphalia introduced nation-state sovereignty and its political dominance over religious authority. Yet, as Hobsbawm writes, it was not before the 19th century that these institutions were actually identified. Taking as sources major European dictionaries of the time, Hobsbawm notes that the *Dictionary of the Royal Spanish Academy*, for example, uses the term 'nation' in the modern sense only after its 1884 edition. Until then, the *gobierno* (government) was not linked specifically with the *nación*. Similarly, the *New English Dictionary* of 1908 underlined that the concept of nation designating political unity was recent, and the established meaning until that time was that of an ethnic unit. As Hobsbawm underlines, '. . . in its modern and basically political sense the concept of nation is historically very young'.[45]

Thus, European Modernity established an identification of state, nation and the people which were connected, as Edgar Morin puts it, in family-like relations: the citizens are the children who are expected to love their 'mother', the nation, while the state as the authoritarian 'father' calls them to their duty and, occasionally, to weapons to protect the 'family'.[46] This bond was particularly promoted by nationalism, which, according to Ernest Gellner, poses that the nation is a natural and sacred way of classifying human beings and their activities and that it should be congruent with a political authority.[47] Or, as Guibernau and Rex put it:

> The nation-state was created as a political institution with a territorial base which utilized the doctrine of nationalism in its foundational moment to generate a common culture and a sense of belonging amongst its members. Most of these nation-states had a multinational character since they were established through dynastic unions and by conquest and annexations. Once the nation-state was created, however, whether out of one nation or as a multinational or imperial entity, it actively promoted the cultural homogenisation of its members and even appealed to a new common ethnicity which had to be constructed in a symbolic manner.[48]

True, nationalism was not to be merely expressed as one's adherence to one's language, customs and habits (Herder's or Rousseau's perception); in the hands of the state, it became the ethical ground to promote cultural homogenisation as well as political and economic domination, but also aggression against those of a different nation or ethnicity within or outside the nation-state's borders.[49]

Aggressive nationalism has been very often an expression of racism, an ideology that draws on the signification or 'race'. Racism is certainly not a European invention, but a characteristic of many societies across history. Racism, as devaluation, exclusion and ultimately destruction of the 'other', simply because of their genetic heritage, has been associated with various other significations and justified on different grounds. God's will has been a rather common ground for ethnic as well as for racist exclusion: from the Old Testament's designation of the Jews as a 'chosen people' down to persecution and expulsion of the same people by Catholics (e.g., Spain in the 15th century), the massive extermination of Christians (e.g., Armenians and Greeks) by Turkish Islam or the Hindu and Buddhist assaults against Muslims in contemporary India and Burma, racism has been galvanised by religion numerous times in history. The idea of progress (see last section), but also science, have also provided grounds to racism. 'Scientific racism', drawing on biology and physical anthropology, rationalised colonial expansion in the 19th and the Nazi atrocities in the 20th century. The same period, which saw the extended institution of nation-states, was accompanied by several cases of 'ethnic cleansing' around the world, i.e. racist assaults guided by the principle of nationality for the sake of establishing national homogeneity. In short, although the modern idea of nation indicates mainly the political classification of societies under the authority of the state, race, as a biological or phenotypical classification of humans, has often been associated with nation, to constitute the bellicose expression of 'national determination'.

The appropriation of the nation by the state has taken place since the 19th century, but the state and bureaucracy, its complementary institution, have their origins much earlier. As Creveld points out, what distinguishes the modern state is that it can be identified neither with the rulers nor with the ruled. It is not a person but acts as if it were a person. It is an invisible being with sovereignty and authority to exercise violence in a bordered territory. The state incarnates the Western European signification of rationalistic mastery and control, undertaken by its bureaucratic mechanism, which, in fact, gave rise to the Modern state. Bureaucracy was generated out of the absolute monarchy's attempt to consolidate political and military control, by means of an impersonal administrative mechanism, staffed by salaried officials and aimed at gathering information and collecting taxes to support the monarchy. Over time, bureaucracy acquired its own life, reducing the power of the ruler and spawning the state as an impersonal apparatus. Thus, the state emerged as an institution separate from the citizenry, setting up infrastructures for statistical information, transportation, police, army, prisons, printing of money, taxation, welfare provision and an education system. Crucial for the establishment and enhancement of state power was the harnessing of specialised knowledge, science and technology, something that was advocated also by main state theorists and philosophers of the time (e.g., Hobbes and Bacon). The state was to be not only a mechanism for imposing law and order but the very embodiment of rationality, which was to bring progress and prosperity to the nation.[50]

Hence, the pivotal role of bureaucracy in policymaking, implementation and control. Modern bureaucracies, according to Weber, are 'rational-legal' authorities characterised by hierarchy, impersonality, continuity and expertise. Their prime feature is expertise – their capacity to organise information and use specialised knowledge. As Weber writes: 'Bureaucratic administration means fundamentally the exercise of control on the basis of knowledge . . . Bureaucracy is superior in knowledge, including both technical knowledge and knowledge of the concrete fact within its own sphere of interest . . .'.[51] This superiority is also manifested by bureaucracy's capacity for precision, continuity, unambiguity, functionality and means-ends calculation. Weber's insightful analysis of bureaucracy underlined particularly its ability to provide instrumental efficiency and calculability of results, because it eliminates emotional engagement (such as love, hatred, sadness, or passion). Bureaucracy is successful when it is 'dehumanised', he noted, and he underlined the pivotal role of capitalist enterprise in fostering it:

> Though by no means alone, the capitalistic system has undeniably played a major role in the development of bureaucracy. Indeed, without it capitalistic production could not continue and any rational type of socialism would have simply to take it over and increase its importance. Its development, largely under capitalistic auspices, has created an urgent need for stable, strict, intensive, and calculable administration. It is this need which gives bureaucracy a crucial role in our society as the central element in any kind of large-scale administration. Only by reversion in every field – political, religious, economic, etc. – to small-scale organisation would it be possible to any considerable extend to escape its influence. On the one hand, capitalism in its modern states of development strongly tends to foster the development of bureaucracy, though both capitalism and bureaucracy have arisen from many different historical sources. Conversely, capitalism is the most rational economic basis for bureaucratic administration and enables it to develop in the most rational form, especially because, from a fiscal point of view, it supplies the necessary money resources.[52]

Similarly, Hannah Arendt pointed out that the emergence and dominance of bureaucracy in governance brought about a new complex system of authority where neither a single person, nor a few nor the many, can be held responsible and account for their practices. Modern bureaucracy is the 'rule by nobody', as Arendt notes, where there is no ruler to be identified, where individual components are powerless but whose power can be overwhelming.[53] Bureaucratic administration was adopted not only by the state and the capitalist enterprise but also by the Church, the army, the political parties, civil society associations and other institutions, including education.

These are, in broad terms, the institutions of European Modernity. The centuries-long domination of religion was fought against by the emergence of a historical movement that foregrounded collective and personal autonomy, drawing largely on Greek Antiquity. However, Christianity bequeathed some of its core significations to a novel and very different form of heteronomy, economic in its logic, but similarly intending the totality of life. The two antithetical central imaginary significations of rationalistic mastery and autonomy, clashing and mutually 'contaminated', gave rise to a web of new significations, incarnated in a host of interrelated institutions that marked European Modernity and the world thereafter. The most characteristic ones are progress, representative democracy, as a form of liberal oligarchy, the nation-state, bureaucracy and capitalism with its relentless quest for techno-scientific innovation, labour control and market expansion. One of these institutions is also the education system.

The institution of education

The institution of education in Modernity was associated to a significant extent with the project of collective and personal autonomy, exemplified in the questioning and critique of established representations and institutions, the pursuit of truth through rational communication and scientific knowledge, and democratic citizenship. The change took place mainly during the Enlightenment, when a great stream of freedom debouched throughout Europe, calling into question whatever until then was considered sacred and allowing people to examine and judge rationally, on the basis of lived experience rather than with divine or royal doctrines. The advent of the idea of democratic citizenship, as Rousseau wrote in his *Discourse on Political Economy*, 'dictates to each citizen the precepts of public reason, and teaches him to act according to the rules of his own judgment'.[54] No authority was to be immune to critique. 'Our age is the genuine age of criticism, to which everything must submit ', Kant wrote in 1781.[55]

The central postulate of the time was that knowledge liberates. The freeing of knowledge was expressed through scientific advancements, the appearance or further development of various disciplines (e.g., physics, biology, sociology, anthropology and psychology) and the dissemination of knowledge through specialised publications and encyclopaedias. The demands for free education for all were an integral part of the Enlightenment project and advocated by its ardent authors and leading actors, including Rousseau in the 18th century and Victor Hugo in the 19th century. Hugo, for example, in his fervent speeches before the International Peace Congress, named ignorance as a more serious problem than poverty and urged for the creation of schools, libraries, academic chairs, theatres and museums that enlighten the citizens, calling for an intellectual movement that, along with universal suffrage and peace, would bring about a prosperous, unified Europe.[56] It was the same period that N.F.S. Grundtvig and his followers founded Folk High Schools and independent primary schools across Denmark. Grundtvig, even though a priest himself, rejected the primacy of religion and initiated a major educational movement which explicitly focused on the study of the living world and the development of democratic citizenship, expressed by his concept of *folkelighed.*[57]

Yet, as Tzvetan Todorov remarks, the ideas of the Enlightenment were not originated in the 18th century, but in Antiquity, the High Middle Ages and the Renaissance.[58] This includes ideas on education, too. Renaissance humanists questioned the medieval status quo and recovered Greek and Latin knowledge, which they translated into vernaculars, organised in a pedagogic fashion (from grammatical introductions to the reproduction of whole treatises of Aristotle and Plato) and disseminated by means of the printing press. This was the time that the idea of the school appeared. In the Middle Ages, there were not really schools, apart from training establishments for scribes and priests, assembling indiscriminately children, young people and adults, regardless of their learning background. Religion grasped the opportunity to proselytise the population through schools when Catholicism lost its supremacy. The rise of Protestantism ended the Catholic (i.e. 'universal') authority of the Vatican and threw the two Christian Churches into fierce conflict, which, in the course of the following centuries, desacralised and weakened their power. In order for them to secure this power and promote their doctrines, they established teaching congregations and set up schools, colleges or 'academies'. On the Catholic side, the Jesuits created a highly centralised system by means of a hierarchical and bureaucratic structure and disciplinary surveillance stemming from *Ratio Studiorum*. Religious indoctrination and 'lettered piety' were the main pedagogic aims of both Catholic and Protestant establishments.

Nevertheless, the establishment of religious schools was accompanied by a process of secularisation, which was stimulated by a return to Antiquity and the quest for empirical knowledge. Jesuit schools taught works of Ancient Greek authors, albeit cut off from their context of cultural freedom, and appropriated them in a way that justified the Christian faith.[59] Secularisation was more pronounced in Protestant Europe. The 'dissenting academies' included in their curriculum scientific subjects, but also placed in the service of faith. Nevertheless, it was in these academies that the term 'research' (*ricercare* or *recherch*) was born, which meant 'to really find out'. Many of them, especially in England, taught Descartes, Newton, Locke and others and sought to implement the theories of the innovating educationists of the time.[60]

Such educationists appeared from the 17th century, but the wave of questioning of the established educational status quo across Europe started in the 16th century. For example, Francis Bacon in England criticised the Latin-based curriculum and the coercive teaching methods of his time and advocated the teaching of science and technology in the vernacular. In France, Rabelais rejected formalism and advocated immersion into Ancient knowledge, but also knowledge drawing on real life, taught in the vernacular. The *Poligrafi*, a group of essayists in Italy, opposed scholastic learning as responsible for keeping teachers and students cut off from their surrounding reality. Similarly, Montaigne, again in France, criticised, in his renowned *Essais*, the pedantry and pretention of scholastic learning as redundant erudition and, drawing on ancient authors, he proposed that education should cultivate judgement and moral character. In the early 17th century, the German reformer Wolfgang Ratke, following the Baconian theory of induction, advocated a teaching system that proceeded from the particular to the general and from the simple to the complex. Ratke, as well as August Francke, influenced heavily the reform movement in Germany, which led to the emergence of the *Realschule* intended to study the *realia*, substances and evidence from the external world, through the activities of the learner. Comenius, the renowned Czech educational reformer, distinguished stages of human growth and suggested that knowledge should be organised according to them. In his immensely influential *Didactica Magna*, published in 1657, he proposed a system of knowledge organisation progressing from simple to complex contents by means of graded schools and textbooks, which followed the language development of the child. He also wrote himself the first picture textbook for children. An advocate of universal education, Comenius argued that everything can be taught to everyone (what he called the 'pansophic principle'). Comenius, as well as Bacon, influenced strongly, amongst many others, the English educational reformers (e.g., Samuel Hartlib, John Milton, William Petty and John Dury) who advocated the tailoring of learning to stages of growth and particularly the adoption of scientific, technical and practical knowledge by educational establishments. The most influential English author of the time, though, was John Locke, who, with his treatises *Some Thoughts Concerning Education* and *Essay Concerning Human Understanding*, proposed that children are capable of reasoning and that upbringing and education should develop this capacity – instead of imposing on them the memorisation of prohibitions – and they should identify their aptitudes and nurture their interests.

This is the epoch in which the signification of childhood re-emerged in Europe for the first time after Classical Antiquity, and it was associated with the creation and generalisation of the school in Modernity. Already in the 17th century, we have the first laws for compulsory schooling in Protestant Germany, in the Scandinavian kingdoms of Denmark and Sweden and the Netherlands provinces, which, however, remained largely on paper until the 18th century, when compulsory education was established in Prussia and, during the 19th century, across Europe. The signification of childhood emerged in the 17th century, although its first signs appeared in the 13th century. Until the 13th century, as Philippe Aries tells us in his classic study on the history of childhood, there were no children, but simply human beings of a small size.[61] This does not mean that people did not love and look after their children, but that there was no sense of child particularity. There was no distinction, for example, between games or ways of dressing for adults and for children. When the child was able to somehow take care of him/herself (around the seventh year), he/she was included in the world of adults. Aries, who surveyed a number of paintings created during the Middle Ages and the Renaissance, observed that it was the first time during the 13th century that one could see cute and smiling infants portrayed in intimate moments with their parents. Later, in the 15th century, paintings also depicted nude infants, with a connoted reference to Ancient Greek Eros or guardian angels; in the 16th century, portraits with dead children appeared; and in the 17th century, paintings showed children alone, without their parents. From the 16th century, books were published with stories tailored to children, conceived now as innocent and sensitive beings subject to protection and guidance. The denial of childhood until, essentially, the 17th century is usually explained by reference to the high rates of child mortality of the time, namely that people would not establish special emotional bonds with their children since they were likely to die. But, as Aries observes, childhood started to be appreciated when the demographic conditions were still very negative for children.[62] It appears then, in spite of the biological conditions, that childhood re-emerged, after Antiquity, as part of the central imaginary signification of autonomy, which foregrounded the nature/nurture distinction and the consequent attention to the particular developmental traits of infancy and childhood.

Hence the focus of educational critique from the 18th century – the Age of Enlightenment – on children and their socialisation and learning. It was the century in which Western societies recognised increasingly that they are instituted by themselves. The Americans underlined this in their Declaration of Independence: 'Governments are instituted among Men, deriving their just powers from the consent of the governed . . .'.[63] In this context, education acquired growing importance. Contemporary philosophy was in line with this development, drawing heavily on Antiquity, as, for instance, German Idealism (e.g., Kant, Fichte, Humboldt and Schelling). Kant stressed particularly the idea of autonomy, which he identified with freedom ('What else can the freedom of the will be but autonomy, that is, the property of the will to be a law to itself?')[64] and argued for the use of the Socratic method as a condition for the cultivation of reason by the learners. Yet, the breakthrough in the educational thinking of the time came from Rousseau and his treatise *Emile*, published in 1762. Rousseau posited that human beings are born free, but social institutions suppress them, and thus, politics should aim to bring them back to their natural freedom and equality. He called on the recognition of childhood as a special stage of human development, which is subject to cultivation, and he associated education with freedom and the democratic rule. Rousseau proposed the abolition of all existing educational establishments and the creation of a single education system affordable by all or free of charge.[65] Pestalozzi, the great Swiss pedagogue and reformer, applied Rousseau's ideas, emphasising the cultivation of imagination in learning and what he called *Anschauung*, meaning learning through sense perception, observation, intuition and awareness in the study of the external world. Herbart, the German philosopher and psychologist, and amongst those influenced by Pestalozzi, devised a sequence-based system of instruction aimed at bringing the scientific method of inductive inquiry into the classroom. And Froebel, a student of Pestalozzi and a creator of the concept of *kindergarten*, argued, as the above educationists, for the individuality of children as well as of free play as a connection between the child and their natural and material environment.[66]

Following this tradition, the 20th century witnessed a major movement of 'progressive education', with prominent educationists such as Maria Montessori, who, following the legacy of Rousseau and Froebel, introduced a child-centred pedagogy, which tailored the material surroundings of the child to their stage of growth in order to stimulate learning; and John Dewey, who emphasized autonomous learning within a democratic school community through a teaching methodology that follows a scientific process of discovery. The movement expanded across Europe and North America with the establishment of schools by renowned reformers (e.g., by Rudolf Steiner and Émile Jaques-Dalcroze in Germany, Franz Cizek in Austria and Alexander Neil in England) and by many pedagogues and community initiatives that created a variety of school-types (e.g., 'free' or 'independent' schools) and methods (e.g., the 'project method' or the 'Dalton Plan') with the main aim of socialising pupils and students in self-reliant and cooperative learning.

Apart from the historical wave of critique and reform in the school system, the imaginary signification of collective and personally autonomy was manifested also in the establishment of universities through the rise of academic autonomy. As the previous chapter pointed out, the idea of academic autonomy was generated in Ancient Athens, when Plato established his Academy. Plato transferred the democratic ethos of the polis in an institution destined to produce 'wise men' – the only ones, according to his conviction, entitled to have a doxa on public matters. The second landmark of the emergence of academic autonomy coincides with the founding of the first universities in the context of the European town which rose in the High Middle Ages. The medieval town allowed the first *studia generale* to be founded as *universitas*, that is, guilds or corporations of scholars and students, according to the legal norm applied to other professions, such as craftsmen and merchants. A corporation (deriving from *corpus*, meaning a body) was a community or an association (a 'body of people') which had an existence independent from its individual members and which was legally recognised as a person – a juristic person. In this sense, the *universitates* were legally communities engaged in learning, which, notwithstanding the surveillance exerted on them by the local bishops or their dependence for status on the Papacy, they could elect their authorities (i.e. a rector), define their pedagogic and examination procedures, issue formal degrees, exercise, within limits, judicial authority and even go on strike – a form of action invented, not by worker movements, as Jacques Le Goff tells us, but by scholars.[67]

The legal status of the first European universities made a crucial difference from similar institutions in other parts of the world. The Chinese *Guozijian*, for example, belonged to the imperial education system, while the *Shuyuan* were initially private establishments and later (during the 13th century) were placed under state control to function as preparatory schools for the imperial examinations.[68] Moreover, in the Islamic world, there was no legal framework that would recognise associations as juristic persons. The legal status of the madrasas was, according to the Islamic Law, that of a religious endowment (*waqf*). The madrasa, as George Makdisi, the renowned scholar in Islamic Studies, points out, designated a building, unlike the university which designated a community. His comparative study of the two institutions concludes that 'the university, as a form of social organisation, was peculiar to medieval Europe' and that 'in the middle ages, outside of Europe, there was nothing anything quite like it anywhere'.[69]

The next time in European history that academic autonomy was foregrounded, and in fact regarded as an integral feature of the university, was at the end of the 18th and the beginning of the 19th centuries. It is the epoch in which the university became a matter of philosophical consideration by the major adherents of German Idealism as well as of political reform, with the establishment of the University of Berlin in 1810. The common view amongst the prominent German philosophers was that the university is a community of teachers and learners devoted to free thinking, philosophical enquiry and scientific discovery. A main advocate of this idea was Wilhelm von Humboldt, the initiator of the University of Berlin. Humboldt argued categorically that any interference by the state would be deleterious for the university as well as for the education system at large – an issue that he discussed extensively in his treatise *The Limits of State Action.*[70] He defined as the purpose of education the creation of self-determined personalities, individuals who draw on their own energy – a unique virtue of mankind. In order to develop themselves, individuals should be able to act in freedom and through voluntary social relations. The state's activity must be confined because it tends to mollify individual energy and generate uniformity. In the university, the content of knowledge, the scientific inquiry and the teaching should be matters defined freely by the academic community. Only in this way would teachers and students realise themselves as thinking individuals, with independent judgement and, as an extension of this, as true citizens. The state should exercise a 'negative' role: it should make available to the university the resources necessary for its existence and the employment of its staff and keep its hands off its educational and scientific work. Humboldt was quite emphatic on this in a memorandum that he wrote when the University of Berlin was being founded, in which one can also notice his concern that state material support may be accompanied by bureaucratic functions which downgrade academic work:

> The state must always remain conscious of the fact that it never has and in principle never can, by its own action, bring about the fruitfulness of intellectual activity. It must indeed be aware that it can only have a prejudicial influence if it intervenes. The state must understand that intellectual work will go on infinitely better if it does not intrude. The state's legitimate sphere of action must be adapted to the following circumstances: in view of the fact that in the real world an organisational framework and resources are needed for any widely practiced activity, the state must supply the organisational framework and the resources necessary for the practice of science and scholarship. The manner in which the state provides the organisational framework and resources can be damaging to the essence of science and scholarship; the very fact that it provides such organisational structures and

resources, which are quite alien to the nature of the activity which they are to serve, can result in the degradation to a basely material level of what should be intellectual and lofty.[71]

Through the establishment of the University of Berlin, Humboldt and the other reformers promoted a perception of the university as a self-governing academic body which is characterised by *Lernfreiheit* and *Lehrfreiheit*. As Metzger put it, in his study of the German contribution to academic freedom in the USA, 'by Lernfreiheit they meant the absence of administrative restraints in the learning situation', and Lehrfreiheit 'denoted the paucity of administrative rules in the teaching situation: the absence of prescribed syllabus, the opportunity to lecture on any subject that engaged the teacher's interest'.[72]

The German reforms sought to consolidate academic autonomy as a European inheritance but also as a sine qua non characteristic of the European university from then on, as well as of any institution of higher education that claimed the title of a university. The Humboldtian proposal, part of the movement of German Idealism and, more broadly, of the European Enlightenment, met these traditions and instituted academic autonomy as an integral feature of the university, mainly, though, as an *entwurf*, i.e. a project – part of the overall project of collective and personal autonomy that characterised European Modernity – pursued from then on along with the institution of the university. The project of academic autonomy was to be manifested in three dimensions: the creation of knowledge, the imparting of knowledge, and governance. Knowledge creation should be characterised by the autonomous research endeavours of the scholar. Neither the state nor any other force is to intervene and define the content of knowledge or the criteria of its creation. Scientific knowledge is not to serve any external interests or even the specialised requirements of particular professions. Scholars should pursue the research they are interested in beyond any constraints except their commitment to truth. Secondly, the university's pedagogy indicates that knowledge is not to be merely transmitted by the master and be ingested by the student; the student should be discovering knowledge by developing their ability to think, to reason and to question, exactly as the master is expected to be doing in their own research. The teacher, therefore, should want the student's autonomy. Fichte, in his writings and lectures, was particularly concerned with this, and, in fact, this was what he meant by 'academic freedom': 'a liberty [of the student] to do all that is right and becoming by their own free determination' and 'leaving him to his own judgment as to what is becoming, seemly, and appropriate, and to his own superintendence of himself'.[73] Thirdly, academic autonomy is manifested as politics, not, of course, in the vulgar sense of intrigues that the term has acquired in today's university life, but as the explicit activity of the academic community to reflect and deliberate on the purpose, the contents and the pedagogic mode of learning in the university and to govern their institution in accordance with their decisions. Crucial for the rise of politics in the university was the development of students' movements, the engagement in which is facilitated by the relatively independent phase of student life. The political dimension of the university's operation has to been seen, in the course of the 19th and 20th centuries, in the establishment of a set of decision-making institutions such as elected authorities (i.e. of rectors, deans and department heads), general assemblies of staff and students, voting procedures and academic unions. At a deeper level, through these three dimensions, the project of academic autonomy has been seeking to establish the university as a space of eros and logos, consisting the foundation of genuine learning in Greek Antiquity: eros, as passion to inquire, to discover, to learn and to know the truth, and as emotional energy invested in or, more precisely, cathected by, the learner, on the teacher, the knowledge or the very investigative activity; and logos, as speech and reason, as rational argumentation and critique, which characterises scientific research, philosophical inquiry but also political activity based on open deliberation. In this way, the university becomes a space constituted by freely thinking, studying and speaking individuals.

However, as no institution can exist outside of its social-historical context, the university could not operate in *freiheit und einsamkeit*, as a free community of scholars in isolation, as Humboldt, Fichte and the other reformers wished for[74] – unless there was a form of political organisation in place which allowed for it, as the Athenian polis did with Plato's Academy. European Modernity, though, was the era of the state. Humboldt was aware of this when he insisted that the state should stay away from the university's affairs and that it should be the nation which should undertake education.[75] But in Modernity, the nation was appropriated by and identified with the state, and thus, the nation-state became the supreme form of political organisation which took over the main social institutions, including education. 'A new phenomenon! The state as the guiding star of education!' young Nietzsche exclaimed in his public lectures on the *Future of Our Educational Institutions* in 1872 in Basel.[76] In referring to the university, Nietzsche said graphically that the state now stood behind professors and students with an overseer's mien, reminding them that it is the ultimate purpose of the educational process. And in a similarly graphic phrase, that could express the entire historical course of the establishment of state education systems, both in his century and the following, he noted:

> . . . a state strives here and there, for the sake of its own existence, after the highest possible expansion of education because it always still knows itself strong enough to be able to clamp under its yoke even the strongest emancipation belonging to education, and it has been found reliable whenever the most expanded education comes to good for its officials or its armies, finally always only for it itself – for the state – in rivalry with other states.[77]

Indeed, education from the 19th century onwards was secularised, expanded and became a crucial mechanism for the construction of the nation-state, the consolidation of its power and its competition in the international arena. The university was to provide the industrial economy with technical-scientific knowledge and to train administrative, professional and specialist elites whose qualifications were certified by the state. The state would control universities' resources, turn scholars to dependent wage-earners, establish hierarchies, regulate access in accordance to the new social class structure and draw the expertise necessary to grant scientific legitimisation to official policymaking. The university, in short, became, from the 19th century on, part of the education system and the state bureaucracy and drawn into the process of capitalist development.

The class structure to which capitalism gave rise was reflected in the organisation of the entire education system. As James Bowen writes, the main question for the dominant classes across Europe in the 19th century was 'how little could be conceded to the working classes to keep them assuaged, yet quiescent in the condition of servitude to which providence had properly ordained them'.[78] This meant limited education provision for the masses, focused on basic and technical skills. 'Reading, writing, and reckoning, that is all that they should be taught; as for the rest, it is superfluous', Adolphe Thiers proclaimed (the French historian, left-wing politician and head of state who cracked down on the Paris Commune).[79]

The basic curriculum was to be delivered in warehouse-like schools, regulated by the organisational principles of industry, directly applied to schools already from the end of the 18th century, and for several decades by means of the 'monitorial method', which was devised by Andrew Bell and developed further by Joseph Lancaster. Bell called his method an 'intellectual and moral engine', and he paralleled it with a 'steam engine, or spinning machinery, [as] it diminishes labour and multiplies work, but in a degree which does not admit of the same limits, and scarcely of the same calculations as they do'.[80] The monitorial or Lancasterian system satisfied the principle of 'utility', praised by liberal philosophers of the time, and of industrial efficiency. In the words of the British social reformer Sir Thomas Bernard, 'the principle in schools and manufactories is the same . . . [it] is the division of labour applied to education'.[81] The Lancasterian school was spread around Europe and around the world for several decades as part of state education systems but also promoted by religious missionaries, military officials and civil society agencies.

Later on, education became mainly an affair of the state, especially of its bureaucracy. In the 19th and 20th centuries, the increased potential of bureaucracy to mobilise information and knowledge recourses enhanced its role and placed it practically at the core of educational governance: ministries, directorates, inspectorates, governmental and quasi-governmental bodies, statistical services and evaluation agencies were and are the main mechanisms that regulate education systems. Bureaucracy, along with the techno-scientific and the capitalist significations, also seized school pedagogy by means of textbooks, mechanical teaching methods, formalised objective-based lessons, grading, discipline and performance controls, reminiscent of the industry assembly line. For example, Herbart's proposal to introduce inductive inquiry in the classroom was turned into the so-called 'Herbartianism' – a process of routinised stages (i.e. 'preparation', 'presentation', 'association', 'generalisation' and 'application') intended to discipline the mind so that it follows taken-for-granted knowledge and masters the natural environment. As the American Herbartian educator Charles McMurry described this purpose: 'All the forces and bounties of nature are to be made serviceable to us, and it can only be done by understanding her facts and laws. The road to mastery leads through patient observation, experiment and study'.[82] Herbartianism dominated classrooms and textbook writing in Europe and the USA for several decades.

All this regulatory apparatus over the school removed from the term the positive meaning (leisure or learning time) that had in Antiquity. 'Schooling' or to be 'schooled' acquired the connotation of having children warehoused, classified according to age and performance and required to learn knowledge defined by the state and organised and examined according to bureaucratic rules.

But the state in Modernity was instituted as the managing authority of the nation, a crucial signification that was incarnated in education, perhaps more than in any other institution. The school undertook the role of inscribing 'national consciousness', turning, as Bernstein put it, a common biology into a cultural specific in a way that it came to have the force of a unique biology.[83] The national imaginary has been reproduced by state education systems through curricula, rituals, celebrations, symbols and teaching practices – often, during the 20th century, associated with racism and fascism.

But while nationalism was to establish a sense of homogeneity, capitalism was to bring about differentiation. Social class segregation and the control of social mobility was to be secured by the establishment of dual systems, namely technical/professional and academic paths, following the primary school. The ideological basis of this was expressed in quite a clear-cut way by Comte Destutt de Tracy, aristocrat and philosopher, creator of the term 'ideology', in his *Observations sur le système actuel d'instruction publique*: 'in every civilised society there are necessarily two classes, one which works with its hands . . . the other with its mind . . . the first is the working class; the second is that of the intellectuals'.[84] The academic paths (e.g., grammar schools, gymnasia or lycées and university studies), and their predominately classical curricula were to be accessed by the economic elites. With the Enlightenment, and under the influence of German Idealism, Antiquity authors became an essential part of a *liberal education, culture générale* or *Bildung* but appropriated by and identified with elite formation. As Bowen again writes, 'the fundamental problem of the bourgeoisie, throughout Europe, was their inability to accept working people as equally deserving of access to the possibilities of good life'[85] – and, consequently, of good education.

In fact, the overall exclusion pattern in education, established by the ruling classes, was associated with the emergence of both central significations of autonomy and rationalistic mastery and control. The dominant elites excluded as much and as long as possible large parts of the population (e.g., poor, working classes, minorities and women) from the emancipatory potential embedded in education as well as in politics. Exclusion from politics was effected, besides the very institution of 'representative democracy', which prevented citizens from taking part in political governance, by selective exemptions from the exercise of civil rights, such as suffrage, under a set of discrimination categories (e.g., income, gender and origin). Exclusion from education was to take place primarily through barring the access of the mass population to selected educational types, levels and contents and through the overemphasis on skills-oriented curricula. In other words, exclusion from politics and education was (and is) inhibition from accessing personal autonomy, but also from accessing resources related to social control, as the education system was to certify the 'merit' of those taking positions of authority and secure class reproduction. The latter function of the education system was extensively analysed throughout the 20th century by sociology of education, which, however, paid little attention to the possibilities for autonomy inherent in the European educational legacy as well as to the fact that political activity can break established patterns of social reproduction – as it actually has since the 1960s (see the next chapter).

In summary, education systems in Europe were instituted under the conflict and symbiosis between the project of collective and personal autonomy with, initially, the medieval status quo and centuries-long religious heteronomy, and later on with the rise of the state and capitalist economy, which set out to industrialise knowledge and learning for the masses and introduce novel forms of social control. Similarly, the university was instituted in Modernity as a bureaucratic mechanism destined to serve social and economic reproduction, state building and policymaking through specialised knowledge. Nevertheless, autonomy in education, manifested as self-governance, free thinking, rational communication, research that intends the truth and critical learning, is deeply rooted in the social imaginary of Modernity. It is also rooted in its comparative gaze towards other societies.

European comparative gaze and educational 'lending' and 'borrowing'

The comparative gaze of a society is also an institution itself, as it incarnates social imaginary significations. The Western European comparative gaze of the Modern Era can be traced in a variety of cultural forms, such as traveller tales, philosophical treatises and novels, as well as in the emergence of specialised cross-cultural and comparative studies in universities – including the knowledge branch of comparative education.

As in Ancient Greece, the rise of the central imaginary signification of autonomy in Europe was associated with the awareness that 'our' idea of the world should not be identified with the natural order of things, nor should it be expected that other societies share this idea. Western Europe recreated the significations of universality of the human condition as well as of the diversity and uniqueness of cultures, breaking with the cognitive closure that characterised the Middle Ages. This awareness arose basically in the Enlightenment Age, which followed the Renaissance and the 'Age of Discovery' – the epoch of explorations and conquests of distant lands by the Europeans. Until then, other peoples and their cultures were still considered inferior and thus subject to derogatory and cruel treatment.

Bartolomé de las Casas, a 16th-century historian and Dominican friar, was one of the first known authors who criticised openly the offensive stance of the Europeans to other civilisations. In his *A Short Account of the Destruction of the Indies*, written in 1542, he castigated the atrocities that indigenous peoples endured in the hands of the Spanish *conquistadores* – something that led to the prohibition of the enslavement of the Indians by the Spanish. Bartolomé de las Casas had first to convince the Catholic Church that the Indians were actually human beings with souls, something that the Church denied because Jesus Christ had never travelled to South America.[86] To hear the same criticism about the Africans, we have to wait for two more centuries, when Montesquieu mocked the Catholic Church for identifying adherence to Christianity with the very quality of being human: 'It is hardly to be believed that God, who is a wise Being, should place a soul, especially a good soul, in such a black ugly body . . . It is impossible for us to suppose these creatures to be men . . .'.[87] Nevertheless, it was remarkable for the time that las Casas condemned the perception by which the Church justified the conquerors' assaults against the Indians, but also its claim that the Indians were barbarians because their customs included human sacrifices. Las Casas counter-argued that savage behaviour can be found in all parts of the world, as well as in the acts of the Spanish invaders:

> The Spaniards penetrated, certainly with great audacity, this new part of the world, of which they had never heard in previous centuries, and in which, against the will of their sovereign, they committed monstrous and extraordinary crimes. They killed thousands of men, burned their villages, took their cattle, destroyed their cities, and committed abominable crimes with not demonstrable or specific cause, and with monstrous cruelty against these poor people. Can such sanguinary, rapacious, cruel and seditious men be truly said to know God, to whose worship they exhort the Indians?[88]

The main argument in Las Casas's writings about the cruelties of his compatriots against the Amerindians was that the Europeans took for granted their own beliefs and representations and viewed people around the world and their cultures as non-human or barbaric, thus justifying their own barbarism. We find this open critique of the European worldview, a few decades later, by Michel de Montaigne, a highly influential author in the Renaissance, in his collection of *Essays* published in 1580. The *Essais* were short treatments of a great variety of topics, including education and childhood, whose author drew on philosophy and literature (but, remarkably enough for that era, not on religion), and especially on his own judgement. In one of his essays, titled 'Of Cannibals', Montaigne discusses the view of the Europeans that other civilisations are barbaric. He questions openly this view by pointing to the fact that societies tend to take their own significations for granted and characterise the peoples that don't share them as barbarians:

> . . .I find that there is nothing barbarous and savage in this nation, by anything that I can gather, excepting, that every one gives the title of barbarism

> to everything that is not in use in his own country. As, indeed, we have no other level of truth and reason than the example and idea of the opinions and customs of the place wherein we live: there is always the perfect religion, there the perfect government, there the most exact and accomplished usage of all things.[89]

Montaigne, in other words, underlined the cognitive and representational closure that characterised the European societies of his time, which considered their institutions as perfect and all the rest as barbaric. This did not mean that he overlooked the cruel habits and acts that humans around the world inflicted upon others or they were subjected to, but he invited his European readers to also see their own:

> I am not sorry that we should here take notice of the barbarous horror of so cruel an action, but that, seeing so clearly into their faults, we should be so blind to our own . . . We may then call these people barbarous, in respect to the rules of reason: but not in respect to ourselves, who in all sorts of barbarity exceed them.[90]

Montaigne's essays were one of the early examples of cultural self-reflectiveness in European literature. It is mainly during the 18th century that we see the development of a comparative gaze towards other cultures, which serves as a mirror in which European societies could see themselves. One of the most prominent examples of this is Montesquieu's epistolary novel *Persian Letters* (*Lettres persanes*), published in 1721. The novel recounts the views of two Persian noblemen who are visiting France. During their stay in Paris, they exchange letters with their friends back in Persia commenting on what they see – from political institutions to social life in general. Through this novel, Montesquieu manages not only to illustrate how the French see the 'others' but also how the 'others' see the French society and its institutions, thus inviting the reader to engage in self-reflecting considerations, in a wonderful satirical way.

For example, Rica, one of the two travellers, writes in one of his letters about the attention that his presence attracted wherever he went in Paris, something that forced him to change his Persian look and wear European clothes. However, if someone happened to know that he was Persian and informed the company, people around him would murmur: 'Oh! ah! A Persian, is he? Most amazing! However can anybody be a Persian?'[91] In another letter, Usbek, the second Persian traveller, is impressed by the intense debates on the significance of Ancient Greek poetry (i.e. Homer) between its admirers and its opponents as well as the debates between theologians in Latin, which he finds barbaric:

> But that which shocks me most in these geniuses, is, that they are quite useless to their country, and amuse their talents with puerilities. For example, when I arrived at Paris I found them warm to dispute over the most trifling matter imaginable. It was all about an old Greek poet, whose birthplace and

> time of dying no one has known for two thousand years. Both sides agreed that he was a most excellent poet: it was only a question of the degree of merit to be ascribed to him. Each wished to fix his rank; but among those apportioners of praise, some carried more weight than others . . .
>
> Those of whom I have told you dispute in the vulgar tongue; and must be distinguished from another set of disputants, who employ a barbarous language, which seems to increase the fury and the obstinacy of the combatants. There are places where these people are to be seen struggling as in a battle, dismal and confused; they are fed upon subtleties, they live upon obscure arguments and false inferences. This profession, although one would think its followers would die of hunger, must pay in some way. A whole nation, driven from their own country, has been seen to cross the sea and establish itself in France, carrying with it no other means of providing for the necessities of life, than a notable talent for debate. Farewell.[92]

Through *Persian Letters*, arguably the first great popular work of the Enlightenment, Montesquieu makes a brilliant critique of monarchy, Catholicism and in general the French culture of his time and simultaneously gives a remarkable example of cultural relativity and reflection.

A similarly notable example of reflection through cultural comparison we find in the same period in England, in another satirical novel, which became even a more popular reading, as it was read widely by adults and children, right after it was published in 1726. It was *Gulliver's Travels*, by Jonathan Swift, who called on his compatriots, through the adventures of his main character, Gulliver, to reflect through his fictional descriptions of other cultures on their own.

Swift tells his fellow countrymen that, when it comes to might, 'nothing is great or little otherwise by comparison':[93] Gulliver is a giant over the Lilliputians, but he is tiny before the Brobdingnagians, who treat him like a pet. He also shows them the relativity and diversity of social institutions and the very fact that what looks strange or horrible to 'us' can be natural to 'them' and vice versa. Gulliver's physical features, smells and needs made him look repulsive to the Lilliputians, just like the gigantic Brobdingnagians seemed repulsive to him. The Lilliputians write neither like the Europeans (left to right), nor like the Arabs (right to left) nor like the Chinese (downwards), but aslant (from one corner to the other).[94] For the Houyhnhnms, a lie is impossible, and thus, they do not have a word for it.

What is most remarkable in Swift's novel is the juxtaposition of the institutions of those fantastic lands with the ones existing in his home country, a method that allows him to make his readers see their institutions afresh and critically. Political authority can look so petty (e.g., the Lilliputian kingdom in the eyes of the 'giant' Gulliver); it can be abusive and humiliating (e.g., a Luggnaggian king wants his subjects to lick the floor crawling before him) or paranoid (e.g., the Governor of Glubbdubdrib seeks to bring back the dead in order to . . . govern them); it can be based on social class division, manipulation of resources and 'science of government', intended to keep the population under control (e.g., Laputa and Balnibarbi); it can rely on reason and exercised by all those who are merited (e.g., in Houyhnhnmland); or it can even be missing altogether amongst our species (e.g., the savage and repulsive Yahoos/humans have no organised society).

Through Gulliver's discussions and observations in the distant lands to which he travels, Swift criticises the European and particularly the English institutions and status quo, such as academic knowledge and its credulous adoption, the dishonesty in the justice system, the mistreating practices of doctors, the political intrigues and secrets of the state against its own people, the preoccupation of those in power to enhancing the means of violence and the various monstrosities committed for the sake of domination. The Brobdingnagian king was astonished listening to Gulliver describing the violent history of the English and 'struck with horror' when Gulliver proposed to teach him how to make and use gunpowder to keep the kingdom's population fearful and controlled.[95] The king, who was appalled by Gulliver's descriptions and propositions, burst by saying that the English must be the 'most pernicious race of little odious vermin that nature ever suffered to crawl upon the surface of the earth'.[96] It is hard to imagine an author addressing with such a phrase his own people outside of the emerging self-critical spirit of Western Europe.

Jonathan Swift drew also critical parallels, through Gulliver's descriptions, between the educational institutions of his travel destinations and those at home, highlighting the relativity of the aims that education serves in different societies. Education in Lilliput, imparts the principles of honour, justice, courage and clemency, but it is provided unequally: the children of cottagers and labourers do not attend a school, and girls are educated less than boys. In Houyhnhnmland, however, with the exception of the learning of some household tasks, it was considered monstrous to give females a different education from the males. Both genders were taught cleanliness, industry, exercise and temperance.

Houyhnhnmland is the society that Gulliver admired most. Swift tells thereby his compatriots, challenging the emerging imaginary of his time, that a society can be advanced without possessing technological and military might. Rather than seeing Houyhnhnmland's deficiency in means of violence as an opportunity to conquer it, the author proposes that the Europeans should be taught by the Houyhnhnms all those values that Europe lacks:

> The Houyhnhnms indeed appear not to be so well prepared for war, a science to which they are perfect strangers, and especially against missive weapons. However, supposing myself to be a minister of state, I could never give my advice for invading them. Their prudence, unanimity, unacquaintedness with fear, and their love of their country, would amply supply all defects in the military art . . . But, instead of proposals for conquering that magnanimous nation, I rather wish they were in a capacity, or disposition, to send a sufficient number of their inhabitants for civilizing Europe, by teaching us the first principles of honour, justice, truth, temperance, public spirit, fortitude, chastity, friendship, benevolence, and fidelity.[97]

The above are distinctive examples of the self-reflective function of comparison that appeared in the European literature of the time, but not the only ones. One could also mention Horace Walpole, an art historian and politician from England, who followed Montesquieu's literary device by publishing in 1757 a similar satirical work. It was a pamphlet recounting a Chinese philosopher who supposedly visited London and wrote a letter to a friend of his back in Peking. Through the letter, Walpole satirised the social conditions of his time in England.[98] We find this again in 1901, by another British author, Goldsworthy Lowes Dickinson, philosopher and political scientist, who criticised the dehumanising effects of industrialisation in the USA, employing Montesquieu's literary pattern of seeing a society through the eyes of someone who comes from another society. Dickinson published a volume of letters that he attributed to a Chinese official who visited the West and was negatively impressed by the prevalence of 'material ends' amongst people and the mechanisation of their life.[99]

In short, the Enlightenment gave rise to a comparative gaze that relativised European cultures by adopting the viewpoint of the 'other', thus inducing self-examination. The Enlightenment meant the regeneration of the project of personal and collective autonomy, and this entailed the recognition that individuals and societies have both universal and particular characteristics. Universality was associated with the signification of equality, which was a central aim of the democratic movement that rose in the same period, exemplified in demands such as: slavery should be abolished, the poor must be recognised as human beings with dignity, women must be equal with men and children must be seen as individuals. Universality in the international space meant that all residents of a country should be recognised as its citizens and that the common characteristics of humans are more essential than what makes them differ.[100]

Yet, the Enlightenment acknowledged also cultural multiplicity and, in fact, saw it as essential for the development of critical thinking, on the ground that it allows detachment from one's own worldview by enabling one to see things from the perspective of the 'other'. Indeed, there were Enlightenment authors who regarded the rise and proliferation of nation-states as positive just because they created a space of diversity, which for these authors meant freedom, and thus critical reflection and creativity. David Hume, for example, compared the great number of poleis in Ancient Greece, separated by its peculiar geographical morphology, with the wide variety of countries in Europe and considered this multiplicity in both cases a necessary condition for the development of sciences.[101]

This combined recognition of the universality and diversity of the human condition was at the heart of the Enlightenment project, which Voltaire expressed in his *Essay on Manners*, published in 1759, quite succinctly:

> . . .it is clear that everything which belongs intimately to human nature is the same from one end of the universe to the other; that everything that depends on custom is different, and it is accidental if it remains the same. The empire of custom is much more vast than that of nature; it extends over

> manners and all usages, it sheds variety on the scene of the universe; nature sheds unity there; she establishes everywhere a small number of invariable principles. Thus the basis is everywhere the same, and culture produces diverse fruits.[102]

It is this perspective that stimulated the interest in other societies, beyond one's own birthplace, and formed largely the European comparative gaze in the Enlightenment Age. As Todorov points out, travellers and intellectuals did not stop from the following day judging other peoples by the criteria of their own culture, but they became conscious of the multiplicity of cultures, about which they started to collect information and conduct analyses, which changed the European perception of mankind.[103] The interest in other civilisations is confirmed by the great popularity of travel and missionary books in the first half of the 18th century, which were exceeded only by theological works. For example, between 1700 and 1750 there were four times more books published on Africa than in the entire 17th century. The publications were more informing and detailed and less 'judgmental' than earlier writings, but also more accepting of cultural differences between overseas and European peoples – accounts that very often fuelled philosophical and political debates back home on key issues, such as the abolition of slavery.[104]

However, the impartial attitude towards other civilisations was not to prevail in the formation of the European comparative gaze. Viewing other peoples through the signification of techno-scientific progress, and considering this progress as supremacy and justification of domination over them, was something that is indicated already in Bacon's *Novum Organum*, as noted above. Nevertheless, this signification took precedence from the 19th century, both in the way the Europeans saw the rest of the world and in how they wanted it to be. Peoples not following the pathway of progress, as conceived by the Europeans, would be considered primitive, barbarians or savages, depending on the part of the planet they resided in.[105]

As Lévi-Strauss remarks, early anthropological accounts identified peoples which did not share the Western course of techno-scientific progress, essentially, with nature. This is indicated by the etymology of the word *sauvage* (stemming from the Latin *silva*, meaning *forest*) and in a more explicit way by the German term *Naturvölken* (people living in natural conditions). Moreover, anthropology, as he pointed out, by calling other peoples 'primitive' or 'archaic', placed them essentially outside of history, thus removing from them a substantial element of their human condition.[106]

From the European perspective of progress, the 'primitiveness' of other cultures was seen during the 19th and early 20th centuries either as the tranquil natural state that the West was increasingly losing or, predominantly, as inferiority and backwardness, and thus as justification for exploitational and colonial enterprises. For instance, Amerindian, Tahitian and sometimes African populations were often imagined as living in an idyllic communion with their natural instincts and the environment, as opposed to the allegedly over-mannered and decadent way of living of the Europeans. In the early 20th century, part of anthropology as well as literature resurrected a kind of Rousseauean image of primitive civilisations where people lived away from the dehumanising effects of industrialisation. Bronislaw Malinowski claimed, in an essay on anthropology and colonial rule, that anthropologists saw cultures in Africa and the South Pacific as places for 'romantic escape' from the standardised life that science and industry brought about in Europe. The British writer Richard Austin Freeman, in one of his non-fiction books (titled *Social Decay and Regeneration*), compared an idealised 'African negro' with the 'British sub-man' who was stripped of his capacities and self-esteem by industrial mechanisation.[107]

But the idealisation of the peoples who did not follow the Western paradigm was not the prevalent stance. The dominant position in the West from the middle of the 19th century was to associate scientific and technological stagnation with barbarism and to regard poor material development as a feature of primitive and savage culture. As Michael Adas remarks, in a seminal study that reviews a wide range of political, scientific and literary sources from Modernity, most authors of the time would lump together Africans and Melanesians as primitives and savages, as they lacked the 'skilful industry' that was for the Europeans the proof or the very condition for a civilisation to be considered superior. The Chinese and the Indians, who were once advanced, were now considered barbarians, as their civilisations were seen to be in decline and stagnation. As a matter of fact, early travellers would extol the virtues of China and even consider it an ideal society ruled by 'philosopher-kings'. However, when scientific achievements and technological applications in Europe grew, authors and commentators castigated the Chinese failure to develop further its earlier inventions and attributed this failure to corruption and the rule of the mandarins. Similarly, the admiration of the Indians' earlier accomplishments in arts, philosophy, literature and mathematics did not last long; India's subordination to the British was regarded as proof of the country's fundamental deficiencies in comparison to the organisational and technological superiority of the colonialists. Africans were also praised, particularly by opponents of slavery, for their innocence, sense of freedom, hospitality and kindness, while often, in poems and novels, 'noble slaves' were extolled for their loyalty and courage in rescuing their masters. Nevertheless, the industrial revolution marginalised these accounts and the Africans were from then on evaluated negatively for their assumed lack of scientific and technological potential, which was attributed to an innate absence of inventiveness and scientific curiosity. In the case of Africans, in particular, racist views were applied as well, drawn from their history of enslavement and 'scientific' and anthropological accounts.[108] Nevertheless, Africans, too, as other peoples, were measured chiefly by the techno-scientific standards of Europe. In fact, European authors coined a variety of terms to indicate the supposed divergence of non-Western societies from the unquestionable historical pathway of progress: 'day', 'twilight' or 'night' peoples; 'improving' or 'stationary'; 'active' or 'passive'; and 'male' or 'female'. As Adas notes, 'the history of civilised peoples was a tale of progress, of continuous advance; that of barbarians, a dreary chronology of endless cycles of decline and recovery'.[109]

The Africans – usually grouped together with the Amerindians and the Polynesians – were regarded as primitive and lacking the intelligence to comprehend and create the scientific and technological wonders of the West. Therefore, what was considered appropriate for them, by Western governments and educationists, was primary education for 'basic skills' and, at most, vocational training to transmit practical skills to domains taken to be in demand in colonial economies (e.g., carpentry, ironworking, machine repair etc.). The Indians and the Chinese were considered worthy of higher education in advanced sciences and mathematics because their history had to show high achievements in these knowledge domains. As Adas points out: 'Thus the burden of the material measure of human worth, now concentrated in a combination of scientific and technological accomplishments, continued to weigh much more heavily on the Africans than on the Indians or Chinese'.[110]

In short, the imaginary signification of progress, and broadly the central signification of rationalistic mastery and control, characterised from the 19th century the European comparative gaze towards other civilisations, but also the establishment of education systems internationally, as part of colonial domination or of the historical process of educational 'lending' and 'borrowing'. The case of the university is characteristic. The European university, as pointed out in the previous section, is marked by the idea of academic autonomy, in terms of free knowledge creation and impartation and self-governance. However, academic autonomy was much less 'lent' and 'borrowed' during the university expansion of the 19th and 20th centuries, outside of the 'European sphere' (i.e. America, Australia and New Zealand). The university, as the education system as a whole, was placed in the service of nation-state building, technical-scientific advancements and economic development.

Indeed, academic autonomy was expanded in Western Europe since, as remarked in the multivolume *A History of the University of Europe*, the so-called 'Humboldtian model' 'prevailed across the whole of continental Europe at the end of the nineteenth century and influenced the other two models, the French and the English'.[111] In Britain, the preservation of the corporations of medieval *universitates* and, by the end of the 19th century, the adherence of Oxbridge to the 'German model' created the conditions for remarkable levels of autonomy in research and teaching.[112] Through Britain, academic autonomy was bequeathed to Canada, Australia and New Zealand – countries which, until the recent past, were reported to be amongst those where universities had the least state interference.[113] In the USA, the move towards academic autonomy dates back to the mid-19th century, when the German reform proposal was gradually embraced by the academic profession and over the years became an integral part of the American university tradition.[114] As Metzger writes, the German influence redefined from the mid-19th century the very meaning of university in the USA: 'Neither the term [university] nor the institution referred to represented scholarship freely pursued. The German paradigm gave new value to both'.[115]

This influence, as the same author notes, is explicitly recognised in the 'Declaration of Principles on Academic Freedom and Academic Tenure', signed by the American Association of University Professors in 1915.

The transfer of academic autonomy in other parts of the world was much more uneven. In Latin America, where the European colonial heritage of the *Ancien Régime* left by the Spanish and Portuguese empires gave its place to strong state control, universities did not achieve any form of academic autonomy until the 20th century. A landmark for this was the 'Cordoba Reform', a student movement in 1918 at the University of Cordoba in Argentina and the demands it put forward (e.g., secularisation, wide and tuition-free access to university, student participation in university governance, freedom in teaching and research for all academic staff, non-intervention of the state in university affairs and full-time employment for academic staff and studies for students, as conditions to create a community experience in the university). Academic autonomy was given formal status in the same year in Argentina and in the following years in the educational legislation of most Latin American countries.[116] While legislation did not always reflect the reality, in some cases (e.g., Argentina and Uruguay in the post-WWII period), it marked a 'golden age' of autonomy for universities, which was characterised by extensive student participation. Nevertheless, the wave of authoritarian and dictatorial regimes which spread in the region from the 1960s interrupted this period (often in a violent way, e.g., through closing down departments, persecuting academics or declaring illegal the student unions).[117]

The European university was diffused during the 19th and early 20th centuries to other parts of the world, either through the form of missionary colleges or through concerted colonial strategies intended to 'modernise' occupied territories and to satisfy the aspirations of local elites for professional training and social status. This was the case in countries where mainly a colonial power was in control, e.g., Britain in South Africa, India, Burma and Hong Kong; France in North West Africa and Vietnam; the USA in the Philippines and the Netherlands in Indonesia. As well as these cases, it was also diffused through combined strategies and influences, e.g., French and Anglo-American in Lebanon, Egypt and China and British and German in Palestine. The 'lendig' of academic autonomy was quite limited and scattered in terms of countries and institutions according to particular colonial policies and local conditions. In the French colonies in Africa, for example, there was hardly any such 'lending' because hardly any universities were established, and thus prospective students had to go to France to study. Academic autonomy became possible mainly in those African institutions which were affiliated to the University of London, e.g., Sudan (Khartoum), Nigeria (Ibadan) and Uganda (Makere University), but, after independence, scholars were often persecuted by authoritarian regimes.[118] Things were better in those establishments where liberal arts were taught, e.g., the American Universities of Beirut and Cairo and the university colleges in India, as well as in the Hebrew University of Jerusalem in Palestine.[119] In most cases where academic autonomy became possible, it was not due to official policies, but because it was an integral element of the European university legacy.

For example, in India, the establishment of universities was a political decision of the British authorities in the mid-19th century which wanted to create anglicised local elites for the effective control of their colony. As the British official Thomas Macaulay famously promulgated in 1835: 'we must at present do our best to form a class who may be interpreters between us and the millions who we govern'.[120] The plan was put into practice initially through the establishment of three universities (in Calcutta, Bombay and Madras) on the model of the University of London, minus its main formal elements of academic autonomy – e.g., elected authorities and free research. However, liberal education in the core curriculum and some sort of collegial life, integral features of the British university of the time, contributed to the gradual opening of a space for argumentation and critique in colleges. The inquiring pedagogic methodology, inherent in the British university, prompted the students to question both the colonial rule as well as the established cultural and religious status quo in Indian society. As Sliwka's analysis of exam papers in the subjects of Political Economy, History and English, taught by the first Indian universities, shows, students were able to question British rule but also to scrutinise the traditional power structure of their society, such as the caste system and the role of women in Hinduism. This was also the case in extracurricular activities (e.g., drama and debating groups) and the activities of student associations. Despite the dominant presence of privileged social groups (such as high-caste Brahmins and wealthy Parsees) in the university, associations were open to students from different social backgrounds and to various social and political issues, thus contesting in practice the established power structure and inducing a sense of a common, public sphere. Thus, as the same researcher points out, by the end of the 19th century, the first Indian universities had not only produced English-speaking elites looking for official positions but also the first public intellectuals and active citizens seeking social reforms and national independence.[121]

In the two major states of East Asia, however, the project of academic autonomy had hardly any success. In China, the first modern universities were founded soon after the country's defeat in the Sino-Japanese war of 1895–1896, which in fact legitimised the creation of an education system directed towards asserting state power. Both before and after the war, Chinese scholar-officials travelled to Europe (mainly Germany, France and Britain) and observed the operation of universities. Amongst the most recorded aspects were faculty and department organisation, subject specialisation and an emphasis on applied sciences. Yet what particularly attracted their attention was the culture of free inquiry amongst academics. In witnessing, for example, that in Germany, one could study areas (e.g., Oriental Studies, Sinology or Mongolian languages) with no practical intent but out of pure academic interest, Li Fengbao, a Chinese scholar-official and ambassador to Germany and other European countries in the late 19th century, wrote with admiration: 'those who are fond of learning, no matter male or female, assiduously search for knowledge and regard learning as their lives, regardless of time and place, no need to push and no concern about use'.[122] An attempt to transfer this culture to Chinese higher education was made during the republican years by the renowned educator Cai Yuanpei, who studied in Germany and who was the chancellor of Peking University from 1917 until 1927. Both during and prior to his chancellorship, when he was involved in the forming of the university legislation of 1912, Cai Yuanpei attempted to establish academic autonomy in terms of research, course development and governance, but with little success.[123] Chinese 'educational borrowing' on the establishment of universities focused on those elements of the European pattern (e.g., applied sciences and technology, subject specialisation, professional training and generation of expertise) which would contribute to state power and economic and technological development. Hence, attention was paid to the so-called Japanese model – considered to have contributed to Japan's technological and military superiority – because of its emphasis on centralised control, specialised knowledge areas and training, and the state-worshipping culture within universities. Indeed, after the Meiji restoration, Japan accelerated industrialisation and set about establishing Imperial Universities as a means of bringing in Western scientific and technical knowledge. With this priority dominating Japan's strategy for higher education institutions, 'the reception of the Western academic ethic and the academic freedom which is so integral to it was to have a hard passage in Japan's reception of the model of the European universities'.[124] In China, this reception was inhibited more explicitly. As Cheung and Fan write, 'since universities serving the nation-state became a focus of attention and were widely accepted by the Chinese, the idea of university autonomy never took root in China'.[125]

In summary, academic autonomy, albeit a core characteristic, became the least diffused signification of university expansion during the 19th and 20th centuries. The university was rendered a main instrument for the nation-state's 'modernisation', economic development and progress and pursuit of domestic and international domination. It is this project that prevailed in the 'lending' and 'borrowing' of the European university worldwide, rather than the project of autonomy.

In general, although the European educational legacy included an emancipatory potential, policy transfer in the 19th and early 20th centuries, was concerned mostly with constructing education systems as part of nation-state building. This was the epoch in which officials, advisors, observers, writers and intellectuals travelled to study educational laws, to meet members of foreign governments, to visit schools and to submit on their return reports and proposals to their governments. For example, Victor Cousin investigated the Prussian education system and submitted a report on which the so-called 'Guizot Law' on primary education was based; Horace Mann's report after his visit to Europe influenced heavily the formation of the first educational structures in Massachusetts; Matthew Arnold investigated the French and the German education systems and based his proposals to the English authorities on his experience; Leo Tolstoy scrutinised and criticised the ideological and institutional basis of the Prussian education system; and John Dewey was invited to China, Russia, Mexico, Chile, South Africa and Turkey to diffuse his ideas and take part in committees assigned to design educational reforms – which eventually, in most cases, reduced Deweyan educational philosophy to a set of pedagogic techniques that would not disturb the principal aim of utilising education for nation-state building.[126]

Comparative education as a field of study was created in the specific context of educational 'lending' and 'borrowing' during the 19th and early 20th centuries. In the broader terms delineated above, comparative education was amongst the knowledge forms that expressed both the extrovert gaze spawned by the European Enlightenment to know and understand other societies and their institutions as well as the signification of progress or development as a universal gauge.

Michael Sadler, for example, asserted in 1900 that the 'practical value of studying, in a right spirit and with scholarly accuracy, the working of foreign systems of education is that it will result in our being better fitted to study and to understand our own'[127] – thus considering educational comparison appropriate to instigate reflection and self-knowledge. At the same time, he underlined the close association of educational institutions with their cultural context and warned, in another of his much-quoted phrases, against a simplistic view of 'educational borrowing'.[128] Isaac Kandel makes this point too in an eloquent way: 'The comparative approach demands first an appreciation of the intangible, impalpable spiritual and cultural forces which underlie an education system; the factors and forces outside the school matter even more than what goes on inside it'[129] – a phrase that expresses the task of the present study.

However, in 1817, Marc-Antoine Jullien, regarded as the founder of comparative education, had claimed, in his essay *Outline and Preliminary Views of a Work on Comparative Education*, that this subject area must be a 'positive science', which collects international data and identifies determinants appropriate for policy-making.[130] This standpoint prevailed in comparative education from individual scholars who constructed the field during the 20th century to governmental agencies and international organisations. In short, the prevalent characteristics of comparative education as a field of study have been: the identification of culture with the nation-state and the adoption of the latter as a unit of analysis; the focus on the functional/instrumental aspects of education; the pursuit of causal explanations and of determining factors; the assistance to policymaking, regarded, in accordance to the dominant role of knowledge production since Modernity, as a matter of epistēmē rather than doxa; and the explicit or implicit assumption that education systems are means of nation-state building, techno-scientific progress and economic development.

Comparative education was created at a time when knowledge expanded dramatically and new subjects, specialisations and departments were established in universities. Already from the 18th century, philosophy had been divorced from science, giving rise, from the following century, to what has been called the 'two knowledge cultures', i.e. the humanist and the scientific.[131] Comparative education, as well as the area of education studies in general, subscribed from the start to the scientific 'camp' by drawing largely on the methodology of natural sciences, through which it tried always to support the validity of its proposals. Part of the 'scientific culture', and in fact part of the entire regime of knowledge production since Modernity, has been a process of constant division of knowledge to more and more specialised areas. Most disciplinary areas after the 19th century established a comparative branch, which developed further specialisations. The same has happened in comparative education, which, after all, has been one branch among the various divisions within education studies (philosophy of education, sociology of education, history of education, anthropology of education etc.). The institution of specialised knowledge areas (through departments, journals, academic societies and their internal hierarchies, 'gatekeeping' practices and self-referential discourses) has given rise to new forms of heteronomy, as the prime aim has become not to know and to understand but to serve and preserve the subject area in question. Today, the managerial university is enhancing heteronomy, as the next chapter will demonstrate, by forcing academics to subordinate their research interests to external funding agencies and thus independent scholarship has become a limited reality in comparative education, as much as in other knowledge areas.

Overall, the social imaginary of the European Modern Era was both an adoption and a departure from Classical Antiquity. European rationality inherited Greek logos but developed mainly as *Zweckrationalität.* European science took further the Greek scientific thinking, fighting medieval superstition and cognitive closure. Nevertheless, European scientific thinking prioritised not the understanding and the symbiosis with the natural world, but the domination of it by means of technological advancements. The signification of progress also emerged in opposition to medieval perseverance on tradition and religion, but kept from Christianity the perception of God's omnipotence and infinity, turning it to a man-driven project of mastery and control of nature and society. This became possible by the simultaneous emergence of capitalism and the new ruling classes, which realised rationality as economic efficiency and sought to infuse it in all domains of social life. Capitalism arose in a symbiotic relation with 'representative democracy', a regime of liberal oligarchy, which became after the Enlightenment the legitimate form of political organisation. Although it drew on Ancient Greece, the new political form departed from democracy as a regime of power-sharing and established a separation between government and the citizens. Citizens were to be subject to individual benefits through a 'social contract' with the government, which was to rule them by means of expert knowledge and bureaucracy. Bureaucracy was embedded in the function of the state, which in its modern form appropriated the nation, a novel European institution.

The Greek legacy was also a source of inspiration in the institution of education in Europe. The Renaissance, drawing on Antiquity, called into question the medieval status quo and foregrounded the appreciation of knowledge and education in the vernacular. During the 16th century, social, philosophical and educational critique emerged across Europe against religious indoctrination, seeking to establish childhood as distinct stage of life and organise learning accordingly. The Enlightenment revived the nature/nurture distinction and advocated the establishment of education for social, political and personal freedom. An entire educational movement developed thereafter, advocating exploratory and autonomous learning, which, depending on time and country, has had a widespread impact on the making of school systems. Moreover, European Modernity established academic autonomy as a *sine qua non* characteristic of the university, drawing on the Ancient Greek legacy of free contestation of ideas and Plato's Academy and the early Renaissance tradition of *universitas*, as a community of scholars. As in Ancient Greece, education in Europe emerged as something fundamentally different from mere training or indoctrination: it pursued scientific exploration, logical reasoning and critical disposition, and it was closely associated with the democratic movement that changed the face of the continent after the 18th century. But education in Europe embodied also the web of significations associated with capitalism and the nation-state, which pursued domination and instrumental control of people and of nature. The education system became an affair of state bureaucracy, organised under the principles of industrialism and 'scientific management', followed the new social class structure, glorified the nation and was placed in the service of capitalism – whose goals in education have been, however, constantly questioned.

In short, education systems in Modernity were instituted under the interaction and conflict between the central imaginary significations of autonomy and rationalistic mastery and control. The fundamental antinomy and conflict between these two central significations constitutes the very particularity of the institution of education in Europe since Modernity, but also of its comparative gaze.

Indeed, the Enlightenment marks the break of cognitive and representational closure in Europe and the awareness that, while people share the same human characteristics, different societies are instituted differently. The first ruptures in European monocultural perception appeared in the Renaissance when the racist views of the Church against non-European populations were publicly criticised. In the Enlightenment, self-reflecting accounts became more inventive and more popular, criticising domestic institutions from the perspective of the cultural 'other'. The Enlightenment recognised both the universality of the human condition and cultural multiplicity, which was welcomed as freedom and as a condition for impartial and critical reflection. Comparative studies, including comparative education, embodied this perspective and set out to understand education institutions in their cultural context.

Nevertheless, especially from the 19th century, the cultural 'others' were seen through the signification of progress. Overseas societies were to be gauged in accordance with their capacity to be/become like the Europeans (or the Westerners), a perception that drove or legitimised colonial and imperialist interventions. Either through these interventions or through influence, universities throughout the world were placed principally in the service of constructing nation-states and industrial economies, while the spread of the idea of academic autonomy was limited.

Thus, the central imaginary signification of rationalistic mastery and control prevailed in the 'Europeanisation' of the world, the process of education policy transfer in the 20th century, as well as the comparison of education systems, as the next chapter will argue, with particular reference to the role of International Organisations.

Notes

1 Castoriadis (1987: 77).
2 By 1500, there were already 20 million books printed throughout Europe, while in 1600, they became 200 million. See Anderson (1983).
3 Burckhardt ([1860] 1995).
4 Bury ([1914] 2006a: 93).
5 Hobsbawm (1975: 288).
6 Hobsbawm (1962: 255).
7 Dunn (1992).
8 Kant (1784).
9 See Habermas (1986).
10 Leibniz, G.W. ([1677] 1989: footnote 323).
11 Paz (1993).
12 Hume (1739: 217).
13 See Castoriadis (1987; 1991; 2007).
14 Descartes ([1637] 2010–2015: 24).
15 Quoted in: Rich (1994: 208).
16 Bacon (1627).
17 Bacon ([1620] 2010–2015: Book 1, 129). (The word 'art', as the book's preface explains, refers to 'any human activity that involves techniques and requires skills'.)
18 Bury ([1920] 2006b: 190).
19 Arendt (1969: 27).
20 Castoriadis (1991).
21 See Rich (1994).
22 Castoriadis (1991).
23 See Marx (1861–1864); Weber ([1930] 1992); Castoriadis (2007).
24 Weber ([1930] 1992: 17), original italics.
25 Weber ([1930] 1992: 24–25), original italics.
26 Michéa (1999).
27 Polanyi ([1944] 2001).
28 Polanyi ([1944] 2001: 37).
29 Fulcher (2004: 32); Bayly (2004: 170).
30 Bayly (2004: 177).
31 See Nye (2013).
32 Bowen (1981: 302).
33 Hobsbawm (1998).
34 Mossé (1989).
35 Mill (1861: 69).
36 Rousseau (1762: 74).
37 See Arendt (2005).
38 Macpherson ([1962] 2011: 263–264).
39 Constant ([1819] 2010–2015: 6).

40 Smith ([1776] 2007: 16).
41 See Michéa (2013).
42 See Morin (1987).
43 Orwell (1941: 36–37).
44 Orwell (1945).
45 Hobsbawm (1992: 14 and 18).
46 Morin (1987).
47 Gellner (1983).
48 Guibernau and Rex (1997: 4–5).
49 See Creveld (1999: 201).
50 Creveld (1999).
51 Weber (1947: 339).
52 Weber (1947: 338–339).
53 Arendt (1969).
54 Rousseau (1755: 5).
55 Kant ([1781] 1998: 100-101). From the preface of the first edition of *Critique of Pure Reason*.
56 Hugo (1849–1869).
57 Jespersen (2004: 103–113).
58 Todorov (2006: 3).
59 Durkheim (2009).
60 Bowen, (1981: 64 and 137).
61 Aries (1973).
62 Aries (1973).
63 Declaration of Independence (1776).
64 Kant ([1785] 2005: 103).
65 See: Rousseau (1991); Bowen (1981: 196–197).
66 Bowen (1981).
67 Le Goff (2005: 124).
68 Mak (2009a).
69 Makdisi (1970: 264).
70 Humboldt ([1792]1854).
71 Humboldt ([1810] 1970: 244).
72 Metzger (1955: 217–218).
73 Fichte (1873: 188 and 192).
74 Humboldt ([1810] 1970: 243). See also Lawler (1991: 18).
75 Humboldt ([1792] 1854).
76 Nietzsche ([1872] 2004: 78).
77 Nietzsche ([1872] 2004: 38).
78 Bowen (1981: 283).
79 Quoted in: Bowen (1981: 317).
80 Bell (1808: 36).
81 Quoted in: Bowen (1981: 298).
82 McMurry (1897: 43).
83 Bernstein (2000: xxiii).
84 Quoted in: Bowen (1981: 251).
85 Bowen (1981: 308).
86 Morin (1987).
87 Montesquieu ([1750] 1911: 238–239).
88 Quoted in: Wallerstein (2006: 10).
89 Montaigne ([1877] 2006: Chapter XXX).
90 Montaigne ([1877] 2006: Chapter XXX).
91 Montesquieu (1721: Letter XXX).

92 Montesquieu (1721: Letter XXXVI).
93 Swift (1726: 102).
94 Swift (1726: 65).
95 Swift (1726: 168).
96 Swift (1726: 165).
97 Swift (1726: 377–378).
98 Walpole (1757).
99 Dickinson (1904).
100 Todorov (2006).
101 Hume ([1777] 1987: I.XIV.22).
102 Quoted in: Cassirer ([1932] 1951: 219).
103 Todorov (2006).
104 Adas (1989: 69).
105 Adas (1989).
106 Lévi-Strauss (1983).
107 See Adas (1989: 70 and 392).
108 See for example Hunt (1863).
109 Adas (1989: 196–197).
110 Adas (1989: 338 and 335–337).
111 Charle (2004: 33).
112 Rüegg (2004).
113 Anderson and Johnson (1998).
114 Shils and Roberts (2004: 164–177).
115 Metzger (1955: 222).
116 Academic autonomy became a legal provision in Argentina in 1918, in El Salvador in 1927, in Guatemala in 1928, in Paraguay in 1929, in Bolivia 1930, in Peru in 1931, in Cuba in 1933, in Colombia in 1935, in Venezuela in 1936, in Ecuador in 1938, in Panama in 1946, in Uruguay in 1951, in Honduras in 1957, in Nicaragua in 1958 and in the Dominican Republic in 1961. See: Levy (1986: 219–238).
117 Levy (1986).
118 Mohamedbhai (2011: 17–18).
119 Shils and Roberts (2004: 187–208).
120 Quoted in: Sliwka (2004: 13).
121 Sliwka (2004).
122 Cheung and Fan (2009: 27).
123 Mak (2009b).
124 Shils and Roberts (2004: 226).
125 Cheung and Fan (2009: 24).
126 See Jones (1971); Bruno-Jofré and Schriewer (2012).
127 Sadler (1900: 4).
128 Sadler (1900: 4).
129 Quoted in: Blake (1982: 3).
130 Jones (1971: 36–37).
131 Morin (1991).

4 Total capitalism and the (de-)Europeanisation of education and cross-cultural comparison

The third historical moment to explore is our own, the era of Postmodernity and globalisation. Europe remains the main locus of this inquiry, but the analysis encompasses also the global impact that the West, in general, has had in the 20th century, again, without focusing on some specific country. Following the same approach, the chapter will place education and educational comparison in the European social-historical field and its alterations in Postmodernity. Postmodernity is the era of 'total capitalism', of the unprecedented penetration of capitalist significations in social and individual life. It is the era that realises economic liberalism, which was implemented first in Western Europe in the 19th century, disrupted in the 20th century, re-generated since the 1970s and has been globalised at the turn of the millennium as *neo*liberalism. According to its main tenet, expressed by Hayek, '. . .anybody should be free to produce, sell, and buy anything that may be produced or sold at all'.[1] And this is what is happening, both in terms of the dramatic expansion of the capitalist territory around the world, but also in terms of the extraordinary penetration of the market in essentially all institutions, forms and activities: medicine, health, housing, social services, infrastructure, food, media, publishing, arts, traveling, sports, leisure, love, education, research and everything one can think of are now subject to the demands, strategies and discourses of the market.[2] By designating almost everything as a commodity, capitalism is disintegrating social institutions, thus undermining severely the potential of individuals to ascribe meaning to their actions and lives outside of the sphere of production and consumption.

Under these circumstances, as it will be argued, notwithstanding the 'free choice' ideology, sponsored by neoliberal capitalism, the European project of autonomy is in decline. Autonomy means the awareness of societies and individuals that they themselves give meaning and form to the chaos, with their own thinking and activities. Autonomy is the potential to question the institutions of society and, if considered necessary, to change them and in general to usher in other forms or *eidē*. The last major instance in which this project was politically foregrounded was the social uprisings of the 1960s, which questioned the existing status quo in Western societies. The Parisian May and the movements it sparkled had a tremendous impact in Europe, the USA and beyond. They promoted the autonomy of hitherto undervalued or repressed categories of the population, such as youth, women and ethnic minorities, transforming social institutions – most prominently, the family, gender relations, as well as the media of communication.[3] Nevertheless, since the late 20th century, we have witnessed, as this chapter will argue, in concurrence with the observations of Castoriadis and a number of other contemporary social theorists to be discussed here, the pervasiveness of the central imaginary signification of rationalistic mastery and control across institutions. It is manifested primarily in the dramatic expansion of technique, techno-science, information and data manipulation, which render dominant the functional-instrumental dimension of society at the expense of its poietic aspect and its potential to create new forms. It is also manifested in the transnationalisation of the state, the expansion of managerial bureaucracy, the weakening of 'representative democracy' and citizenship and the globalisation of capitalism, in geographic and cultural terms.

As the title of the chapter indicates, it will be also argued that education and cross-cultural comparison have been 'Europeanised', in the sense that they are permeated by the imaginary of unlimited mastery and control, but at the same time they are 'de-Europeanised', as the critical and self-reflective spirit of Modernity has retreated. Particular reference will be made to higher education which, as it will be suggested, is abandoning the project of academic autonomy that marked the genesis of the European university. The last section focuses on the globalisation of capitalism and the institutions shaping transnational education policy and comparison.

Capitalist domination and de-socialisation

One of the driving ideas of European Modernity, as the previous chapter showed, was progress, understood as the unlimited accumulation and application of techno-scientific knowledge and increase of production and productive forces. The idea of progress was discredited by the catastrophic world wars, genocides and totalitarian regimes of the 20th century, but it was revived in the 1950s by the 'developmental' policies that the West started promoting around the world. Today, progress is seen, as Taguieff points out, as nothing more than a perpetual movement for the sake of movement (a *mobilisme*) and a continuous quest for and adornment of the new (a *neophilie*), or, essentially, an idea empty of meaning other than business making.[4] To be sure, European societies, and now societies around the world, celebrate, as their main aims, productivity, consumption and scientific and technological achievements, which are considered to be progressing on an exponential, rather than linear, pace.[5] Nevertheless, liberal capitalism, by proclaiming the 'end of history,' removes societies' historical perspective towards both their past and their future. Postmodernity establishes the sense of a recurrent present or an inescapable destiny, as the future no longer promises utopias or contains any major expectations, beyond the invention of new technological gadgets.[6] Most importantly, the environmental crisis hardly allows one to envisage the future of the world in bright terms. We are facing global warming, extreme weather phenomena, extensive droughts, the heating and acidity of the oceans, the ice melting in the poles, rising sea levels that threaten life on islands and coastal cities and the massive extinction of flora and fauna, which may reach 50% of the species by next century.[7] Environmental degradation is challenging the imaginary signification of progress in its various versions (as 'development', 'growth' and 'prosperity'), which all have been associated with the economy and consisted the legitimation ground of most political regimes. Although transnational initiatives pledge to detain the foreseen devastating effects of capitalist expansion on the natural environment by means of 'green' technologies and industries, the promise is hardly credible as long as the current drive for wealth accumulation and domination, through, also, advanced and nuclear arms race, continues. The signification of unlimited rationalistic mastery and control, which emerged in Europe and has been incarnated by capitalism, in all its stages and types, has generated a major *hubris* against the environment (now naturalised as *Anthropocene*). Climate change and its consequences are appearing as the *nemesis* against human beings.

Part of this hubris is the unlimited and unrestrained expansion of techno-scientific applications in the social space. Throughout the 20th century, and especially during its last decades, the significance of technology and science, as well as technique in general as a mode of organisation and control, has been overwhelmingly enhanced in Europe, as in the West overall, and more recently around the world, thus expanding the functional-instrumental dimension of society. Technique is not necessarily an application of science to practical life, as Ellul showed in his classical study.[8] Technique and science should not be defined in relation to each other, as he pointed out. Historically, technique preceded science, though in order for the former to develop, it had to wait for the latter. Since the 20th century, technique has become independent from machine, thus transforming 'everything it touches into a machine'.[9] In other words, technique has taken over not only productive activities but essentially all human activities, and it is fully integrated in society.

This has led to the rise of 'technopoly' and dominance of 'scientism', in Postman's terminology.[10] Scientism means that science has been elevated to the status of a faultless moral authority which has answers to all questions – about life and death, right and wrong, and good and bad. The same status is granted to technology. Before Modernity, cultures were, as Postman writes, 'tool-users': tools solved the practical problems of life (windmills, water power etc.) without contradicting significantly people's worldview. Modernity gave rise to 'technocracy', in which tools were not merely integrated into culture but 'attacked' it: everything should give in to technological development. Today's 'technopoly' entails the total prevalence of technology in social institutions and the elimination of alternatives; alternatives are not made illegal, immoral or unpopular, but invisible and thus irrelevant. This is a world that includes the belief that efficiency is what matters most of all in the action of humans; that judgement is too ambiguous and complex to be trusted; that what cannot be measured does not count; and that citizen's affairs must be guided by experts. Individuals in a 'technopoly' are driven to fill their lives with the quest of information. The processes of generation, storage and distribution of information constitute both the means and the end of human creativity.[11]

In our age, four centuries after Descartes and Bacon, the drive towards rationalistic mastery and control, through technology, science and perpetual accumulation of knowledge and information, is fully realised. If wisdom for the Greeks and the Western Europeans of the Enlightenment Age lay in judgement, critique and the quest for truth, for their contemporary descendants, wisdom results from the accumulation of data, information and knowledge. Harnessing information and knowledge aspires at mastering existence, a privilege of God for 17 centuries, bequeathed to the Modern Man, who is trying today to actualise it by merging information and communication technologies (ICT), artificial intelligence (AI), robotics, genetics, nanotechnology and brain research.

The current brain research paradigm, as pointed out in Chapter 1, does not see humans as possessing a psyche, as belonging to a society nor even as parts of social relations. Most neuroscience regards taste, ethics, religiousness, aesthetic experience and essentially all modes of conduct as epiphenomenal of biochemical processes that are locatable in the cerebral cortex. While some of neuroscientific research is aimed, in synergy with ICT, to improve the quality of life of handicapped people, most activity in this domain is directed towards manipulating human capacities and feelings: 'smart soldiers' who can activate military equipment through neural messages and can stay awake for longs hours, drugs that incapacitate without killing, memory erasing, attention or cognitive enhancement for learners etc.[12] As Taylor writes, 'the growing power of neuroscience to manipulate human brains directly offers capacities beyond the dreams of the most totalitarian government. Your skull is not the fortress it once was'.[13]

Indeed, the brain becomes the target for controlling behaviour and the means for enhancing the individual's performance. This is not only the storyline of science fiction movies.[14] There is, actually, a branch of techno-science that is seriously envisaging the so-called 'human transcendence' or 'Singularity'. Inventor and futurist Ray Kurzweil, who made these terms widely known, prophesies that, from the mid-21st century, human life will be transformed irreversibly, because: ICT capacity is expanding exponentially; brain scanning is mapping out the regions of the brain in detail; AI is accessing all of the information and knowledge available on the internet and is able to record and 'remember' all facts; nanotechnology is enabling the construction of nanorobots designed to manipulate physical reality at the molecular level, the brain included, in which they will be interacting with neurons to create virtual reality and extend 'intelligence'.[15] The convergence of these technologies will bring about the era of the 'Singularity':

> The Singularity will allow us to transcend these limitations of our biological bodies and brains. We will gain power over our fates. Our mortality will be in our own hands. We will be able to live as long as we want (a subtly different statement from saying we will live forever). We will fully understand human thinking and will vastly extend and expand its reach. By the end of this century, the nonbiological portion of our intelligence will be trillions

> of trillions of times more powerful than unaided human intelligence [. . .] In the aftermath of the singularity, intelligence, derived from its biological origins in human brains and its technological origins in human ingenuity, will begin to saturate the matter and energy in its midst.[16]

The dreams of the 'Singularitarians' are deeply rooted in the social imaginary of European Modernity, which set out to realise the attributes of the Father Almighty, i.e. omniscience, omnipotence and immortality, through techno-scientific inventions. In fact, there are already neuroscientists proudly working to 'upload the mind to a computer', aspiring to see these aims achieved.[17] Two centuries after the publication of Mary Shelley's novel, the Victors Frankensteins of today are not actualising their passions in isolation and suspicion. They are acclaimed researchers in neuroscience, genetics, biotechnology, or bioengineering and related areas, supported generously by corporate and state funding and collaborating in transnational academic networks to modify existing life or to create new life (through bio-tech hybridisation, cloning, genome editing etc.) available for mass production and consumption.[18] If Modernity generated the drive to dominate nature and living beings, the world of Postmodernity, under the dominance of capitalism, is creating new beings, while causing the massive extinction of species that have existed on earth for millions of years.[19]

Precisely because of its heavy emphasis on techno-scientific inventions and applications, contemporary capitalism has been called *knowledge capitalism*. This is, rather, a pleonasm, since capitalism has always been based on production and manipulation of new knowledge. Nonetheless, knowledge (or *post-industrial, informational, cognitive* and *flexible*)[20] capitalism indicates its reorganisation under the rapid advancements in information and communication technologies and a set of measures taken by governments and big corporations in dominant states in the 1980s and, mainly, in the 1990s. In that time period, major corporations shifted away from traditional modes of labour regulation by initiating new ICT-based organisational models. Governments introduced policies of privatisation, liberalisation and deregulation of the economy, and main International Organisations promoted these policies throughout the world. Recurrent organisational and technological restructuring, aimed at increasing productivity and profitability through the use of applied information and knowledge, has been the main feature of capitalism in Europe and around the world.

The new capitalism has been instituted by 'absorbing' demands promoted by the 1960s social movements, which foregrounded collective and personal autonomy. As Boltanski and Chiapello have shown in their major study *The New Spirit of Capitalism*, the demand for liberation was useful for the market to promote the lifting of established prohibitions and moral reservations to create new commodities and services (related to entertainment, tourism, fashion etc.). The demand for authenticity was used to differentiate the homogenised mass production of traditional industries and diversify and customise commodities. The demand for creativity led to the fading of the opposition between business and the intellectual domain giving rise to new market niches, especially in services and cultural production, and, overall, to the 'knowledge economy'. And the demand for worker autonomy was used to devise methods of self-control that reduce supervision costs and increase task engagement.[21] With the expansion of ICT, this new mode of employee control was actualised by what has been called 'digital Taylorism', namely the turning of innovation into routinised tasks, which de-skill and tighten performance controls over 'white-collar' workers.[22] Considering extensive digital work routinisation, and given the advances in AI, large shares of both 'blue collar' and 'white collar' jobs are expected to be robotised, increasing severely unemployment and underemployment.[23]

Overall, capitalist reorganisation in Europe since the last quarter of the 20th century has altered occupational structures and work arrangements. Services, particularly information and knowledge-based, have been diversified and expanded, traditional manufacturing employment has been, to a large extent, outsourced to newly industrialised countries and employment in agriculture has shrunk in most major economies. The new technologically driven production and management strategies have individualised labour, eroding job stability and breaking established social contracts between employers and employees. The traditional pattern of a stable, lifelong, linear career after one's formal education is now less typical, while part-time, 'short-term' and 'zero-hours' contracts, job changes and involuntary re-training and re-skilling are part of many people's reality. Work segmentation has shifted individual experience from more or less stable courses of life to continuously negotiated and revised life arrangements.

Restructured labour markets entail alterations in the institution of social classes. There still is a working class, which relies on wage income and has no control over the means of production, and there are small business owners, too, striving for a living. But there is also a new low-income class: the *precariat.* It is comprised of people who oscillate between insecure jobs and unemployment (which in the EU averages at 10% of the workforce) and have uncertain access to housing and public resources. In Standing's analysis, the precariat has mainly a working class background, and it is comprised mostly of ethnic minorities, immigrants or asylum seekers, as well as holders of higher education degrees, who expected to make bright careers in the 'knowledge economy'.[24] Underpaid and 'flexible' digital labour behind computer screens is now the type of occupation for much of the working class and the precariat.[25] These classes, and especially the unemployed and the 'underclass' (people living at the socio-economic margin), are the main victims of income inequality, which has been growing across Europe and other member countries of the Organisation for Economic Cooperation and Development (OECD).[26] Inequality in income share, which was sharply decreased by the welfare state policies of the mid-20th century, has started rising since the 1980s.[27] The widespread expansion of higher education, followed by vacuous policy promises such as 'the more you learn the more you earn', has not withheld this trend: qualification levels have moved upwards, meaning that higher education degrees have the value that upper secondary school diplomas used to have and that degree holders are likely to join the precariat for extensive periods.[28]

The main beneficiaries of unequal wealth distribution worldwide are a tiny minority of the population of less than 1%, which controls the means of production and owns about half of all wealth.[29] This is where the 'transnational capitalist class' is found, (business moguls, executives of transnational corporations, big property holders, globalising politicians, bureaucrats, and professionals, merchants, media owners etc.) whose allegiance, as Lawrence Summers, former US treasury secretary, pointed out, 'is to global economic success and their own prosperity rather than the interests of the nation where they are headquartered'.[30]

Between the above two categories stands the middle class, with different origins and amounts of wealth and influence. There is the middle class whose roots go back to the epoch of nation-state capitalism, and there is a newly emerged middle class, which includes various types of affluent professionals that appeared out of the neoliberal policies of the last decades (i.e. de-industrialisation, expansion of banking and finance and privatisation of public services).[31] A significant part of these socio-economic strata is engaged in activities which are by definition transnational due to the globalisation of economy. In this economy, as Heiman et al. point out, the middle class is more insecure, but, at the same, its role has become more central in the efforts of capital to develop new markets and new forms of labour, promote consumption, reduce social welfare and expand surveillance.[32] In other words, the middle class is now more power-focused in serving the goals of capitalist economy and securing its own prosperity, thus losing, as Fusaro observes, its traditional 'unhappy consciousness' (i.e. torn between the promotion of its own class interests and social and economic justice). The middle class, as he notes, now adopts the 'happy unconscientiousness' of the transnational capitalist class, which cynically promotes the commodification of everything.[33]

As recent studies testify, 'upward' social mobility within the new class structure does not extend out of the range of middle class occupations.[34] However, mobility is a signification that marks contemporary societies – promoted also officially by the EU as a condition for economic competitiveness.[35] There is geographical mobility, within and across countries; mobility for education; mobility for economic survival; mobility for career advancement; mobility for tourism and shopping; and virtual mobility within the global audiovisual and digital space, that leads many people, as Dufour remarks, to a 'process of becoming ubiquitous and practically free from all spatio-temporal restraints, whilst others are losing the ability to inhabit any space at all'.[36] Contemporary capitalism favours nomadic lives in its quest for performative and pliant employees and supple personalities readily available for the consumption of new commodities.

In fact, personalities receptive to commodity flows are celebrated by capitalism as free because they can choose between all sorts of products and life styles. The ideology of 'freedom of choice' is a distortion of the signification of personal autonomy, which has its roots, as the previous chapter showed, in Modernity. European Modernity generated the idea of liberal or possessive individualism that interpreted freedom as the pursuit of self-interest and private pleasures within a market society, under the auspices of the state. However, it is our era that is realising this inextricable link between liberal economy and individualism. The ideology of 'free choice' presents the individual as the definitive master of his/her life, which is identified with consumption. People are called on to 'be themselves' and 'live for the moment', as Salecl remarks, but always in the realm of consumption and its unlimited possibilities.[37] In other words, freedom or empowerment is reduced to one's right to choose between different commodities, services and lifestyles. But of course, the market can create neither free nor empowered citizens, as this is possible only when individuals are able to question, through rational argumentation, the directions and institutions of society and form them accordingly. The market, instead, creates privatised, narcissistic and infantilised individuals, occupied constantly with their personal desires, as never before.[38] While individuals aspire to achieve fulfilment through consumption and lifestyle choices, they are subjugated by the strategies of capital, which in our days is focused on commodities produced for their *exchange value* (i.e. intended to increase the capital invested on their production) rather than their *use value* (i.e. corresponding to necessities).[39] Thereby, instead of bringing about personal fulfilment, the market 'casts the gigantic shadow of consumerism on the whole of the *Lebenswelt*'.[40]

Yet the shadow is 'illuminated' by another dimension of consumerism – a signification and institution that are closely associated with contemporary capitalism: the spectacle. According to Debord's classic analysis, the spectacle is a form of commodity intended to rule all of human experience. 'The spectacle is capital accumulated to the point where it becomes image', as he wrote; it is 'the perfect image of the ruling economic order'.[41] Through this image, capitalist societies exercise economic and cultural hegemony, but they also keep their citizens appeased: 'the spectacle is the sun that never sets on the empire of modern passivity . . . [it] is the bad dream of modern society in chains, expressing nothing more than its wish for sleep'.[42] Taking into account the testimony of Martin and Schumann, it appears that the globally networked ruling elites are aware that the constant supply of entertainment and spectacles act as the 'bread and circuses' of our times, capable of keeping the masses of the underpaid and unemployed in good spirits.[43]

'Bread and circuses' is mainly what the television specialises on – an institution which is at the heart of the spectacle society. Ever-present today through all sorts and sizes of screens, television, a dominant institution since the last third of the 20th century, is fully permeated by the signification of entertainment. 'Entertainment' as Neil Postman writes in *Amusing Ourselves to Death*, 'is the supra-ideology of all discourse on television. No matter what is depicted or from what point of view, the overarching presumption is that it is there for our amusement and pleasure'.[44] Television has the double function of bringing people together as an audience while at the same time keeping them isolated through their one-way relation to a transmitting centre: 'The spectacle thus unites what is separate, but it unites it only in its separateness', as Debord remarked.[45]

The invention of the internet with its capacity for horizontal connectivity broke the mono-directional function of the television and the other traditional media. The so-called Web 2.0, especially, has facilitated online interaction and provided platforms for free publication and production, thus allowing any form of digital content to be uploaded and inducing the practice of 'search 'n share'.[46] But it is hard to argue that, in the epoch of *connectivity*, the above point by Debord is not still valid. Connectivity, a concept that initially denoted computer transmission, has replaced human connectedness and related significations rooted in social life (such as 'collaboration', 'sharing', 'community' or 'friends').[47] Connectivity signifies the perceived need of the individual to be online continuously, but also to the rise of a form of artificial sociality that network technologies and their various gadgets have given rise to, through the 'social media'. The social media engineer and marketise connections amongst people (including love relations) through algorithms, making sociality not only technical, but also quantitative, as social relations are valued for their quantity rather than their quality.[48] They are also valued economically, as online platforms are businesses selling their services or their clients' personal information for targeted advertising and other marketing strategies. Thus, the discourse on social media notwithstanding, they are essentially a business product, which further dismantles rather than restores the feeling of belonging to a community.

The sense of belonging to a community or, in broader terms, the process of identification in contemporary societies, has been a main issue in philosophical and sociological thinking in the recent decades. Castoriadis observed a process of simultaneous 'external' over-socialisation, mainly due to the ever-presence of the media, and 'internal' de-socialisation, due to the withdrawal of individuals to their private lives.[49] Michéa notes that the combination of liberal economy and atomisation produces moral relativism and, through the proliferation of the new media, a form of asocial sociality. The outcome is a society in which people live together without the others.[50] Dufour has underlined the widespread unleashing of egoisms and personal desires, across all social classes, that creates a 'de Sade-ish' culture, in which the other person is seen as a tool to serve one's own goals and individual satisfaction.[51] Fusaro, drawing on a metaphor by Marx, speaks of Robinson Crusoe as the living image of the new separated individual, who copes with a social landscape dominated by the market, where relationships are established with the main purpose of carving one's own acquisitive selfishness.[52] Similarly, Pforde offers an account of de-socialisation manifested by the widespread collapse of social bonds:

> Society is thus moving down the road (although only a part of that journey has been travelled so far) of becoming an aggregation of separated individuals where dominant rules come to be informed by the idea that people are to follow their own personal gain. In this way of living, people tend to act in competition with each other, use each other, and in a way which involves treating their fellows as objects . . . Perhaps they key dynamic of this whole development is an impulse towards nothingness. Atomisation and separation, distance and detachment, isolation and alienation, fracture and dislocation, impersonality and anonymity – these are the goals towards which desocialisation works.[53]

At a deeper level, the current trend towards de-socialisation indicates a general dilapidation of imaginary significations that bind society together. As pointed out in the first chapter, following the Castoriadian theory of psycho-genesis and socio-genesis, the socialisation process takes place as the psyche sublimates meanings available in the social-historical world. These meanings or social imaginary significations designate how a society views itself. Thus, for example, the Ancient Athenians imagined themselves as free citizens, the Jews as 'chosen people', the medieval Christians as children of the Church Fathers or subjects of the King. Contemporary societies lack a self-representation, a collective 'we', from which individuals can create meaning for their life and death, beyond sustaining and enhancing productivity and consumption. This entails an identity crisis, which induces conformity, and in turn, conformity makes the formation and preservation of an identity impossible.[54] Identity crisis, as Bauman observed, 'has become more than a rare condition of mental patients or a passing condition of adolescence', as '"sameness" and "continuity" are feelings seldom experienced nowadays either by the young or by adults'.[55]

The crisis is manifested in social institutions (the individual being one of them) which incarnate imaginary significations in their triple role of structuring representations, setting characteristic affects and indicating the aims of social doing. As capitalism permeates social institutions, it collapses existing significations and replaces them with its own values and significations (productivity, consumption, cost effectiveness, profit, competition, investment, performance etc.). Or, as Dufour puts it, liberal capitalism runs on de-institutionalisation; it simply defines everything as a commodity 'and then waits for the inevitable to happen: for human beings to transform themselves while they adapt to the commodities, which are henceforth promoted as the only reality'.[56] Under these conditions individuals are disabled from cathecting on their activities, beyond the profit-making and instrumental logic pervading institutions. Thus, the type, for example, of the conscientious professional (e.g. teacher, researcher, judge or doctor), created by earlier forms of society, is being destroyed, as he/she is institutionally disabled from acting through inner commitment and instead is controlled by surveillance techniques designed to ensure conformity.[57]

If desocialisation impacts human psyche in terms of its capacity to make meaning, there should also be consequences for its very health. In Modernity, the individual was threatened mainly by neurosis, divided between what was permitted and what was forbidden. In Postmodernity, the individual deals with psychotic tendencies induced by being incessantly plugged into all sorts of commodity and communication flows and the pervasive 'telepresence' which transforms the 'over there' into an 'over here'.[58] Especially, though, it is the alternation between anxiety and depression that threatens individuals today, as they face a world of employment and multiple consumption and lifestyle choices, where success and failures are considered solely a personal responsibility. According to official figures, anxiety or depression characterise the psychic reality of about a quarter of the European population each year.[59] Alain Ehrenberg has examined the emergence and spread of depression as psychic pathology embedded in contemporary society. As he remarks, depression portrays 'the style of the uncontrollable in the age of limitless possibilities'.[60] If neurosis was a likely condition of the person torn between what is allowed and what is not (the tragedy of guilt), depression threatens the individual who, free of his/her taboos, is divided between the possible and the impossible (the tragedy of inadequacy). Thus, in full contrast to the image of the motivated, visionary and energetic subject celebrated by liberal capitalism, the depressed person has severe difficulty in forming and carrying out plans, is unable to communicate meaningfully with the others and lacks energy to move and express him/herself. In Ehrenberg's words, depression 'is the familiar shadow of a person without a guide, tired of going forward to achieve the self and tempted to sustain himself through products and behaviours'.[61]

However, as it was noted above, the limitless possibilities amongst which the individual loses orientation have to do with the realm of consumption and life-style, rather than with his/her capacity to form and reform the terms under which society and its institutions operate. Postmodernity reduces this capacity through new modes of conformity. If in Modernity, conformity was expressed by the patient execution of orders, today it is manifested by the insecure and willingly surveilled employees, working under personalised performance targets, the narcissistic and infantile ethos of the consumer, the physically and digitally nomadic subjects, floating between different commodities, pleasures and realities, the extensive identity crises and the consequent psychosomatic disorders. The crucial difference with Modernity is that the expansion of capitalism undermines severely the potential for critique toward these new modes of conformity.

Undoubtedly, questioning and critique, as significations embedded in the Greco-European project of collective and personal autonomy, are presentified in institutions such as arts, education, publishing, journalism, media, the internet and civil society organisations. Nevertheless, we are witnessing the severe decline of critique due to the extensive penetration of these institutions by capitalist significations.

This is evident, for example, in music, film, literature and publishing, which are now largely run by industries and according to marketing strategies, but also in painting and sculpture. Works of art in the 19th and early 20th centuries were at the spearhead of critique towards religion, aristocracy, industrialisation or the political status quo, and they were unique expression of the artist's autonomy and free experimentation with different styles. In the 21st century, painting and sculpture have become assets and objects of speculation by rich individuals. The market has impacted fundamentally the way art is produced and circulated.[62] Moguls, speculators, major auction houses and mega galleries have turned works of art into colossally priced commodities and are making vanguard artists extremely rich. The dominance of global market is dragging art, as Adam's inquiry suggests, into 'an era of duplication and conformity, where the focus is on repetition of form supplied by a few hundred "bankable" names [. . .] rather than on a broad range of artistic creation at all levels'.[63]

Even more extensive is the commodification of the media. The media are largely connected with political and economic power and belong to corporations functioning in accordance to entrepreneurial plans and market strategies. Audio-visual media, especially, have acquired a central role in political life through electoral campaigning, information management, public opinion polls, image making and marketing of policy measures, transforming 'representative democracies' to 'mediacracies'.[64] Dialogue, contestation of ideas and critique in the media-dominated public space are lost amidst commercialised information and show-like news broadcasts, aiming mainly at high rates and high profits. A characteristic example is the 2016 presidential election in the USA, where the political, economic and media system promoted two candidates, one sponsored by the billionaire class and the other being a member of this class and a TV performer who ran a campaign as a vulgar 'reality show', highly profitable for the media. In the end, the 'insane clown' won the show, and took office with an entourage of 'alt-right' nationalists, militarists, and fellow-billionaires set to greater business.[65]

Contemporary media are or function largely as capitalist enterprises permeated by and promoting the significations of spectacle and perpetual amusement, thus rendering real dialogue impossible. Entertainment displaces articulate, critical discourse and has dissolving effects on serious exchange of views, as Postman and Bourdieu pointed out in their studies on television.[66] And as Debord remarked in his theses, there can be no dialogue in the spectacle, because the spectacle is the opposite of dialogue.[67] But more than critical dialogue, perpetual entertainment and enjoyment, celebrated in our times as conditions of happiness, absorb the very possibility of political action, which lies at the heart of the European tradition of citizenship. In fact, it is this European 'culture of revolt', as Julia Kristeva points out, drawing on Freud, which is a companion to the inner experience of happiness and constitutes an essential element of the principle of pleasure. The weakening or absence of this revolt culture, as she suggests, is an indication that a society is stagnating and turning to barbarism, namely to corporal or ethical violence.[68]

The advent of the internet would expectedly open pathways for critique and political activity breaking the monopoly of the mono-directional media (television, radio and newspapers). The internet has indeed decentralised electronic communication and allowed for the interactive circulation of information, knowledge and ideas. The proliferation of networking devices has made the internet an accessible tool for organising political action and communal initiatives, given voice to activists and independent journalists, encouraged horizontal communication between citizens and facilitated electronic voting for referenda and elections. More importantly, the internet has allowed individuals to be informed and learn independently, to an unprecedented extent in human history, bypassing institutions that have been controlling knowledge for centuries (e.g., the education and medical systems).

Yet, technology is embedded in the social-historical field. The internet today, especially after the proliferation of mobile gadgets and all kinds of 'apps', embodies primarily significations associated with contemporary capitalism and its emphasis on production and consumption, information, spectacle and entertainment, rather than with active citizenship.[69] Political organisations have changed the channel of communication from the traditional media to the internet rather than the nature of this communication.[70] 'Network governance' has been primary used to replace traditional forms of bureaucracy with new modes of 'pubic management', i.e. to reorganise the public sector on a business-like basis.[71] Apparently then, the early enthusiastic predictions about the revival of democracy through the internet have not come true. The same holds for all electronic media, whose introduction to everyday life has been traditionally accompanied by wished-for correlations between informed listeners/viewers/users and participating citizens.[72] In fact, even more than the traditional media, the extensive absorption of the public by digital technologies has turned, as Lovink remarks, the virtual into real and has established 'networks without cause' – time eaters, in which 'we're only being sucked deeper into the social cave without knowing what to look for'.[73] More so than ever before, the everyday immersion into the digital worlds of superficial communication (often anonymous and irresponsible), incessant flows of information and audiovisual spectacle, severely undermines attentiveness, the capacity to read major literature and monographs and the potential for thinking and critique. T.S. Eliot's lines in *Choruses from the Rock* sound timelier than never before: 'Where is the wisdom we have lost in knowledge? Where is the knowledge we have lost in information?'[74]

What is most remarkable, however, is how the personal computer and the internet, which would supposedly be the means to escape the gaze of 'Big Brother', have finally become the tools of generalised surveillance. We are denizens in the 'empire of surveillance', as Ramonet calls it – a state of affairs unprecedented and unimaginable even for the 20th century's dystopic literature on totalitarian societies.[75] Whereas a totalitarian regime would set up the mechanism to monitor citizens, now, as Ramonet remarks, this happens by the citizen's own initiative, when they simply buy a mobile device, which is essentially equivalent to electronic tagging. Moreover, whereas under dictatorial rule, it is the state which gathers surveillance data on its subjects, now it is a handful of global corporations that do this, sharing, of course, information with agencies of the state, but also making major profits from exploiting people's personal data and manipulating the public's decisions and choices.[76]

To be sure, surveillance can now be exercised by the state, by private business, as well as by individuals. From high-definition cameras installed on the international space station, available for renting to companies and private persons, down to face recognition apps that can identify the exact details of photographed people in a crowd, the inventiveness and expansion of surveillance technologies are inexhaustible.[77] The 'Big Brother' metaphor is now irrelevant: surveillance is ubiquitous and associated with the penetration of information processing in all spheres of life. In our 'post-panoptical' world, as Bauman calls it, network digital technologies and 'social media' have essentially abolished the distinction between the private and the public, which is crucial for democratic citizenship to function. Now, 'the private is public, to be celebrated and consumed by countless "friends" as well as casual "users"'.[78]

Citizenship is also weakened by capitalist reorganisation, at the historical phase, following the collapse of the communist rule in East Europe, that 'representative democracy' has become the prevalent political regime. Privatisation of public companies in many countries, along with the shift to individualised work patterns, has fragmented organised labour and reduced participation in trade unions.[79] Political activism is extensively corporatised and absorbed by what it supposedly criticises. Many Non-Governmental Organisations (NGOs) operating in the domains of human rights, gender equality, animal treatment or environmental protection are funded by major corporations which are hardly interested in these issues but very much like to appear 'ethical' in order to promote their products.[80] Funding comes also from the state or intergovernmental organisations with which many NGOs cooperate in policymaking projects (e.g., to 'raise awareness' amongst a local population) along bureaucratic and corporate standards (carrying out 'stocktaking reviews', defining inputs and outputs, lobbying with 'stakeholders', monitoring results etc.).[81] Bureaucratic and market values and rules have penetrated the discourse and the operation of a great array of public institutions, from transportation and communication to post offices and hospitals. Citizens in many countries have been rendered customers of state services, eligible to market 'accountability' rather than to public responsibility. The welfare state, the cornerstone of the legitimacy of the European nation-state in the 20th century, has been under a recurrent process of 'restructuring' since the 1980s, by both conservative and social democratic governments, which have weakened socio-economic safety nets.

At the core of economic restructuring in the last decades has been the subjection of governments and citizens to transnational financial markets, and this has had consequences for national sovereignty. States have relinquished their monetary sovereignty – i.e. their authority to create money – to the private sector and to global financial capital, thus shifting to debt-based economies. Debt creation or credit has become the engine of contemporary economy and a technique which establishes new power relations between creditors and debtors (i.e. states, citizens, consumers or users of welfare services).[82] As Lazzarato remarks, the European citizen, as a consumer, must spend money in order to sustain production and satisfy fashioned needs by putting him/herself in debt, and, as wage earner, he/she must earn less and use fewer social services to keep the costs of labour and social security low so that the economy is more competitive and the state pays back its sovereign debt. The debt economy deprives the majority of the Europeans from the wealth distribution that they had achieved throughout the 20th century but also from exercising, through their governments, political authority.[83]

Political authority has also been weakened by the transnationalisation of the state and its decision-making mechanisms. The modern state, as noted in the previous chapter, is a historically specific form of political organisation. Conventionally, it was born with the Treaty of Westphalia, and it has been associated with the demise of the medieval world, the appropriation of the nation and the building of impersonal bureaucracies, financial mechanisms, apparatuses of violence and a set of institutions, including the education system. Territoriality and sovereignty have been the characteristic features of the nation-state. But now the majority of European nation-states are parts of a historically unprecedented political form of a transnational 'super-state' or 'network state',[84] comprised of a variety of nations, with a single economy and with a set of powerful policymaking mechanisms: the European Union.

The Union has its origins in the six-member 'European Coal and Steel Community' (ECSC), which was created in 1951 in order to control mutually the production of these two materials, necessary at that time for the military industry, and thus to avoid a new war. In 1957, the 'European Economic Community' (EEC) was established by the Treaty of Rome, destined to facilitate trade and investments between the same members. With the accession of more member-states in the 1970s and 1980s, the EEC started building up a distinct economic and political presence on the global scene. That was also the time business enterprises started getting actively involved in the EU mechanisms to shape the Community's agenda for economic restructuring as a response to the then perceived Japanese and USA scientific and technological superiority. To organise a competitive response to this challenge, political and business elites joined forces to bypass national sovereignties and establish a common economic policy.[85] The concentration of both economic and policymaking command was accelerated in the 1990s under the conditions created by the collapse of the communist bloc, the re-unification of Germany and the rise of global capitalism. With the Maastricht/Amsterdam Treaty, the Lisbon Strategy and the introduction of the single currency, the process of 'European integration' has been decisively expanded, giving rise to a European transnational 'network state' – whose foundations though are currently being shaken by its debt crisis and the reactions amongst national constituencies against its excessive concentration of power.

European integration does not mean that nation-states have been eliminated, but that they are bypassed by the EU's decision-making mechanisms, which have been promoting intensively, in the last decades, neoliberal economics across the continent. Such a priority can hardly create a feeling of belonging capable of replacing citizens' commitment to their nation, notwithstanding the Union's attempts to use symbols and practices similar to those used by nation-states (flag, anthem, maps, statistical reviews, cultural events etc.).[86] Language, a crucial institution, cannot be used for this purpose either, as the widespread use of English is not only a European phenomenon. And despite the fact that the 12 stars of the EU flag refer to St John's Apocalypse, Christianity cannot be a source of European identity, as religion is no longer a dominant institution, and the EU includes non-Christian populations. In other words, the EU's multinational character has not allowed for the formation, through these materials, of a new 'imagined community' based on the past. Yet, it has allowed to keep in this past the nationalistic animosities and catastrophic wars in which the European states have been engaging against each other for centuries.

The EU functions like a network, whose nodes are member-states, governments, bureaucracies and businesses, connected with unequal power relations, in accordance to their role in the operation of the network. The current roles of Germany and the European Central Bank in the Eurozone are obvious illustrations of this power asymmetry.[87] This is also the modus operandi of the European Commission and its directorates, services, and agencies, the 'Eurogroup' and mechanisms such as the Open Method of Coordination (OMC), which engage member-states in the mutual pursuit of policy goals (by means of fixed guidelines, timetables, indicators, benchmarks, performance comparisons, monitoring, peer review, diffusion of 'best practices' etc.). This is a 'netocratic' mode of decision making, rather than a democratic structure.[88] It combines the functions of bureaucracy (e.g., long-term strategies, hierarchical relations and homogeneity) with those of the market (e.g., decentralisation, competition and short-term action).[89] In this context, political questions are replaced by technical issues elaborated through data production and presented by the EU institutions as objective solutions to objectively identified problems – set by experts, appointed committees, business agents and officially registered lobby groups. Thereby, the decision-making authority of national parliaments, a main creation of European Modernity, is seriously weakened and often completely displaced.

National political authorities, after all, are occupied with implementing in their countries neoliberal economics, which transcends state borders and ideological boundaries, under the pretext that 'there is no alternative' – thus rendering the Right/Left division, which marked traditionally parliamentary regimes, obsolete. The general consensus between most political forces on the absence of alternatives removes, on the one hand, the ground for critique and contestation of ideas on the part of citizens, while it induces them to turn to their private lives and their individual striving for survival or success. On the other hand, this consensus had fed the electoral power of forces, which invest politically in the weakening of nation-state sovereignty (hence, the notable success of exclusionist political parties and demagogues since last decade across Europe and now in the USA),[90] seeking to manage capitalism under neonationalistic or neofascist ideologies.

This latter phenomenon is associated with the crisis of another pivotal European signification: interculturality. Interculturality has its origins in the Greco-European tradition which acknowledged the particularity of cultures as well as, since the Enlightenment, universality, as a principle according to which all human beings should be free and equal citizens. However, the cultural 'other' has been seen predominantly through the signification of progress, intermingled in many cases with those of nation and 'race', which drove or legitimised imperialist interventions and exploitative immigration policies. Nonetheless, this dual acknowledgment of cultural multiplicity and universality lies at the root of the institution of contemporary multi-cultural societies and has allowed European countries, to use Gadamer's words, 'to learn the art of living with others' through a 'fusion of horizons'.[91] Today, Europe (as well as North America) contains some of the most multicultural cities in the world, and immigration from within and outside Europe is now a familiar reality across the continent.[92]

Facing cultural otherness challenges, however, established imaginary significations. The present crisis should be seen in the context of the displacement of the project of autonomy that accentuates citizenship, critique, reflectiveness and free contestation of ideas by liberal capitalism which 'tolerates' 'or 'respects' or 'accepts' cultural particularities while it levels them through the promotion of productivity and consumption in all sectors of life. Part of this context has been the so-called 'politics of difference' or 'identity politics' which has been advocating, over the last decades, social groupings around ethnicity, 'race', religion, language, sexuality etc., while it has been downplaying the universal quality of citizenship as open critical dialogue and power-sharing. The state has been carrying out these policies by undertaking the role of managing cultural differences through its institutions and primarily through the education system. In Modernity, the European state assumed the role of the nation's leader, discrediting local customs, identities and ethnic minorities as 'premodern' or 'parochial' in order to inculcate a unifying national identity.[93] Today, the state is managing interculturality while it prioritises successful integration into global capitalism. This condition induces reactions, for instance, by social forces which cannot 'respect differences' that encroach upon the premises of individual and collective autonomy (e.g., the case of minorities living under religious heteronomy); by those who see unfettered worker mobility used by businesses as an instrument to undermine established employment rights; by those who scapegoat the cultural 'others' as a reaction to domestic and own problems; or by believers in the 'purity of blood', i.e. nationalist and racist forces. Very often, these different positions and significations are confused (unintentionally or intentionally), as, for example, when opponents to religious heteronomy are considered intolerant to cultural differences or when the defence of human rights of minority members is used as a disguise by neonationalist (or neofascist) ideologies to advance exclusionism.

In short, democratic citizenship in our time is weakened by identity-based exclusionism and economic instrumentality, as well as their interaction. This interaction is also manifested by the attacks of Islamic terrorism against civilians and civil freedoms in Europe, since the last decade. What was a limited, geographically, phenomenon until recently has expanded dramatically across countries, following the recurrent Western military interventions in the Middle East, before and, especially, after 9/11.[94] Islamic fundamentalism, with horrific brutality against its own believers, extensive recruitment amongst the European youth, and the latest digital and spectacle technologies, has brought to Europe the barbarism that transnational capital, in its unstoppable quest for energy resources and market expansion, helped wake up.[95] Old and new forms of barbarism cooperate or clash, depending on economic and geostrategic interests, at the expense of democratic citizenship in Europe, but also at the expense of innocent lives in and mostly out of the continent. Barbarism, in its various forms, is forcibly displacing people at record levels, many of whom are seeking, through dreadful and uncertain journeys, refuge in Europe.[96]

In this Europe, in summary, capitalist significations have pervaded essentially all social institutions, absorbing or collapsing the project of collective and personal autonomy, expressed in democratic citizenship, questioning, critique and self-realisation and hindering the making of meaning beyond the domains of production and consumption. The outcomes are generalised heteronomy and conformity in times which celebrate 'free choice' in society, as well as in education.

The decline of the project of autonomy in education

The project of autonomy in European education has been expressed as knowledge seeking the truth, empirical observation, logical reasoning and argumentation, as well as emotional energy (*eros*) cathected on the pedagogic relationship and the act of learning. Moreover, closely associated with politics and democratic citizenship, autonomy in education has been manifested as equal access, organisational self-governance and critical disposition to established knowledge.

Ours is the age of universal primary and secondary education and of massive tertiary and higher education, as well as of digital technologies which have enormously expanded the possibilities for independent learning. Nevertheless, as it is argued here, the project of autonomy in education is in decline, and this can be observed, indicatively, in the fading or collapse of pedagogic spaces and relations, the waning of the signification of childhood, the extensive technologisation and bureaucratisation of learning, the 'vocationalisation' of curricula, the proliferation of surveillance techniques and the making of education policy under goals and mechanisms related with transnational capitalism. Special attention will be paid, as in the previous chapter, to higher education, which has been under extensive reforms aiming to eliminate the European legacy of academic autonomy.

The project of autonomy made its way in education, about half a century ago, through 'external' (e.g., abolition or weakening of school differentiation and examination barriers) and 'internal' reforms (e.g., relative independence in curriculum planning and classroom pedagogy), following the 1960s movements. The New Education movement or 'progressive' education had a widespread, though uneven, influence in Europe. The evolution and development of this movement has a long history, as the previous chapter showed, but it is especially from the 1960s on that education systems – particularly, pre-school, primary and, partially, lower secondary education – endorsed and applied 'progressive' practices.

Bernstein, who devoted much of his work studying these practices, remarked that in the 1960s, there was a convergence between linguistic, sociological and psychological theories which, under the impact of the social movements of the time, foregrounded the autonomy of the pupil with respect to learning. The main aim of progressive education is that pupils should live their childhood and express themselves freely without much teacher intervention and without concern about their future school performance and career. The learner's work, in this context, is regarded as an expression of the particular stage of cognitive, social or personal development that she/he is going through, rather than something which indicates their performance. The function of evaluation is to show what is present in the pupil's work, rather than what is missing or what has to be corrected. Similarly, emphasis is placed on the process of teaching rather than on its results. Learners are given a measure of control in content (choice according to their interests), in the sequence and pace of teaching, and in space (relatively free movement in the classroom). The teacher is considered a facilitator of pupils' learning, rather than its exclusive source. Curriculum planning favours weak boundaries between subjects and cross-thematic projects, while delivery through the exclusive use of textbooks is not favoured. The overall purpose of pupil-centred education is personal emancipation, empowerment and self-fulfilment of the learner, and it is opposed to the use of learning for economic aims.[97]

However, as no institution develops in social vacuum, progressive education has to been seen in the magma of significations characterising European (and Western) societies, particularly in relation to the expansion of liberal capitalism and possessive individualism since the mid-20th century. Bernstein highlighted the 'therapeutic' mode of control exerted by liberal/progressive pedagogic methods, as opposed to the imperative controls characteristic of traditional education.[98] Hannah Arendt, observed, already in the 1950s, in her essay *The Crisis in Education*, that the withdrawal under child-centred education of teacher authority, on the ground that it is, by definition, tyrannical, has deprived children from an important aspect of their socialisation. This would lead, as she suggested, to their subjection to a truly tyrannical authority, that of their peer group. The child, as Arendt reminded, is a newcomer to a world that is strange to him/her, and he/she must be gradually introduced to it. The teacher, even though he/she did not create this world, is there as a representative of the society of adults who assume responsibility for the child's development. With the relinquishment of pupils' learning to extensive interaction with their peers, the teacher no longer assumes this responsibility and the pupils are left out of a vital part of their socialisation. Since there is no longer authority to either rebel against or escape from, the pupil ends up adopting compliant or delinquent behaviour, or both.[99] The fact that today 'bullying' has come to be one of the main pathologies of school life in many countries[100] would vindicate Arendt's insight about the excesses of child-centred pedagogy. The same phenomenon would vindicate contemporary authors who draw attention to the role of the audiovisual media in incapacitating children from taking part in dialogic relations at school and thus from developing themselves as listeners and speakers. In other words, violent behaviour at school becomes possible, as the discursive space, where teacher authority is exercised and meaning is made through patient deliberation and discussion, is weakened or collapses.[101]

Apparently, the development of 'progressive' or, as it was later renamed, 'postmodern' education, in the context of liberal capitalism and its consumer ethos, has undermined, instead of advancing, the pedagogic relation in the school, a relation of logos and eros in the Greco-European tradition. In fact, there have been critical educationists who granted intellectual support to this development. For example, Aronowitz and Giroux, in their book *Postmodern Education*, express their satisfaction with the cultural industry and the television shaping and promoting 'popular culture', because, as they argued, it brings pupils and students in touch with their surroundings and with pleasure. '. . .Popular culture both reconciles us to the social order and threatens it because it puts us in touch with pleasure, even when we have to buy it', the two authors write, and they suggest with emphasis: 'So critical pedagogy is amongst other virtues, a *discourse on pleasure*'.[102] This is a good example of how many 'progressive' (or 'postmodern' or 'critical') educationists welcomed into the school classroom the products and strategies of neoliberal capitalism while appearing to criticise it at the same time.

But, as all creations, intellectual activity too is immersed in the magma of imaginary significations dominating a society and a historical era. Our era is marked by the advent of the spectacle industry and perpetual entertainment – something which has had profound effects on the institution of childhood and the function of the school. As it was shown earlier in this study, the signification of childhood emerged in Ancient Greece along with the creation of the school, but it was mainly during Modernity that childhood was institutioned as a distinct phase of human life. Childhood was associated with a host of meanings, such innocence and shame, and it was attributed developmental traits that derived from psychology and educational studies. The society of spectacle, information, entertainment and old and new media is also the society where childhood is in process of dissolution as we have known it so far. The commercialised and ever-present media have lifted the 'veil' from the world to which, until the recent past, adults introduced children, and from which they could protect them, through social institutions such as the school and the family.

The family as an institution has been dramatically transformed over the last decades. The success of the feminist movement, part of the European project of autonomy, has essentially put an end to millennia-long patriarchal domination. A diversity of familial types and arrangements now co-exist with the remnants of Modernity's 'nuclear family model'. Children are being raised in families where roles are negotiable, rather than taken for granted. The collapse of the patriarchal family has brought about liberation, but also, in conjunction with changes in production, consumption and the very meaning of childhood, an identity crisis, which, as far as children and adolescents are concerned, is also an authority crisis. Children are introduced to the world largely by the media and the advertising industry, whose prescriptions are followed by their parents, too. Postman remarked in *The Disappearance of Childhood* that the increasing 'adultification' of children, but also the 'childification' of adults, associated with widespread consumerism, entertainment and unrestricted access to media contents. As he pointed out 'we are in the process of exorcising a two-hundred year-old image of the young as child and replacing it with the imagery of the young as adult'.[103] He observed that children appear on the media frequently as miniature adults, as in 13th- and 14th-century paintings, while child clothing and playing are disappearing, replaced by competitive games. The emphasis placed in recent years on pupils' performance and career-oriented schooling are additional manifestations of children's' adultification.[104]

The everyday exposure of children to the media, especially the television, is part of this transformation. The contents of the television constitute a 'curriculum', as Postman remarks, as it also teaches and shapes the mind of the young.[105] Nowadays, these contents have to do primarily with violence, power, money-making and consumption, all presented as entertainment. Moreover, while story-listening and book-reading allow the pupil to create their own mental images and meanings, TV-watching, as Dufour points out, exposes children, as everyone else, to relentless televisual images that cause constant disruption of meanings – let alone symptoms such as difficulty in concentration, memory loss, insomnia, or aggression. In comparison to watching TV, teaching appears 'boring' unless it resembles a televised chat show and uses heavily audiovisual technologies.[106]

Television has had a massive impact on learning, and so does now ICT. ICT allows access to information and knowledge as well as interactive communication on a global scale. Never before has it been so easy for pupils and students to access educational material (maps, experiment demonstrations, recorded presentations etc.) available in such a graphic and realistic mode as today. Children and adolescents are fully immersed into the audiovisual and digital environment of 'virtual, 'augmented' or 'mixed reality', provided by numerous types of electronic devices: computers, laptops, iPads, tablets, phablets, smartphones, videogame consoles etc. These devices and their plentiful 'apps' have combined education and entertainment establishing the so-called *edutainment* as a mode of learning, which can take place at anytime and anywhere, thus undermining severely the authority of schools and teachers in knowledge communication. As well as the 'television children', the 'screen-agers' or the 'digital natives' of today live in a 'know-it-all state of mind', where there is nothing new to discover or to learn from their teachers or from adults in general.[107] In this regard, as Dufour remarked, teachers are no longer *instituteurs* (meaning 'primary teachers' in French), since they do not institute children as pupils any more, and thus, children are no longer pupils.[108]

Pupils and students are called on everywhere by companies of educational technology to 'learn while having fun' through various devices and applications. As a consequence, curricula are being commercialised and standardised under the claim that they become technologically more efficient and pedagogically more attractive. Good education is increasingly identified with updating hardware and software and the capacity to retrieve, reproduce and present information and knowledge, thus displacing critique towards its actual content. Students are being accustomed to the so-called 'multitasking', which in essence means distraction by different activities performed simultaneously (information retrieval, video watching, communication, shopping, social networking etc.) and reduced concentration on their main undertakings. Moreover, students are now massively registered as members of 'social media', which, although they have allowed for networked communication and for the bypassing of the traditional state or corporate media, have subjected the young to their surveillance and marketing strategies, and keep them attached to all sorts of screens throughout the day.

Overall, digital learning and edutainment provide now a major field for profit-making, for software and hardware corporations, despite the fact that widespread ICT use in schools not only has not improved learning attainment, but, in fact, has damaged it. The OECD, for instance, which urged originally its member-states to close the 'digital divide' through ICT use in education, has finally discovered that students who use most frequently computers at school demonstrate the worst learning outcomes.[109] In the meantime, for-profit educational technology firms, private foundations and governmental and inter-governmental agencies, the 'education-industrial complex', promoted educational hardware and software into schools and universities as an undeniable necessity for 'effective education' – which also means the recurrent measurement of everyone and everything involved in education.[110] Indeed, the pervasive presence of ICT in educational establishments is augmenting their monitoring and control. Universities, schools, teachers and students have been turned into data and they are subjected to detailed surveillance (examination results, performance measurement, test scores, attendance rates etc.).[111] The invention of the so-called 'affective computing' threatens to insert surveillance in the very teaching process by monitoring students' engagement through facial-expression recognition.[112]

Although the extensive use of digital technologies is very recent, the new modes of performance surveillance in schools appeared in the 1990s, when education policies shifted from traditional bureaucratic controls to outcome-driven regulation. Taking advantage of the critique towards bureaucracy, neoliberal policies castigated, already from the 1980s, 'red tape' in the public sector, for stifling personnel's initiative and creativity and troubling citizens, and set out to replace it by a 'new public management', orientated to outcomes. Undoubtedly, schools have traditionally been subject to bureaucracy, operating under formal circulars, prescribed material and uniform practices. Uniformity and routine that disallow professional initiative and socialise students into hierarchical power relationships have been characteristic traits of schools. With the introduction of 'new public management', those constraints were to be removed: hierarchies would be flattened, 'red tape' would be diminished and schools would be flexible and could control their strategies and practices. 'Educational restructuring' spread across Europe, aimed, supposedly, to enhance professional autonomy by delegating authority and financial resources to schools for their day-to-day needs. However, what these reforms were about was the introduction of market principles in the discourse, policies and organisational practices of educational establishments and the turning of students and parents into customers. Measures such as school-based budget schemes have forced schools to look for extra funding from private resources; 'free school choice' has instigated competition between schools for students, funds, and higher performances; and schools' and teachers' public responsibility has been turned into market 'accountability' through detailed performance monitoring and evaluation.

Evaluation, as Foucault has shown, has multiple regulative effects (i.e. correcting, training, categorising, normalising) over the evaluated.[113] In education, it can impose hierarchical visibility in the way establishments operate and perform, which allows for public comparison and classification. Evaluation stresses outcomes, but it can alter pedagogic practices by refocusing them on the outcomes expected. In the last decades, evaluation mechanisms (standardised tests, evaluation boards, performance indicators, comparative data, monitoring schemes etc.) have been used across Europe (as well as in North America, Australia and New Zealand) to monitor performances and control pedagogic practices. As a consequence, the potential of institutions, educationists, teachers and communities to reflect on the way knowledge should be organised and taught, a fundamental aspect of autonomy in/through education, has been displaced. In short, this entire 'managerial revolution', with its supposed aim to set educational establishments free from bureaucracy and make them autonomous, flexible and innovative organisations to work and learn, has replaced or merged one mode of bureaucratic control with another, thus enhancing conformity.

The augmentation of bureaucracy and related monitoring techniques are manifestations of the expansion of the signification of rationalistic mastery and control, including capitalist significations, such as productivity, competitiveness, and consumption. Parents of schoolchildren and university students are now customers, learners are human resources, and knowledge should serve production and labour market demands. One could remark a process of 'vocationalisation' of study programmes in selected European countries since the 1990s.[114] In higher education, traditional distinctions between universities and non-universities have been abolished or weakened, and a common system has arisen in which the two types function as competitors, seeking private funding and constructing modularised programmes of study responsive to labour market needs. Secondary education systems have been brought closer to the economy under education reforms seeking to introduce content related to future employment and reducing or abolishing classical studies.[115] For the same purpose, there has been an increasing emphasis on the detailed specification of competences as a central principle for organising educational knowledge and teaching.[116] Similarly, there has been an expansion of recurrent, formal and non-formal training as a condition for employability in the increasingly volatile European labour markets. Education has been permeated in these last decades by the priorities and the language of the economy to an unprecedented extent. 'Knowledge should flow like money to wherever it can create advantage and profit', as Bernstein observed. 'Knowledge is divorced from persons, their commitments, their personal dedication, for these become impediments, restrictions on flow, and introduce deformations in the working of the market'.[117]

Although the takeover of education by the economy has been promoted by governments, in various degrees, in selected countries, the EU has played a vital role in spreading this policy across Europe, proclaiming as its main goal to: 'develop and make the best use of human resources and achieve maximum investment efficiency . . . otherwise, the likelihood is that the gap between the Union and its main competitors will become even wider'.[118] The EU has been making policies in education through provisions and ministerial initiatives, mainly in vocational education, since the early times of the EEC. Later on, the 'European Community' developed its major educational programmes and actions in order to promote mobility and cooperation between students and institutions. From the Maastricht Treaty (1992) onwards, educational programmes promoting a 'European dimension in education' proliferated. Since 2000 (at the Lisbon summit), the EU has activated a whole set of mechanisms and methods to steer its member-states' education systems towards the realisation of so-called 'Europe of knowledge'.[119] Thus, European states decided, at the turn of the century, to both give an end to their exclusive national education policy and to subjugate their education systems to the commands of the economy. Education systems and practices remain, of course, deeply rooted in their national histories and conditions. But education policies follow largely a common agenda, not by means of traditional 'policy borrowing', but through transnational policymaking networks and bureaucracies. Member-states engage, through unequal power relations, in mutual pursuit of policy goals which rely heavily on data produced by public and private research agencies, most often sponsored by the European Commission. These data provide 'scientific' support to what is diagnosed as a problem or agreed upon as a goal, thus legitimising the proposed measures.

This state of affairs in decision making has fundamental repercussions for the function of democratic politics across Europe and consequently for the entire project of collective and personal autonomy in education. For politics to exist, there should be a distinction between expertise and political opinion, and political decisions should be the outcome of public deliberation. At a deeper level, for politics to exist, societies should be able to call into question the social imaginary significations (the fundamental locus of power) incarnated in their institutions, projects and policies. Accordingly, *education politics* is possible only when there is activity by citizens – parents, teachers/academics and students – capable of putting explicitly into question and reflect and deliberate on the purpose, the contents and the pedagogic mode of learning, and, if deemed necessary, alter them. This should be distinguished from *education policymaking*, which is a hierarchical and expert-driven process of decision making that is based on a taken-for-granted or implicit political opinion about the purpose, the contents and the pedagogic mode of learning. This kind of decision making, which has characterised policy under the nation-state, is now the modus operandi of the European 'network state', which thus supersedes the potential for education politics within the space of its member-countries.

Indeed, education politics is displaced by transnational policymaking networks and steering mechanisms of objective setting and performance measurement as well as by the penetration of the economy in education systems which, thus, diminish the project of autonomy in education. This is clear in universities, which have been subject to a series of reforms around Europe, including those promoted by the so-called Bologna Process.

As suggested in the previous chapter, the university as an institution of higher education was 'Europeanised' when it was defined as, and identified with, a self-governing community of scholars and learners who decide, as an academic body and as individuals, about the knowledge they create and the way it is communicated. The landmark for this was the early 19th-century German reforms, whose historical precedents were two, independent from each other, traditions of higher education in Europe: Plato's Academy in Ancient Athens and the founding of *universitas* in the High Middle Ages. The Academy created a space of free contestation of ideas amongst scholars, adopting and utilising the spirit of political freedom prevailing in the polis. The universitas established the corporation of scholars and students as a legal person entitled to elect its authorities and designate its educational practices, within the limits posed by the dominance of religion. These traditions were synthesised in European Modernity, during which self-governance and freedom in research and teaching, namely academic autonomy, were established as the indispensable properties to regard an institution of higher education as university. No doubt, the university has been highly bureaucratised, functioning under hierarchical control of knowledge and scholars and has reflected the dominant social class structure. However, the project of academic autonomy has always accompanied universities, and it has been an essential part of the critical spirit that emerged in Modernity.

Since the end of the 20th century, we have observed the decline of this project across Europe. In more recent years, we have witnessed a concerted pan-European policymaking process to eliminate the legacy of academic autonomy in the continent, but also beyond,[120] in all its three dimensions – politics and governance, knowledge as research and curriculum, and pedagogy as knowledge impartation. This argument is substantiated below through reference to EU policy documents.

Education politics in European universities, as deliberation and decision making on behalf of the academic community and as governance of their institution, is being displaced by transnational policymaking and corporate management. The Bologna Process, led in reality by the EU and with the full commitment of its member-states, renders university reform a matter of policy networks, dominated by major business and bureaucracies, which define the policy agenda and monitor and evaluate its implementation across Europe through massive data collection. The Bologna Follow-up Group (BFUG), the body which oversees the Process, is composed of the representatives of all countries participating in the Process, EU agencies, as well as 'consultative members'.[121] From all these members, the European Commission and its Directorates as well as business associations are the most powerful 'nodes' of the Bologna policymaking network. The European Commission sponsors, financially and organisationally, the ministerial meetings and takes a variety of related initiatives aiming at pulling universities to the EU's 'modernisation agenda', that is, the establishment of a competitive 'knowledge industry'. In other words, the Commission plays a crucial role in realising the Bologna Process in terms of setting mechanisms, promoting measures and diffusing the discourse, part of which is, apparently, 'scolding' universities for having kept, until recently, some measure of autonomy:

> After remaining a comparatively isolated universe for a very long period, both in relation to society and to the rest of the world, with funding guaranteed and a status protected by respect for their autonomy, European universities have gone through the second half of the 20th century without really calling into question the role or the nature of what they should be contributing to society.[122]

The business interest groups have direct involvement in the Process and make detailed proposals for university reform, which are adopted, to a remarkable extent, by the EU and the Bologna Process (e.g., 'quality assurance' and rankings, student mobility, increased research and courses in science and technology and involvement of entrepreneurs in curricula design and the management of universities).[123] These proposals are promoted through the formal meetings of the Process, the various committees in which business representatives take part, as well as through lobbying, for which they are officially registered with the European Commission as 'professional associations', along with hundreds of other associations and companies.[124]

The European Commission pronounces its understanding of 'the role of universities through education, research and innovation, in the transfer of knowledge to the economy and society as a main contribution to Europe's competitiveness and the need for closer cooperation between academia and the world of enterprise'.[125] For this reason, the 'European Research Area' (ERA) has been established, in order 'to ensure "knowledge transfer", namely exploitation of research produced in universities by business and industry'.[126] Under this policy, academics are not considered independent scholars but an industrial workforce or 'brainpower', which the EU aims at 'mobilising' and 'applying it in the economy and society . . .'.[127]

To have their reforms passed, the EU and the Bologna Process are employing a variety of means: legally binding decisions, state legislation, funding-based leverage, assessment mechanisms and recurrent 'shaming/faming' comparisons. Member-states justify ideologically the decisions taken in the transnational settings to their citizens and introduce and enforce the legislation necessary for the implementation of these decisions. Also crucial is the role of EU mechanisms (e.g., the Open Method of Coordination, the EU Directorates and associated 'advisory committees' and 'expert groups' and the European Association for Quality Assurance in Higher Education – ENQA), in which member-states engage in the mutual pursuit of policy goals by means of performance comparison and benchmarking. In other words, evaluation plays a central part in the realisation of the policy agenda by prescribing the rules for 'internal' and 'external' scrutiny of universities' performance.[128]

Indeed, evaluation mechanisms and procedures are of major importance for controlling institutions, academics and their practices, and they are closely linked with the EU's policy to turn universities into competing business units. The European universities should not operate as corporations in the sense of communities of learners, but as corporations according to the later meaning of the term: business organisations led by appointed managers and running with cost-benefit and profit-seeking criteria. This fundamental organisational transformation is accomplished by the member-states which are made aware that 'the development of an entrepreneurial culture at universities requires profound changes in university governance and leadership'.[129] Established divisions in faculties, departments, laboratories and administrative units – where academics traditionally had a say – are replaced by 'new internal governance systems based on strategic priorities and on professional management of human resources, investment and administrative procedures'.[130]

As well as by means of corporate management, the reduction of scholars to 'human resources' is pursued through the enforced involvement of the private sector in higher education. As the Commission proclaims: '. . .the stronger involvement of enterprises in university boards, research agendas, admission panels, curriculum design, course delivery and quality assurance systems can significantly improve universities' teaching, research and innovation'.[131] Universities are being turned into business primarily by means of legislation, but also by being held committed 'through multi-annual agreements' and 'strategic objectives', which include chasing competitive and outcome-based funding.[132] Evaluation mechanisms are crucial for this purpose: 'Competitive funding should be based on institutional evaluation systems and on diversified performance indicators with clearly defined targets and indicators supported by international benchmarking for both inputs and economic and societal outputs . . .'.[133] Scholars should be subject to assessment by indicators such as: 'research outputs per academic staff', 'external research income', 'number and percentage of competitive grants won', 'commissioned reports', 'consultancy contracts', 'number of collaborations and partnerships' and similar gauges that force academics to shape their knowledge and research according to the desires of all kinds of sponsors.[134]

Evidently, under these European-wide university reforms, management-based governance is dissolving the academic community by turning scholars into methodically controlled 'knowledge workers' or 'human resources' with no say for the affairs of their institution. The management system promoted across Europe is changing the relation between the body of academics and the administration within the university. Traditionally, the administration processed the decisions made by the academic body (in which, of course, there were strong internal hierarchies); now, academics are being fully subjected to an increasingly voluminous administration, which exercises (and is subject to) thorough surveillance through digital databases. Moreover, management is exposing academic staff to market relations by involving business agents in governance, removing employment security from academics and forcing them to make their interests and knowledge available for purchase by any potential buyer.

Thus, universities under these reforms are being stripped of their, already, limited autonomy, and academics are being disabled from deciding, not only about the governance of their institution, but also about their research and even their teaching. They are being asked to 'generate *income by selling services* . . . particularly to the business sector, and from *using research results*'.[135] The consequences of obliging academics to sell their research are obvious in the domains of science and technology (e.g., pharmaceutics, medicine, ICT, biotechnology, nanotechnology and nuclear engineering), and they have often been reported. Stephanie Pain, for example, associate editor of *New Scientist* in the 1990s, commenting on the dependence of biological and pharmaceutical research on funding by private companies, testified to these consequences: '. . .where research was once mostly neutral, it now has an array of paymasters to please. In place of impartiality, research results are being discreetly managed and massaged, or even locked away if they don't serve the right interests. Patronage rarely comes without strings attached'.[136] In the humanities and social sciences, scholars must conform to the agendas and pursuits of private or public agencies and research funds, operating in and out of their country, at the expense of their personal intellectual interests. Academics are required to succumb to the aims and the bureaucratic rules and decision making processes of external agencies (e.g., applications, budgeting, anticipation of outcomes, deadlines, procedures of approval or rejection, reporting to sponsors etc.). Thereby, scholars are being institutionally obstructed from creating knowledge following their own intellectual interests and judgement, and they are obliged to produce knowledge which is being, in an unprecedented manner, both marketised and bureaucratised.

Given that universities transmit to a large extent the knowledge that their staff creates, the control of their research has self-evident repercussions to what they teach. However, transnational policy is intervening in the design of university curricula too, on behalf of the business sector: 'The Commission will support business-academia collaborations through the creation of 'knowledge alliances' between education and business to develop new curricula addressing innovation skills gaps'.[137] In fact, this curriculum policy in universities 'should extend beyond the needs of the labour market to the stimulation of an entrepreneurial mindset amongst students and researchers'.[138]

Similar suggestions are promoted through the so-called Qualifications Framework which encompasses all higher education qualifications in the 'European Higher Education Area' (EHEA), consisting of the countries that participate in the Bologna Process. Academics in all member-states are required to design their courses at all levels by defining expected outcomes in accordance with the categories and the language (e.g., 'knowledge', 'skills' and 'competences') prescribed by the Qualifications Framework. These are elaborated by *Tuning Educational Structures in Europe*, a process of curricular and pedagogic standardisation operating across European universities. *Tuning*, since its start in 2000, has aimed: 'to link the political objectives of the Bologna Process and at a later stage the Lisbon Strategy to the higher educational sector'.[139] *Tuning*'s main aim is to design comparable curricula, described in terms of cycles, levels, learning outcomes, competences and workload-based credits. Study programmes should be output-oriented and modularised. Learning outcomes must be stated both at programme level and for every course unit or module. Learning outcomes are formed in terms of competences, which *Tuning* classifies as 'instrumental', 'interpersonal' and 'systemic competences'. Through its detailed technical description, *Tuning* links learning outcomes, competences and workload-based credits. Following this standard procedure, so far, *Tuning* has produced curricula in the subject areas of Business, Chemistry, Earth Sciences, Education Sciences, European Studies, History, Mathematics, Nursing and Physics. An increasing number of universities and scholars whose countries apply the Qualifications Framework are required to plan their courses according to *Tuning's* competence-driven and outcome-based curriculum design. As the European Commission observes contently: 'The new language of learning outcomes is gradually being introduced across the entire life cycle of learning, from curriculum development to teaching, learning, assessment, recognition and quality assurance'.[140]

In short, under the current university reforms in Europe, scholars are required to teach knowledge related to labour-markets and standardise the language and the organisation of their teaching; they are being obstructed from creating the knowledge they wish and are instead obliged to sell off their intellectual interests to all kinds of sponsors, succumbing to competition and bureaucratic rules; and they are placed under productivity surveillance by corporate management methods that disintegrate the academic community and treat students as consumers. Reforms are carried out by transnational policymaking networks that are dominated by business interest groups and mechanisms of objective-based steering and performance monitoring, rendering universities parts of a 'knowledge industry' and subjecting them to the competition strategies of the corporate world.

The extensive acceptance, active or passive, of the EU agenda and the Bologna Process and similar reforms that have taken place across Europe testify to the penetration of higher education by the capitalist imaginary, at the expense of the idea of academic autonomy – a valuable European legacy, notwithstanding its inadequate realisation. The same complex of significations prevails in the field of higher education studies, which, of course, is not exempt from the increasing compulsion placed on other fields to produce externally sponsored knowledge: official documents, policymaking events and claims about the Bologna Process are being reproduced to designate it as the glorious pathway for competitiveness and progress; marketisation is considered a positive challenge that universities should undertake; management theories are employed to study university governance, taking corporate management as its natural and irrefutable reality; and the European university legacy is reduced to a 'Humboldtian model', which simply belongs to the past or is dismissed as a mere 'Humboldtian myth'. The perception underlying contemporary accounts is that what is happening now is good because it is new and what happened or was attempted in the past is simply old and thus outmoded. This perception is reminiscent of Pangloss, the intellectual figure in Voltaire's satirical novel *Candide*; Pangloss, expressing Leibniz, is sure that the new world is the best of all possible worlds and the castle of his noble paymaster the best of all possible castles.

This perception, in other words, is rooted in the social imaginary of progress emerged in European Modernity and spread in the rest of the world, especially as 'development'. This has been the driving force of the globalisation of capitalism, but also of education policy and comparison.

Transnational education policy and country rankings

In Greek Antiquity and European Modernity, as the two previous chapters showed, comparison with foreign societies and their institutions was conceived as impartial inquiry and critical reflection on domestic institutions. Although this intellectual attitude has been inscribed in cross-cultural studies, overseas societies have been primarily gauged, since the 19th century, through the lenses of capitalism and the idea of progress, both associated with the central imaginary signification of unlimited expansion of rationalistic mastery and control, generated in European Modernity.

Since then, progress, economic and techno-scientific development, nation-state, bureaucratic organisation and capitalism have been the main significations and institutions disseminated across countries, through conquering, colonisation, international relations, cultural lending and borrowing and, in our age, through globalisation. The project of personal and collective autonomy, present in social movements and struggles around the world, has hardly taken root in the various 'republics' and 'liberal democracies' that have sprung up in the last decades. Democratic institutions have been the pretext for imperialist interventions or function as a façade of autocratic regimes that suppress even basic civil rights, which are now being weakened in most countries.[141]

Rather than spreading democracy, globalisation has given rise to a world structured by capitalism, which, as the following pages will show, is incarnated in the dominant way by which societies and education systems are compared. Globalisation is distinguished by the abolition of restrictions in cross-border mobility of products, services, information and, especially, by the wide range of action that financial markets and big corporations have acquired, which has weakened severely states' ability to organise production and trade and to control their fiscal policies. This is different from the word economy of the past. As Robinson points out, until the mid-20th century, each country developed circuits of accumulation that were connected through exchange of commodities and flows of capital in an inter-national market. But now, these national circuits are functionally integrated into global circuits of accumulation. Globalisation 'is unifying the world into a single mode of production and a single global system and bringing about the organic integration of different countries and regions into a global economy'.[142] Globalisation operates through digital networks, transcending territorial and institutional boundaries and compressing time and space, thus giving rise, in Castells's terms, to a 'space of flows' and to 'timeless time'. The 'space of flows' indicates a global capitalist territory which networks mega-cities, business and financial functions, sites of techno-scientific innovation and production, and labour and operates through circuits of electronic exchange. 'Timeless time' expresses the incessant hunting for profit in real time and around the clock and the culture of the ephemeral and the eternal induced by consumerism, digitalisation and the audiovisual collages of the media.[143]

Globalisation concerns policymaking, too, as the authority of nation-states as administrative and policymaking mechanisms has decreased, and they now function less as 'sovereign' entities and more as the components of an international 'polity'.[144] This polity constitutes a 'transnational state apparatus', which Robinson defines as a 'network that comprises transformed and externally-integrated national states, together with the supranational economic and political forums . . .'.[145] Education policy and the comparison of education systems are amongst the key priorities of this transnational network, whose nodes are mainly three types of institutions: global business, states and International (or intergovernmental) Organisations (IOs). All together, they constitute a space of 'economic sovereignty', to borrow Beck's phrase, which is actively devising and promoting policies, but it is devoid of politics:

> This represents the first ever manifestation of a (quasi-) state without territory, whose power impacts upon existing territorial states from the outside, but which also creates a new political space beyond their borders. This is an utterly unpolitical state, a state without public sphere, indeed a quasi-state without society, located in a 'non-place', pursuing 'non-policies' which it uses to restrict the power of national societies and to break them up from the inside.[146]

The role of transnational corporations in this context is pivotal, as they enhanced dramatically capital accumulation and the economic control that they exercise over countries. According to figures from 2008, out of 166 economies with sales or Gross Domestic Product (GDP) of more than 50 billion US dollars, only 60 are countries. The other 106 are corporations.[147] Currently, there are more than 43,000 transnational corporations located in 116 different countries. But only 737 of these companies accumulate 80% of the control over the value of all transnational corporations. Even more remarkably, 40% of this control is accumulated just by 147 corporations, 3/4 of which are financial intermediaries – something that testifies to the dominance of financial capital and the 'global casino' they have established over national economies.[148]

Techno-scientific knowledge and therefore education systems are of pivotal importance for global capital because they provide the means for recurrent innovation and thus enhanced profitability. To access and control knowledge as well as the 'human resources' of countries, global capital, as Beck suggests, employs a range of strategies.[149] With its 'autarchic strategies', capital tries to minimise its dependency on individual countries by rendering them easily replaceable and interchangeable, depending on whether they fulfil investment criteria; with its 'substitution strategies', capital places countries in a process of competition by comparing them on the basis of a unitary norm in order to make them streamlined for investments; and with its 'innovation strategies', capital acquires systematic access to the cognitive possibilities of national societies – namely access to the innovatory capacity of science and technology – in order to devise new production methods and new products.

Hence the promotion of reforms across countries which standardise education provision and knowledge generation: they are intended to produce human and cognitive resources relevant to global business and to increase competition between countries and therefore the range of options available for investors to choose from. Nation-states endorse, through their participation in transnational institutions, a policy agenda intending to make education systems more performative and more competitive. The weakening of the sovereignty of the nation-state does not mean that it cannot enforce policies on its citizens. On the contrary, its role is indispensable for the realisation of transnational policies. The nation-state can justify ideologically the decisions taken in global fora to its citizenry (e.g., arguing for the importance of acquisition of productive skills through education as a necessary condition for competiveness), and it can introduce the legislation necessary for the implementation of these decisions.[150] Certainly, there are unequal power relations in transnational policymaking: some 'nodes' are more powerful than others and thus able (e.g., through funding, differential voting rights in intergovernmental organisations, expertise, political or business pressures etc.) to have their own goals adopted by all 'nodes'. However, it is nation-states and their political authorities which accede to take part in this system and adhere to the rules and power relations of its institutions.

Intergovernmental organisations and regional or 'super-state' institutions, such as the EU, constitute the third actor, along with nation-states and global business, that play today a major role in shaping education policy, as well as in shaping their member-countries' comparative gaze towards other education systems. These institutions, as Beck points out, function mainly as the 'midwives' of global markets, undertaking the turning of national states and societies into instruments of capital flows and production-consumption cycles.[151] The EU, for example, calls on national education systems to create the most 'competitive knowledge-based economy in the world', the OECD to present high scores in production-related subjects and skills, the World Bank to focus on human capital production, and the World Trade Organisation (WTO) to become 'educational services' opened up to foreign investments.

The modus operandi of IOs is bureaucratic, and this vests their decisions with 'rationality' and validity. Indeed, as Barnett and Finnemore remind, in a relevant study, IOs are bureaucracies created by states, and they appear, as all bureaucratic authority, according to Weber, as rational, impartial and technical. IOs are 'in authority', as the two researchers point out, and at the same time, they are 'an authority'. They are 'in authority' because they have the role that national societies recognise as legitimate for them to exercise power, and they are 'an authority' because they handle data and demonstrate expertise. Thus, they are valued as superior and neutral agencies of policymaking:

> Bureaucracy is powerful and commands deference, not in its own right, but because of the values it claims to embody and the people it claims to serve. IOs cannot simply say, 'we are bureaucracies; do what we say'. To be authoritative, ergo powerful, they must be seen to serve some valued and legitimate social purpose, and, further, they must be seen to serve that purpose in an impartial and technocratic way using their impersonal rules. The authority of IOs, and bureaucracies generally, therefore, lies in their ability to present themselves as impersonal and neutral – as not exercising power but instead serving the others.[152]

To appear neutral and impartial, IOs rely heavily on specialist knowledge, as it can support scientifically political pursuits and 'solutions' to pre-defined 'problems'. The OECD, for example, is structured in directorates, departments, centres, committees, working groups and expert groups, and it is comprised of networks of specialists, consultants, researchers and policy analysts, which produce more than 250 publications a year about practically all policy domains. In education, the OECD produces 'national reports' and 'thematic analyses' for its 'clients 'about most educational issues and conducts major programmes of comparison of educational attainment. The World Bank is an even bigger bureaucratic organisation, with more than 11,000 staff, including hundreds of economists, financial analysts and technical specialists, structured hierarchically with boards of executive directors, a president and vice presidents, about 150 directors, project officers, tasks managers etc. The organisation is structured in sector-based divisions and technical departments, according to continents and regions, country programmes and project operations and gives more than 20 billion dollars each year in 'development loans' to its 'clients'.

The function of the major IOs is characterised by tremendous asymmetry of power and opaqueness in decision-making. In the WTO, for instance, the crucial negotiations leading to formal decisions are carried out in informal talks and in circles made by representatives from selected major economies and big corporations. Through the WTO, wealthy countries can pressure the poor countries to abolish their trade barriers, while the former can keep their own barriers, so that the latter are unable to export their own products.[153] In other words, investors from powerful states can have access to foreign markets, despite the fact that their governments do not accept investors from abroad. The OECD has 34 member states, but only 7 countries (the G7) contribute almost 80% of the total funding to the organisation, and this translated to unequal balance in decision making regarding research and policy. For example, by utilising their economic control, the American and British representatives pressured the OECD in the 1980s to set 'basic skills' at high priority in its agenda and demanded that the organisation introduces comparative studies using performance indicators, in order to promote competition in human capital formation[154] – as it has finally happened. In the Word Bank, five countries (the USA, Japan, Germany, the UK and France) hold almost 40% of its shares. If one adds the members of the OECD and the EU (the biggest financier of the World Bank), the percentage possessed by the economically powerful states exceeds 50%. Economic power is translated to decision making power. In the 25-member Board of Directors governing the World Bank, 8 states (the 5 mentioned above, followed, more recently, by China, Russia and Saudi Arabia) appoint their own Executive Director, while the other 17 Directors are appointed by the remaining 181 member-states. The president of the World Bank is chosen by the US and the president of the International Monetary Fund (IMF) by the EU, 'behind closed doors', as Joseph Stiglitz, testified, from his inside experience as a chief economist of the Bank. As he also remarked: 'The institutions are not representative of the nations they serve . . . [they] are not dominated just by the wealthiest countries but by commercial and financial interests in those countries . . .'.[155]

The testimony of Stiglitz concurs with that of John Perkins who revealed the existence of companies (by one of which he was employed) contracted by the World Bank, the IMF and other multilateral or bilateral agencies to send off 'economic hitmen' to targeted countries to pressure their governments to accept infrastructure projects funded by the loans of these agencies – usually presented as 'aid programmes'. The projects would be carried out mainly by corporations based in dominant states, while the borrowing governments would be in debt and thus economically and geostrategically controlled by the lenders.[156] But these intentions have hardly been a secret amongst 'donor' governments. For example, as the UK's Overseas Development Administration has proposed: 'By choosing projects carefully we can ensure that benefits go to them [i.e. to 'developing' countries] at the same time as offering valuable opportunities to British firms'.[157] Similarly, Eugene Black, one of the World Bank's first presidents, made clear from the start that foreign 'aid programmes' are beneficial for American business because: they provide 'substantial and immediate market for US goods and services'; they stimulate 'the development of new overseas markets for US companies'; and they orientate 'national economies towards a free market system in which US firms can prosper.'[158] Richard Nixon, the US president in the early 1970s, was more succinct: 'Let us remember that the main purpose of aid is not to help other nations but to help ourselves'.[159]

This purpose has been well served by the ideas of 'progress', 'development' or 'growth' that the West, with the leading role of the USA, utilised since the end of World War II to expand capitalism across countries. The inaugural speech of the US President Harry Truman in 1949 was particularly expressive of these associated significations, which, since Modernity, have been identified with application of techno-scientific knowledge, capital investment, productivity, consumption and the treatment of human beings as 'resources' or 'human capital'. In expressing fully the capitalist imaginary, Truman identified 'greater production' with prosperity and promulgated his country's endeavour to make the rest of the world adopt this idea but also to make profit out of it: 'Experience shows that our commerce with other countries expands as they progress industrially and economically'.[160]

The IMF and the World Bank were the main agencies assigned to carry out this plan. They were established originally (in Bretton Woods of the USA) in 1944 in order to undertake the post-WWII reconstruction in Europe, but soon their policies spread all over the world, particularly in poor countries. Today, 189 states, out of the 193 recognised by the United Nations, are members of the IMF and the World Bank (as acceptance by one entails membership in both). The two organisations promote macro-economic reforms and infrastructural programmes by means of loans and evaluations of governments' creditworthiness, which is crucial for them to attract loans and grants by international investors. Using these tools, and the promises for prosperity through 'development', a legitimation basis for most governments, these organisations have managed to advance the economic and geostrategic interests of their sponsors and promote capitalism around the world. To make this possible, the IMF and the World Bank have often taken advantage of extraordinary conditions (e.g., deep economic crises or natural catastrophes) and cooperated with some of the most oppressive regimes in modern history (e.g., Suharto's in Indonesia, Marcos's in Philippines, Ceausescu's in Romania, Pinochet's in Chile, Mobutu's in Congo-Zaire and the South African apartheid regime).[161]

Economic reforms have been promoted through loans under the notorious Structural Adjustment Programmes (SAPs) of the IMF and the World Bank (now renamed as Memoranda of Understanding). These programmes have allegedly aimed at 'improving the business climate' in the borrowing countries by abolishing restrictions in trade and investments, and by reducing deficits through cuts in public spending. Part of the cuts comes from reduction in real wages, which the IMF designated as a necessary means 'to restore adequate investment incentives.'[162] Since the 1990s, the 'Bretton Woods twins' embarked upon the so-called 'Washington Consensus' policy, joined by the WTO. The expression refers to the promotion by all three IOs of the neoliberal economic agenda which includes three basic sets of policies: privatisation of public companies, liberalisation of international trade and investments and deregulation of domestic economic and financial activity. This economic ideology penetrated all major IOs, either under the direct political pressure of major Western governments in the 1980s or through its advocates who occupied key positions in these organisations.[163] The process of economic 'liberalisation' was accelerated through GATS (General Agreement on Trade and Services), signed today by 164 countries in the framework of WTO. The major function of GATS has been to abolish restrictions in global trade and to open selectively domestic markets to capital flows, by committing legally WTO member-states to not distinguish between national and foreign companies wishing to invest in trade and services. These programmes and agreements, as Castells has also pointed out, have actually brought about economic globalisation:

> The mechanism to bring in the globalisation process to most countries in the world was simple: political pressure either through direct government action or through imposition by the IMF/World Bank/World Trade Organisation. Only after economies were liberalised would global capital flow in . . . The goal was the unification of all economies around a set of homogeneous rules of the game, so that capital, goods, and services could flow in and out, as determined by the judgement of the markets.[164]

But the opening of weak economies entailed the devastation of the sectors that lacked the competitiveness of corresponding sectors in major economies. The result was, in many cases, economic crises that led governments to become more dependent on foreign creditors, including the Bretton Woods IOs, which would demand national economies to adopt the same reform agenda – regardless of local particularities. This agenda is vested with bureaucratic neutrality, rational planning and the supposed expertise of these organisations' economists. Analysts who have witnessed this mode of policymaking report 'hypocricy' and 'disconnection' between the pronounced 'expertise' in these IOs and the actual conditions they dealt with, and 'cold-bloodedness' in destroying economies by removing political controls on capital.[165] Joseph Stiglitz paralleled the indiscriminate imposition of the neoliberal agenda to dropping bombs on a national territory, not from warplanes, but from the luxury hotels where 'experts' reside and 'callously impose policies about which one would think twice if one knew the people whose lives one was destroying'.[166]

This is, in fact, what has happened in many countries under the 'developmental' policies of these organisations. The overall result of the implementation of Structural Adjustment Programmes in more than 80 countries has been, with just a few exceptions, the widening of income disparities between the poor and the rich.[167] For instance, the management of the 1997 economic crisis in South East Asia led to mass unemployment and the 'biggest peacetime transfer of assets from domestic to foreign owners' in the past half a century.[168] The reinforcement of the capacity and role of IMF since 2009 and its involvement in European 'aid packages', together with the European Commission and the European Central Bank, is a repetition of the same 'model': predatory loans that function as steering tools to control national economies and make public wealth available to transnational capital. The demolition of the Greek economy that has taken place in cooperation with the country's unprincipled and submissive political classes is the most recent and well-known example of this economic policy, under which, as Badiou et al. reminded in a public call, 'vulnerable populations are doomed to a programmed elimination while those who work are condemned to the most extreme conditions of impoverishment and precarity'.[169]

Overall, in promoting the 'development' of the world, these major organisations and their sponsors have drastically contributed to plunging it into exploitation, inequality, and misery. In the 1970s, the GDP per capita difference between the richest country and the poorest country was 88:1. Four decades later, this difference became 267:1.[170] The gap between the richest 1/5 and the poorest 1/5 of the earth's inhabitants was 30:1 in the 1960s, and it was widened to 60:1 in 1990 and to 74:1 in 1997. Currently, half of the world's population shares 1% of global wealth, while 1% of the world's population owns half of all global wealth.[171] About 2/3 of city residents in the 'least-developed countries' live in slums under appalling conditions, with the help of the 'adjustments' and 'conditionalities' of the major IOs, which increased massively urban poverty. In 2040, slum-dwellers may reach two billion worldwide.[172] Furthermore, this half a century of intense 'developmental' polices has recorded the highest increase in global temperature since the beginnings of industrialisation.[173]

At the heart of these polices have been education reforms, which have been principally moving along two lines. First, education systems should produce 'human resources' destined to develop 'Third World' economies and to maintain growth in advanced economies. All domestic education policies should be orientated towards increasing productivity and competitiveness in the global economy. This direction has been intellectually justified by the so-called human capital theory, a complete expression of the capitalist imaginary, adopted since the 1960s by the major IOs, which, all these decades, have been performing ideological and decontextualised arithmetic exercises on 'rates of return'.[174] Secondly, educational systems should be marketised, in the sense of handing over parts of education provision to the business sector or/and introduce its criteria into the running of educational establishments. These policies were promoted, initially, by the SAPs. During the 1980s, the percentage of the GDP allocated to education in the Latin American and African countries that implemented these conditions decreased more than half, following the demands of the Bretton Woods IOs to reduce public sector expenditure.[175] In the year 1990, the majority of World Bank's programmes requested reduced funding to secondary and higher education, introduction of tuition fees, and the expansion of private education.[176] During the same decade, the World Bank sponsored a reform agenda whose main elements are now common wherever market-like policies in education are established: the transfer of financial responsibility to educational establishments, 'free choice' of schools, more involvement of the business sector, performance-related payments for teachers and monitoring and evaluation of educational results.[177]

The marketisation of education has been promoted decisively by WTO and the GATS. By describing education as a 'service' and by including it amongst the approximately 160 services to be 'liberalised', the WTO has opened a global market in education.[178] This includes, for example, establishment of overseas annexes of schools and universities (directly or through franchising), studies abroad, investments by private training companies, distance education and 'e-learning' programmes, trade of teaching aids, examination material etc.[179] Domestic policies favouring the access of the business sector to public education facilitate the adoption of GATS. In other words, the more an education system is open to business making, the wider the field of implementation for the GATS provisions.[180] The same applies to the new 'free trade agreements' that follow the pattern of GATS. They aim at extending dramatically the reach of transnational capital by abolishing trade barriers and removing existing regulations with regard to the function of businesses (e.g., food safety rules, labour rights, environmental regulations, digital privacy laws etc.) and by allowing them to prosecute governments in ad hoc arbitration tribunals if investors think that certain national policies act against their interests. The 'commitments' that signatory states would make under these agreements could open up the space for massive investments both in private and public education.[181]

Apart from turning education systems to commodities, IOs have been systematically, for the past half a century, orientating education to production demands. As the World Bank proclaimed from 1960s, 'nothing is more vital to the economic progress of underdeveloped countries than the development of human resources through widespread education'.[182] In the following decades, the World Bank became the biggest external loan provider for education programmes, implemented around the world.[183] Investments in education supported by the Bank have always had to be substantiated on the basis of human capital development. In the period from 1962 to 1980, the organisation prioritised the establishment of technical and vocational training schools, while it inhibited the promotion of educational contents related with pure science, arts or humanities and even the construction of libraries, as these were considered merely unproductive academic activities.[184] Thus, in the 1970s, when Western countries were establishing comprehensive secondary schools, the World Bank would fund only binary secondary education systems and only if sufficient emphasis was to be placed on the teaching of technical skills. Similarly, in the 1980s, when the West started expanding higher education, the World Bank would force countries, through its lending programmes, to expand only primary education because it was said to guarantee 'high rates or return'. However, since the late 1990s, under the globalisation of capitalism and its quest for 'high skills', for consumers of electronic gadgets, as well as for educational markets, the World Bank 'discovered' the value of upper levels of education. Since then, higher education has been made massively available for private investments and the World Bank set out a 'Knowledge for Development' Programme, ranking countries along a performance axis 'in their ability to compete in the knowledge economy'.[185]

Ranking as a means to promote human capital development lies at the core of the OECD's policy, too. Also established in the 1940s, the OECD state members account today for 2/3 of goods and services produced in the world, and it cooperates with another 70 countries and organisations, promoting 'market economies'. With a short break between the mid-1960s and mid-1970s, when social movements in the West demanded the democratisation of education systems, the OECD never stopped viewing education primarily as a provider of human resources destined to feed up the economic development of its member states.[186] Since the 1990s, this policy direction has been even more emphasised. The OECD proposes constantly now that all types and phases of education should serve the rise of productivity through organisational, curricular and pedagogic reforms and through the elimination of boundaries between vocational and general education and between education and work.[187] The International Adult Literacy Survey (IALS) and the Programme for International Student Assessment (PISA) were initiated by the OECD as tools for measuring human capital, an aim which is further pursued through the recently launched AHELO programme (Assessment of Higher Education Learning Outcomes), a kind of 'PISA for higher education'.[188]

The OECD, along with many other organisations and more than a hundred countries, has been promoting a 'culture of evidence-based decision making',[189] realised through 'a world progress monitoring system', namely 'a global web-based technical infrastructure where progress indicators would be made accessible'.[190] This is indicative of the quantification of the idea of 'progress' in our times, which is globalised and subject to accumulation of 'big data' by transnational institutions. Progress now can be defined in detail through indicators and benchmarks, it can be measured, and societies can be compared in accordance to their degree of achieving it (from GDP, foreign direct investments, purchase of smartphones, divorce rates, life expectancy, leisure, 'civic engagement', happiness and whatever else transnational bureaucracies can think of). Progress is remarkably standardised around the world as a set of quantities that must be reduced or increased accordingly.

The same, of course, applies to education. Progress in education means, for example, higher performance scores in science and technology, more students entering higher education, more scientific researchers, more job-related adult learning, more externally funded research, more international mobility, more academic publications etc. The more, the better; the maximum is the optimum. The 'evidence-based' educational policy of transnational bureaucracies is fully penetrated by the logic of quantification which defines their perception of progress in education.

But neither education nor its study, comparative or not, can be subject to progress, unless we refer to their instrumental aspects. Progress, as Weber pointed out in his *Methodology of the Social Sciences*, in concurrence with the Ancient Greek perception, cannot be conceived outside of the domains of technical improvements, quantities, and standards setting.[191] There can be, for example, no progress in the affective and cultural domains and, as he stressed, empirical inquiry has nothing to say about this, let alone to measure it. Cultural creations, aesthetic evaluations or inwardness cannot be subject to progress. Progress refers to the instrumental domain, where solutions to technical problems are sought and where the relation between means and ends is calculated. As Weber put it: 'The use of the term "progress" is legitimate in our disciplines when it refers to "technical" problems, i.e. to the "means" of attaining an unambiguously given end. It can never elevate itself into the sphere of "ultimate" evaluations'.[192] Likewise, progress in education is conceivable and consequently measurable only with respect to its technical and instrumental aspects (e.g., material infrastructure, technological aids, formal qualifications, relation between qualifications and access to labour markets or wages etc.). There can be no progress, and therefore no measurement, if by education we mean cultivation of the inner self, freedom of spirit, search for and creation of personal meaning, in other words, if we mean *paideia*.

But because education is conceived as an instrument of economic survival, success or competitiveness, it is measured intensively, along with various other aspects of social life. Entire domains of social and, by extension, personal life are being quantified, monitored and evaluated by the institutions of globalisation, seeking to standardise societies around the world, under the ideas of progress and development, closely related with submission to global capital. Similarly, entire education systems, with deep roots in the history of their societies, are regarded, for the first time so explicitly and so widely, as means to ends defined by the global production system. Through the international performance measurements this instrumental logic is applied to a variety of social and educational characteristics: socio-economic and national background of students, gender differences, administration of schools, assessment practices, pedagogic methods etc. are all treated as means to the ultimate end of raising scores in selected subjects and skills. Societies, education systems and pedagogic arrangements are scanned by transnational bureaucracies, to identify performing economies and 'best practices' for the production of human capital, incarnating the dominant comparative gaze that characterises globalisation.

The same gaze prevails in comparative education and related areas practiced in universities. Certainly, the critical tradition in comparative studies and overall in social sciences is alive as well as the perspective of universality in terms of the rights that citizens and children should enjoy all over the world. But comparative studies have predominantly embodied, as pointed out in the previous chapter, the capitalist imaginary, under which university knowledge production has been instituted since the European Modernity, and particularly the significations of progress and development. The reform of the university under the aims of transnational capitalism and the concomitant weakening of academic autonomy reinforces this direction. Performance comparisons, participation in the construction of indicators, technical and decontextualised studies, techno-bureaucratic projects under compulsory external funding and the industrialisation of paper publications are some of the features of knowledge production in comparative education, as much as in other areas of social sciences.

In conclusion, Postmodernity is marked by the dominance and pervasiveness of the central imaginary signification of unlimited rationalistic mastery and control, generated in European Modernity. Technique permeates not only productive activities but essentially all human activities, thus expanding dramatically the functional-instrumental dimension of society. Generation, storage and distribution of information are at the core of social and personal activity, and techno-scientific applications proliferate unrestrainedly and are overwhelmingly focused on the manipulation, control and engineering of nature, humans and other living beings. The phantasy of Modernity for omniscience, omnipotence and immortality lives on, heavily sponsored by transnational capital, which seeks endlessly new opportunities for profit.

Capitalism has drawn heavily on techno-science to reorganise itself, through corporations activated and networked across the globe, giving rise to a transnational capitalist class, to highly competitive and power-focused middle classes, and to insecure and fragmented labour forces. The so-called 'free market' favours physically and digitally nomadic lives, conformed and pliable employees and personalities oriented to the consumption of new commodities, largely by putting themselves into debt, which is the basis of financial capitalism. Possessive or liberal individualism, namely the pursuit of self-interest and private pleasures within a market society, functioning under the auspices of the state, is a signification generated by Modernity but glorified in our times as never before. This is creating a social landscape characterised by the widespread unleashing of consumption desires and egoisms and the dilapidation of social bonds.

The central imaginary signification of collective and personal autonomy, the other major Greco-Western creation, is largely dislocated by the capitalist imaginary. Citizenship is weakened by the penetration of economy in social and political life, the bypassing of the institutions of 'representative democracy' by transnational state mechanisms, the bureaucratisation of policymaking and the pulverisation of critique in the whirl of information and spectacles available incessantly on the television and the internet, which has been eventually turned into a global marketplace and a gigantic surveillance mechanism.

Surveillance in all forms and techniques is removing autonomy from education, a project also rooted deeply in the history of Europe. Undoubtedly, since Modernity, education systems have been placed under state bureaucracy, following the principles of industrial organisation, and served social class reproduction, the nation and the economy. Nevertheless, education has evolved and expanded by questioning its own institution and the institutions that it has been called on to serve. It is precisely this signification of questioning or critique that is being displaced in contemporary education systems under a combination of bureaucratic and market norms.

Higher education is the most characteristic case of this move towards heteronomy. As the previous chapter argued, what distinguishes the European university from similar institutions created in other parts of the world was neither its age nor its function to train experts, administrative or professional elites or grant formal certificates. Its particularity was the idea of academic autonomy, according to which the university should be a self-governing community of scholars and learners who decide, as an academic body and as individuals, about the knowledge they create and the way it is communicated. Since the end of the 20th century, we have witnessed a concerted political process across Europe to eliminate this unique attribute of the university in all its dimensions. Politics about the university is displaced by transnational policymaking networks dominated by business interest groups and bureaucracies; corporate management is decomposing the academic community, bringing academics under detailed performance surveillance and positioning students as consumers;

knowledge generation is subjected to business strategies, as scholars are requested to relinquish their research interests to those of various sponsors; and knowledge organisation and communication are extensively vocationalised and technicised.

Comparative education studies are hardly an exception to the new regime of knowledge exploitation. A large share of these studies is conducted or funded by International Organisations and supranational entities which promote an agenda that defines education in economic terms, and they designate the purpose of educational comparison accordingly. Education systems are predominantly studied and compared as means to ends defined by global capitalism. The driving and legitimating idea of capitalist expansion internationally has been the European imaginary signification of 'development', understood as perpetual increase of production and consumption capacity. Having been convinced that productivity and consumerism equals prosperity, Western societies have been unable to see the barbarism that 'development' would bring about both to 'others' and to themselves. No doubt, globalisation has been subject to critique by comparative education, as much as by social sciences in general. But this critique was almost exclusively focused on the injustices and inequalities that neoliberalism has been bringing about rather on the very imaginary signification of development, incarnated by capitalism in all its ideological versions and political expressions. Development, as its foundational idea of progress, has largely been unquestioned and is considered the irrefutable pathway for all societies. Under this idea, societies are viewed as an undifferentiated 'other', subject to hierarchisation based on their level of 'development', and cultural self-reflectiveness has become marginal. The next chapter will suggest that it should be brought to the foreground.

Notes

1 Hayek ([1944] 2006).
2 Michéa (1999); Dufour (2003); Leys (2008),
3 See Castells (2004).
4 Taguieff (2001).
5 Kurzweil (2005: 10). See also Brynjolfsson and McAfee (2014).
6 Fusaro (2015: 89).
7 Kolbert (2014).
8 Ellul (1964).
9 Ellul (1964: 4).
10 Postman (1993).
11 Postman (1993).
12 See: Rose and Rose (2014: 263–274).
13 Taylor (2012: 10).
14 See, for example, *Robocop, Eternal Sunshine of the Spotless Mind, Limitless, Lucy* and *Transcendence*.
15 Kurzweil (2005).
16 Kurzweil (2005: 9 and 21).
17 See: Hooton (2015); BBC (2016).
18 See for instance: Cyranoski (2015); Huang (2015).
19 See Kolbert (2014).

20 Bell (1976); Castells (2000); Burton-Jones (1999); Boutang (2012); Sennett (1998).
21 Boltanski and Chiapello (2005).
22 See Brown, Lauder and Ashton (2011).
23 See: Bank of America Merrill Lynch (2015); Haldane (2015).
24 Standing (2011).
25 See Scholz (2013).
26 OECD (2015a).
27 OECD (2007a); Piketty (2014).
28 Piketty (2014: 484); See also Savage et al. (2015: 66); Brown et al (2011).
29 Credit Suisse (2016).
30 Quoted in Brown, Lauder and Ashton (2011: 115). See also Sklair (2001).
31 Heiman, Freeman and Liechty (2012: 14). Savage et al. (2015).
32 Heiman, Freeman and Liechty (2012: 16).
33 Fusaro (2015).
34 Savage et al. (2015); Piketty (2014).
35 See: EC (2008).
36 Dufour (2003: 106).
37 See Salecl (2011).
38 Barber (2007); Sennett (1977).
39 Michéa (2013).
40 Bauman (2005: 88).
41 Debord ([1967] 1994 : theses 34 and 14).
42 Debord ([1967] 1994 : theses, 13 and 21).
43 See Martin and Schumann (1997: 1–5).
44 Postman (2005: 87).
45 Debord ([1967] 1994: thesis 29).
46 Lovink (2011).
47 Dijck van (2013: 12–13).
48 Dijck van (2013: 12).
49 Castoriadis (2015).
50 Michéa (2013).
51 Dufour (2003).
52 Fusaro (2015: 63–64).
53 Pforde (2009: 22–24).
54 Castoriadis (2003a: 208–230).
55 Bauman (2001: 148).
56 Dufour (2003: 6).
57 Castoriadis (2003a: 220); Dufour (2003).
58 Dufour (2003: 93 and 106).
59 WHO (2012).
60 Ehrenberg (2010: 232).
61 Ehrenberg (2010: 11).
62 Adam (2014).
63 Adam (2014: 182).
64 Castells (2000).
65 See Taibbi (2017).
66 Bourdieu (1996); Postman (2005).
67 Debord ([1967] 1994 1971: thesis 18).
68 Kristeva (1996).
69 Hindman (2009).
70 Norris (2001).
71 Barney (2004: 136–137).
72 Bimber (2001: 57).
73 Lovink (2011: 6).

74 Eliot (1969).
75 Ramonet (2015).
76 See Epstein (2016).
77 See: Urthecast.com and Walker (2016).
78 Bauman and Lyon (2013: 14).
79 Savage et al. (2015).
80 See Dauvergne and LeBaron (2014).
81 Murphy (2001); Shivji (2007).
82 Lazzarato (2012).
83 Lazzarato (2012).
84 Castells (2000).
85 See Streeck and Schmitter (1991).
86 Paasi (2001); Calhoun (2003).
87 See Beck (2013).
88 Bard and Soderqvist (2002); Castells (2009: 44).
89 Messner (1997).
90 See, for example, Mouffe (2005); Mammone, Godin and Jenkins (2012).
91 Quoted in Bauman (2011: 84–85).
92 See: IOM (2015).
93 Bauman (2011).
94 See Chomsky (2016: 225 and 251–255).
95 See Atwan (2015); Pollock (2014); ICM (2014).
96 UNHRC (2016).
97 Bernstein (2000: chapter 3).
98 Bernstein (2000).
99 Arendt (2006: 178).
100 See, for example, Schott and Søndergaard (2015).
101 Dufour (2003: 106–109). See also Postman (1982).
102 Aronowitz and Giroux (1991: 166). Original italics.
103 Postman (1982: 124).
104 Postman (1982).
105 Postman (2005).
106 Dufour (2003: 103 and 113).
107 See Louv (2008).
108 Dufour (2003: 109).
109 See OECD (2001a); OECD (2015b).
110 Picciano and Spring (2013); Spring (2012).
111 Picciano and Spring (2013); Piattoeva (2014).
112 Knight (2013).
113 Foucault (1991).
114 Young (1998).
115 See Quinn (2015).
116 Nordin (2014).
117 Bernstein (2000: 86).
118 European Commission (2003a: 4).
119 European Commission (2002).
120 Launched with the Bologna Declaration of 1999, today the Bologna Process is implemented in 48 countries (the 28 EU members and 20 non-EU countries located in Europe and Central Asia), which constitute the EHEA, effective since 2010. Moreover, there are another 23 countries from all over the world which take part in the Process with observer status. There are also many countries that participate in selected actions (e.g., 19 Latin American countries have joined *Tuning*); there are ad hoc policy fora (e.g., the 'Rectors' Conference of Asia-Europe Meeting' – ASEM); initiatives of the 'external dimension' (e.g. 'Euro-Africa' for the continent's Francophone countries, the

'Euro-Mediterranean Partnership' for Middle East states and the Maghreb region and the 'Lusophone HE Area); and related EU programmes, such as 'Tempus' and 'Erasmus Mundus'. See Robertson (2010).

121 These are: the EUA (European University Association) representing the Rectors; EURASHE (European Association of Institutions in Higher Education) representing the Heads of Polytechnics and University Colleges; ESU (the European Students' Union) an umbrella organisation of 44 National Students' Unions; EI (Education International) representing 100 national organisations of academics worldwide; UNESCO-CEPES (European Centre for Higher Education); ENQA (European Association for Quality Assurance in Higher Education); and 'BusinessEurope', the Confederation of European Business.
122 European Commission (2003b: 22).
123 The main interest groups are BusinessEurope (2009) and Alliance for a Competitive European Industry (2010). BusinessEurope is constituted by 40 central industrial and employers' federations and the Alliance for a Competitive European Industry by 12 major European Industry sector associations.
124 See the website 'Transparency Register' of the European Commission.
125 European Council (2007: 3).
126 European Commission (2007).
127 European Commission (2005: 5).
128 ENQA (2009).
129 European Commission (2009: 5).
130 European Commission (2005: 5).
131 European Commission (2009: 7).
132 European Commission (2005: 9).
133 European Commission (2006: 8).
134 European Commission (2010c).
135 European Commission (2003b: 13), original emphasis.
136 Pain (1997).
137 European Commission (2010a: 10).
138 European Commission (2006: 6–7), original emphasis.
139 *Tuning's* Homepage.
140 European Commission (2010b: 6).
141 See for example Reporters without Borders (2016); Freedom House (2016).
142 Robinson (2001: 159).
143 Castells (2000).
144 Hirst and Thompson (1996: 192 and 171).
145 Robinson (2001: 166).
146 Beck (2005: 146–147).
147 Rothkopf (2008: 33).
148 Vitali, Glattfelder and Battiston (2011).
149 Beck (2005: 121–165).
150 Carnoy and Castells (1999).
151 Beck (2005).
152 Barnett and Finnemore (2004: 21).
153 Stiglitz (2002). See also Mundy and Iga (2003).
154 See Papadopoulos (1994: 181–182); Heyneman: 1993: 375; Henry et al. (2001: 87).
155 Stiglitz (2002: 18–19).
156 Perkins (2006).
157 Cited in: Hancock (1989: 161).
158 Quoted in: Lindenberg (1975: 7).
159 Quoted in: Hayter (1982: 83–84).
160 Truman (1949).

161 Klein (2007). Toussaint (2008).
162 J. de Larosiere, quoted in: Robinson (2001: 31).
163 Harvey (2005).
164 Castells (2000: 140).
165 Weaver (2008); Berkman (2008: 19–20); Castells (2004: 331).
166 Stiglitz (2002: 24).
167 Stiglitz (2002); Beck (2005); Klein (2007).
168 Klein (2007: 276).
169 Badiou et al (2012).
170 Rothkopf (2008: 33).
171 Credit Suisse (2016).
172 Davis (2007).
173 IPCC (2013).
174 See Klees (2016).
175 Reimers (1994).
176 Jones (1992).
177 Alexander (2001).
178 WTO (1998).
179 OECD (2002).
180 Rikowski (2002/2003).
181 An example is the Comprehensive Economic and Trade Agreement (CETA) between the EU and Canada, which was signed in 2016. Other 'free trade' agreements are currently in the process of negotiation, and strongly resisted by social movements, such as the Trade in Services Agreement (TiSA) between the EU and 22 member-states of WTO – altogether accounting for 70% in world trade services. See also European Commission (2015); Hilary (2015).
182 World Bank (2010: 22).
183 Alexander (2001).
184 Heyneman (2003).
185 World Bank (2007: 3). World Bank (2008).
186 Papadopoulos (1994).
187 OECD (2006); OECD (2007b).
188 OECD (2013).
189 OECD (2007c: 1).
190 OECD (2007d).
191 Weber (1949).
192 Weber (1949: 38).

5 From comparison to *syncrisis*

Education and comparative inquiry in Europe

Societies, according to Castoriadian ontology, have a functional-instrumental or ensemblistic-identitary dimension and a dimension of imaginary signification, indissolubly connected with the former. A functional-instrumental dimension exists because there is a natural stratum on which society leans on – a physical and biological reality which society cannot ignore. This reality is ensemblisable and thus subject to an ensemblistic-identitary logic or, more simply, to mathematical logic: there are properties and classes which can be distinguished, categorised or counted. But at the same time, no society can exist without an imaginary dimension by which society gives meaning to a groundless world, or, in other words, it imposes a cosmos on the chaos.

Each society, then, is instituted by creating its own world of imaginary significations and immerses whatever appears into this world. Imaginary significations convey a representational, affective and intentional complex which defines how a society views itself in the past and the present, but also the future that it is pursuing, as well as how it views other societies. To understand, therefore, the particularity of a society and its comparative gaze towards other cultures, one has to access its imaginary world.

Social imaginary significations are intermingled in a magmatic mode and thus they cannot be accessed by following the analytical process pertaining to the study of physical or biological reality. However, they can be identified, as they are organised by the central imaginary significations characterising each society and as they are presentified in its institutions. Institutions are ensemblistic organisations which are nonetheless unthinkable without significations. Education is an institution, too, that takes places officially, but also across institutions.

Significations and institutions constitute the social-historical field, which expresses a symbiosis and conflict between what emerges (the social imaginary) and what is already 'there', the instituted society. The preceding chapters explored pivotal periods of the European social-historical field in order to understand the institution of education and of cultural and educational comparison. The following pages are bringing together the main threads of this exploration and, after they discuss current influential theories and methods in comparative education, draw some conclusions with respect to the meaning and purpose of cross-cultural comparison at the present juncture.

The inquiry started from Ancient Greece, the birthplace of the school, but also of the systematic interest in the institutions of other societies. In Greece, we have historically, in Castoriadis's terms, the first rift to heteronomy and the emergence of the central imaginary signification of social and personal autonomy. Heteronomous societies are not aware of the fact that they are the creators of their institutions, which they usually attribute to transcendental or extra-social sources. In autonomous societies, there is consciousness that it is they themselves who are the creators and reformers of their institutions. The Greek polis, and especially Athens, which was the locus of this research, questioned its own laws, traditions, representations and taken-for-granted knowledge – something which happened through politics, but also through philosophical, artistic and educational activities. In this regard, the cognitive closure and, in general, the closure of meaning, a characteristic of heteronomous societies, were ruptured for the first time there, allowing for the socialisation of autonomous individuals, who were capable of directing their *vis formandi* and *libido formandi* to the creation of new forms – forms which marked the European but also world history.

Pursuing learning for the Greeks was a way of living (*φιλοκαλοῦμεν* and *φιλοσοφοῦμεν*, in Pericles's words), and they opposed the subjection of knowledge to instrumental ends. The founding of the school became possible in Ancient Greece because it was there that epistēmē, as knowledge and inquiry free of practical intents, was created. Education was, for the Greeks, for general cultivation (*οὐκ ἐπὶ τέχνῃ*', not for technical skill, but *ἐπὶ παιδείᾳ*, for paideia, as Protagoras said), which was inextricably connected with one's own capacity to be a citizen in the democratic polis. The democratic and particularly the sophist movement in Athens foregrounded aretē, namely distinction in the domains of politics, knowledge or the arts. At the same time, there was deep awareness amongst the Greeks that education was, what I called, transinstitutional, namely that the very living and acting in the polis had an educative function.

The rise of self-examination in the autonomous Greek polis gave rise to a genuine interest (i.e. free of any instrumental purposes) in the institutions of other societies. Impartiality in the study of the others' institutions starts in Greece, and it is closely associated with the Greeks' distinction between nature (physis) and law institution or convention (nomos). At the core of the Greek social imaginary lay an ontological view according to which the world derived from the chaos. The gods had no role in designing human societies, nor would they provide any hope to mortals. The source of the world for the Greeks was non-meaning, and thus, it was subject to the creation of a cosmos, a world-order made by humans and their institutions. By distinguishing physis from nomos, the Greeks recognised the capacity of every society to establish their own conventions of life. It is in that context that comparative inquiry in history, culture and consequently in education was born in Ancient Greece, which developed an impartial gaze towards the cultural 'other'. Amongst a host of other ancient societies, where the main intellectual activity was to glorify the deeds of their kings and sacred persons, in Greece, a curiosity arose to learn and write about other cultures and through this activity to reflect on home institutions.

This was part of the scientific spirit which appeared from the 6th century BCE but also of a cultural attitude according to which the foreign society under inquiry was considered neither inferior nor superior, but simply different. Cross-cultural exploration was associated with the rise of epistēmē and philosophia, as forms and activities in the field of logos, which ruptured cognitive closure and foregrounded empirical inquiry, logical argumentation and the search for truth. Moreover, behind the Greek comparative gaze lay the philosophical and political questioning which characterised the life of the democratic polis. Philosophical inquiry put into question the representations and the cognitive traditions of the Greeks, and part of this questioning was the research of the institutions of others. Furthermore, the Greeks acknowledged cultural diversity, as they accepted the multiplicity and equality of views in the democratic polis. If there are different doxai about the same issue amongst interlocutors, so there are different cultures, expressing different worldviews.

The central imaginary signification of social and personal autonomy, generated in Ancient Greece, re-emerged in European Modernity, in coexistence and opposition this time with a new imaginary signification, that of rationalistic mastery and control of nature and of human beings. These two central significations, in their conflict and mutual 'contamination', have been incarnated in the then established education systems as well as in the institution of the European comparative gaze towards other civilisations. The project of autonomy in Europe arose in conflict initially with religion and later on with industrial capitalism. European science developed the Greek scientific thinking against medieval superstition and cognitive closure, but it prioritised human domination on nature and society by means of technological advancements. The idea of progress emerged in opposition to medieval attachment to tradition and to religion. However, God's omnipotence was replaced with that of Man, who was destined to pursue progress through techno-scientific development. The simultaneous emergence of capitalism realised rationality as economic efficiency, infusing it in all domains of social life. Capitalism arose in a symbiotic relation with 'representative democracy', a form of liberal oligarchy, which became since Modernity the legitimate system of political organisation. 'Representative democracy' established a separation between government and citizens, the latter regarded as stipulators of a 'social contract' with the former, which was to rule through expert knowledge and bureaucracy. Bureaucracy was embedded in the function of the state, which in its modern form appropriated the nation, a new European creation.

The institution of education systems incarnated the conflicting central significations of autonomy and rationalistic domination. During the 16th century social, philosophical and educational critique emerged across Europe against religious indoctrination, seeking to establish the particularity of childhood and organise learning accordingly. The Enlightenment revived the classical distinction between nature and nurture and advocated the establishment of education for social, political and personal freedom. From then on a major educational movement developed, promoting exploratory and autonomous learning, which had a significant impact on the making of education systems. Academic autonomy was established as a sine qua non characteristic of the university, drawing on the Ancient Greek legacy of intellectual freedom and the early Renaissance tradition of universitas. Education in Europe broke with mere training or indoctrination and foregrounded scientific exploration, logical reasoning and critical disposition, and it was closely associated with the democratic movement which changed the face of the continent after the 18th century. But education in Europe embodied also significations related to capitalism and the nation-state. The education system was to be regulated by state bureaucracy, organised under the principles of industrialism and 'scientific management', and serve the new social class structure. The fundamental co-existence and opposition between collective and personal autonomy and rationalistic mastery and control constitutes the very particularity of the institution of education in Europe as well as of its comparative gaze.

In other words, European Modernity is constituted by a duality of ideas, projects and institutions which has been incarnated in Europe's epistemological tradition with regard to how we see and compare to other cultures. The prevalent part of this duality is associated with the rise and expansion of capitalism. But European Modernity is also marked by the rise of a major democratic movement which instigated critique and reflective thinking, a component of which was the comparison to the cultural 'other'.

Indeed, the Enlightenment brought about a rupture in the cognitive and representational closure in Europe and re-introduced the perception that, while human nature is common, different societies are instituted differently. Self-reflective accounts in literature and philosophy criticised domestic institutions from the perspective of other civilisations. The Enlightenment recognised both the universality of the human condition as well as cultural multiplicity, which was welcomed as freedom and as a condition for impartial and critical reflection. Nevertheless, from the 19th century, other cultures were 'seen' primarily through the signification of progress, and thus, they were either romanticised or depreciated for their 'primitiveness'. The latter was the dominant viewpoint: overseas societies were to be assessed in accordance to their capacity in being/becoming like the Europeans, a perception which drove or legitimised colonial and imperialist interventions. Thus, the central imaginary signification of rationalistic domination was what characterised the 'Europeanisation' of the world and consequently the historical process of educational 'lending' and 'borrowing'. The expansion of the university across countries is an illustrative case: universities throughout the world were placed predominantly in the service of constructing nation-states and industrial economies, while the idea of academic autonomy was hardly 'lent' and 'borrowed' outside of the 'European sphere'.

In Postmodernity, academic autonomy, as the entire project of autonomy, has retreated. No doubt, the Parisian May and the movements to which it gave rise transformed social institutions in the direction of personal autonomy. But the cultural emancipation sparkled by the 1960s was soon absorbed by capitalism and turned into labour precariousness and consumer individualism. Notwithstanding the erosion or collapse of traditional authority and power structures during the last part of the 20th century, rationalistic control has been pervasive across institutions. Postmodern Europe is marked by the transnationalisation of the state and its bureaucracies and dominated by the capitalist imaginary. European societies, as societies around the world, pursue techno-scientific progress and enhancement of production and consumption, and they are immersed into the audiovisual and digital environments of the old and the new media. Democratic institutions are weakened by the penetration of market values and enhanced surveillance through the new technologies.

Indeed, technique, technology and science have been drastically expanded in Europe, as well as in the West in general, thus expanding the functional-instrumental dimension of society. Productivity and consumption are still celebrated as main priorities – something which, given the dramatic environmental degradation, reminds one of dancing in the ballroom of the Titanic.

Capitalist reorganisation has transformed occupational structures and work arrangements, including identity formation, which is characterised by fragmentation, atomisation and weakened social cohesion and citizenship. The widespread expansion of connectivity and interactivity has not enriched democratic citizenship, despite earlier expectations, but it is creating the informational and 'post-spectacle society', part of which is enhanced surveillance over individual and social activities. In addition, widespread digitalisation is inserting technology into, essentially, all segments of life.

Although since the latter part the 20th century, the European project of learning autonomy has been promoted through reforms in school systems and methods, the expansion of capitalism and associated significations, such as recurrent technological innovation, productivity, consumption and commodified amusement, have contributed to the decline of this project. Youth and children are immersed into the audiovisual and digital environment provided by numerous types of electronic devices which have established edutainment as a mode of learning. Digital technologies have provided a major field for profit-making, presented by the education-industrial complex as undeniable necessity for effective learning. Education systems are now under controls exercised at both transnational and national levels through the definition of measurable goals and recurrent evaluations. The changes promoted by the Bologna Process all across Europe, and especially by the EU education reform agenda, have established the idea that progress means economic competiveness and that this is the main aim that education and, most of all, universities, should serve. With the prioritisation of productivity and competitiveness in Europe, education is being largely considered a means for survival or success in volatile labour markets and learners are being seen as 'human resources'. Thus, knowledge is divorced from the learner, and from the European inheritance of paideia or Bildung.

The capitalist imaginary is incarnated also in the way other countries and their education systems are 'seen' in/by Europe, and internationally. The state, the capitalist enterprise and bureaucracy are now operating on a global level and produce education policies – amongst all kinds of policies – but also educational comparisons. IOs play a crucial role in promoting the aims of global capitalism by producing comparative data on education systems in the service of these aims, thereby establishing performance measurements on selected indicators as the dominant comparative perspective.

Reconsidering or redefining educational comparison entails, as it will be argued below, breaking away from the perspective that treats education systems as means to ends defined by global capitalism and re-assuming the scholarly task of studying education within its cultural context.

Redefining comparison

As social sciences, in general, comparative education has been seeing and studying education through the lenses of 'progress' and 'development', significations associated with the capitalist imaginary that emerged in Europe. And as, overall, in educational studies, knowledge fragmentation, adoption of the methods of natural sciences, focus on measurable or instrumental aspects of education and subservience to official policymaking have been some of the main features of comparative education over the past century.

Indeed, the main focus of comparative studies has always been on the functional-instrumental aspects of social and educational phenomena, combined with their reduction to a set of causal factors – a deterministic approach, aimed at assisting policymaking. The quest for determinants and indicators started already from Marc-Antoine Julien, considered by Bereday 'the first scientifically minded comparative educator',[1] although one could well regard him as a forerunner of today's rankings in education conducted by International Organisations. The pursuit of a 'scientific approach' to educational comparison, which can provide tools for policymaking, has characterised most of its 20th-century scholars, regardless of being categorised as positivists or not. Hans and Mallinson, for example, looked for factors or determinants shaping the 'national character' (Hans even tried to construct with them the 'ideal nation') which in turn determined education systems.[2] Brian Holmes advocated the quest of determinants as outcomes of 'ideal typical national models' to be used for prediction and therefore policymaking.[3]

All the above comparative educationists embraced the national education system as a unit of analysis and looked intensively for causal factors or 'normative models' or 'patterns' leading to predictions that can inform policymaking. This approach intends to explain social phenomena across countries by placing them essentially in the 'laboratory'. It goes back to John Stuart Mill and Emil Durkheim, who explicitly identified comparison in social sciences with indirect experimentation.[4] Drawing on these authors, Ragin, in his textbook *The Comparative Method*, writes that 'the ideal social scientific comparison is identical in structure to the simple experiment'.[5] Simply put, it is as if country A is the experimental group which has received the 'treatment', and country B is the control group which has not, while all other factors are common. If differences emerge between the two groups, they are attributed to the factor 'treatment', thus establishing cause-effect relations. In other words, this method aims at approximating experimental design with non-experimental data. It originates in John Stuart Mill's 'method of agreement' (looking for a common factor amongst a series of factors which cause a specific effect on a variety of cases) and 'method of difference' (looking for the absence of this factor wherever the effect is also absent).

The method is also advocated by comparative historians Skocpol and Somers who proposed it as pertinent for macro-causal analysis.[6] Skocpol used it in her comparison of French, Russian and Chinese revolutions with the purpose of identifying causal factors. However, in concluding her study, the author admits that there is 'difficulty' in extending these factors to other social revolutions.[7] Such problems (i.e. identifying the causes that supposedly explain a phenomenon in selected country-cases but with uncertain applicability to other cases) are inherent in comparative studies that are based on causality or this experiment-like methodology. Causal explanation entails reduction – the process of explaining a phenomenon through another phenomenon, which precedes it or it is more general, by inferring rational associations or causal relations. Cause-effect relations that are inferred through reduction are usually converted into means-ends relations for policymaking purposes.[8] This is, for instance, what OECD does in PISA: it identifies the causal factors which supposedly explain student achievements, and then it bases on these data its policy proposals to governments. But, as the OECD admits, it cannot assure that the identified causal factors would be valid determinants for policy transfer. As, for example, PISA 2009 notes: 'the fact that such characteristics are more likely to be found among successful school systems does not mean that they are necessary or sufficient for success'.[9] In other words, the OECD negates the fundamental principle of causality (i.e. that the same effect corresponds to the same cause)[10] on the basis of which it conducts its performance comparisons.

The failures of causal explanation, often admitted by its own proponents, are due to the fact that it pertains to natural sciences rather than to human or social sciences. Its adoption by social sciences indicates an intention to have potentially everything in society explained and determined. Determinacy demands that everything should be subject to full distinction and definition in terms of its properties, origins and causal relations. This leads to reductionism, the doctrine which maintains that all phenomena can be explained through reduction. If this is the case, then reduction can be indefinite, or it should lead to a pattern, a primary element or a universal law which would serve as the source of everything.[11] This logic would point to the assumption that the multiplicity of societies is the result of a determined differentiation of a supposed unity/identity.[12]

This is also the underlying assumption of Eurocentric accounts in history, sociology and comparative studies that see societies around the world as differentiated according to their degree of economic and techno-scientific progress, which is a European signification. Typically, the discourse in these accounts is about the West and the 'Rest', history's 'winners' and 'losers', about which civilisation invented first what, who took what by whom, who is a 'latecomer', who triumphed over whom etc. – always in reference to or with focus on economic and technological supremacy.[13] Fergusson, for instance, in his book *Civilisation: the West and the Rest*, identifies a 'western package' comprised of 'the best available set of economic, social and political institutions' (competition, science, property rights, medicine, consumer society and work ethic). These are six 'killer apps', as he calls them, that allowed the West to dominate the 'Rest', but the 'Rest' have now 'downloaded' them, thus entering too the pathway of prosperity.[14]

Ironically, many opposed analyses, which declare to be anti-Eurocentric, are Eurocentric, too, because they interpret world history also through the lenses of development and progress. The dispute between the two sides is mainly ideological, rather than based on cultural or civilisational analysis of the societies and the institutions under inquiry. It is usually a debate marked by simplistic claims and catchy slogans, where facts are ignored or distorted, and opposing arguments are exaggerated in order to be easily refuted.

A main claim of the anti-Eurocentric camp is that the 'triumph' of the West is based on the appropriation of institutions from other civilisations – with the focus being again on economic and technological progress. Hobson, for example, goes so far as to suggest that the origins of the Western civilisation lie in the East. He suggests that the East pioneered in economic development centuries before the West, which rose because it appropriated the East's 'resource portfolios' (ideas, institutions and technologies).[15] For Jack Goody, and his widely read book on the matter, Western civilisation has stolen its main institutions, including democracy. In an extraordinary demonstration of ignorance, he writes that 'The Greeks, of course, invented the word "democracy". . .but they did not invent the practice of democracy'.[16] Without even searching for a definition of this word, he identifies democracy with 'representation' and, unbelievably, with 'Robin Hood type' of rebels and bandits in Africa and China.[17]

Baseless claims can be found also in much of postcolonial theory, which essentially identifies the entire European epistemological tradition in social sciences with Western imperialism. It is argued, for example, that coloniality is constitutive of Modernity and the knowledge produced out of it is Eurocentric;[18] that Enlightenment-based social sciences constructed totalising theories which express an imperialistic will to power over other societies;[19] that European social sciences constitute a cultural expression of the white male metropolitan bourgeoisie, and that the purpose of comparative studies was to serve colonial domination.[20] It is not unusual to say something which is correct – and the analysis which associates knowledge generation with the mode of capitalist development in the 19th century is correct – in order to reach a conclusion which is false. This happens normally when a truthful argument is intended to represent the whole truth, or when it is simplified or distorted. A characteristic example of this is a book by Connell, who coined a distinction between 'Northern Theory' and 'Southern Theory'. Through a brief review of a handful of sociological texts, the author labels the entire European social-scientific tradition as 'Northern Theory', and to illustrate 'Southern Theory', she mixes up a set of local worldviews in Africa, disputes between Muslim theologians in the Middle East and critical writings of dependency theorists in Latin America and of feminist theorists in India. No attempt is made to substantiate how these examples from diverse cultures and circumstances can possibly constitute a common 'theory', nor does the author see that the critical accounts from the 'South' that she refers to, as well as her own, draw on some version of 'Northern Theory'. More remarkably, the author regards as 'Southern Theory', and as response to the Western imperialist and corporate takeover of social sciences, believe it or not, writings of Muslim preachers too, who declare that: 'Islam is superior to other religions . . . because it is the most rational', and 'everywhere addresses itself to reason' and that a 'new intellectual era' will come in which 'a new breed of Muslim scientists will take over, who feel Islam in their hearts and minds . . .'.[21] Indeed, a book of 'postcolonial sociology' recommends religious heteronomy as alternative to knowledge Eurocentrism. Of course, in an academic world operating as a fashion industry, with its public relations, avoidance of dialogue and pseudo-intellectual rhetoric, 'anything goes' as scholarship and even as 'critical'. But it is precisely this European critical and self-reflective tradition that is displaced by the ideological accounts and, often, thoughtless statements of both Eurocentric and anti-Eurocentric authors.

This tradition is also absent from the so-called neoinstitutionalist theory (or 'world culture theory' or 'Stanford School') which has had a big influence on sociology and comparative education in the last decades. Although this theory has correctly acknowledged the major impact that European institutions have had on the world, the research produced regards this impact as a universal 'model', consisting of a set of yardsticks against which worldwide convergence or divergence is measured. Overall, neoinstitutionalism has rightly moved away from the conventional approach in comparative education that takes the nation-state as the unit of analysis, as national societies are not and cannot be isolated entities; it has also rightly criticised functionalism for associating the establishment of educational systems solely with 'national needs' and social reproduction aims; it has correctly been critical to the economism of 'world system' theories and has looked instead for cultural influences behind the expansion of educational institutions across countries during the 20th century; and, importantly, it has rightly drew attention to the 'legitimating myths' ('individual', 'progress,' 'childhood', 'nation' and 'state') of the European civilisation and their significance for understanding the institution of education during the 18th and 19th centuries.[22]

However, there has not been any further analytical elaboration of these 'legitimating myths' (e.g., their origin, associations or justification of selection) which constitute, according to world culture theorists, the 'European model of national society' – something which is indicated by the multiplicity and the apparent ambivalence of the concepts used (e.g., 'myths', 'models', 'ideologies', 'doctrines', 'cultural frames', 'schemes' and many others).[23] Moreover, the theory has provided no account of historical change or transformation of these myths (the term 'model', after all, which is also used, originates in mathematics and indicates a fixed representation of an actual condition). The lack of any account of change – historical or cultural – is inherent in the Stanford School's theorisation of institutions, which defines them as cognitive and normative principles, while it hardly elaborates on the myths to which it refers. If institutions were solely about cognition and prescription, then they would remain unaltered by history and unaffected by other societies and their own myths. Neoinstitutionalist theory neglects the culture of other societies, as well as politics and power, which fundamentally lie in shared myths.

Thus, neoinstitutionalism has provided no account of 're-contextualisation' or 'translation' or conflict or synthesis of the European/Western influences with other cultures. To address this criticism, neoinstitutionalist scholars have resorted to the terminology of policy or organisational studies and their standard claim that there is always 'gap' between policy and practice or there is 'decoupling' or 'loose coupling' or even 'hypocrisy'. As Meyer writes, 'global pressures to conform to standard models of the modern nation breed hypocrisy' and, thus, 'many policies adopted by countries around the world go unimplemented in practice'.[24] Apparently, while neoinstitutionalism claims that it adopts a 'culturalist perspective',[25] the explanations it offers reduce cultures to disobedient subjects.

Apparently, also, neoinstitutionalism promotes what its authors themselves call the European myth of progress. Their central argument is that the world's institutions have been following, almost by historical necessity, the European 'models', and the outcome is the rise of a 'world culture'. There are 'varying idiosyncrasies' and 'diverse paths to national development',[26] but all countries move towards progress, development and justice, and their education systems are aligned to this process with essentially the same curricula, professionalised teaching and active child-centred learning. The argument is supported by a research methodology which focuses on the instrumental-functional aspects of societies and their education systems (e.g., administration, enrolment rates, curriculum prescriptions, textbooks, school timetables etc.). However, confining comparative research to measurable features and official sources consists a form of legal or administrative formalism, i.e. if something exists in official documents, then it actually happens. This method leads world culture theorists to the conclusion of institutional 'isomorphism' or 'homogenisation' across the world.[27] The two terms are used by the theory interchangeably, despite the fact that their meaning is not the same. Isomorphism is the one-to-one mapping of the elements of different sets. One can indeed speak of isomorphism, if one matches the formal and measurable features of different education systems. But homogenisation is something else. Homogenisation would presuppose the existence of absolutely identical significations, imposed by a single totalitarian authority on societies and institutions which have no history, something which is, of course, impossible.[28]

This last point must be underlined with respect to globalisation theory, too. Globalisation means a shift from a world economy to a global economy and the rise of a 'transnational state apparatus', which, as the previous chapter argued, promotes policies that serve the expansion of capitalism and define the comparative gaze of societies under its terms. But do the domination of the capitalist imaginary and its institutions entail the rise of a global culture or a global society? Castells suggests that there is now a 'global network society'. It is marked by digital networks that have a global reach, transcending territorial and institutional boundaries. Network society is a global social structure where time and space are compressed, giving rise to a 'space of flows' and of 'timeless time'. The space of flows is a networked, a-historical space which tries to impose its logic on fragmented and excluded localities. Timeless time creates 'the universe of forever' through the functioning of the global economy in real time as well as through the global media which scan the planet and the history of humanity incorporating every cultural expression in a major 'hypertext'.[29]

However, as Castells points out, a global social structure does not entail the rise of a global culture. If there is a culture to be considered global, this is 'a culture of protocols of communication' which shares the value of communication but does not necessarily have shared values.[30] If this is the case, then the term 'global society' is an overstatement. To speak of a 'society', we must have the same social-historical field, something, of course, that cannot be argued with the respect to the world as a whole without abolishing history, as pointed out also above. As also Martinelli writes, we can speak of 'global society' only if we mean 'a world association of peoples, nations and transnational communities which share a few core values of cosmopolitan ethics and are integrated and regulated by a polyarchic form of global governance'.[31] What we have, he observes, is a world system, that is an inter-dependent whole, characterised by a single economy and multiple cultures. Global interdependence, notwithstanding the changed experience that time and space compression entails, does not mean that places are becoming identical or interchangeable.[32]

Nevertheless, capitalism has undoubtedly a strong impact on societies around the world. By celebrating 'the end of history', global capitalism tries to 'de-historise' and 'de-culturalise' societies, and regard them as differentiated only according to their degree of integration into the global production and consumption system. No doubt, also, the social imaginary significations that this system conveys have a decisive impact on cultures and the socialisation of human beings, as the previous chapter demonstrated. Productivity, consumerism, competition, profit, power seeking, the identification of personal merit with economic success and egocentrism penetrate all spheres of social life.[33] Moreover, one should take into account that cultures throughout the world have now been directly turned into commodities and become part of the spectacle society. Tourism is a top industry worldwide and has been growing recently faster than world trade (international tourists are currently nearly 1.2 billion and domestic tourists 5–6 billion).[34] Capitalism has transformed cultures into theme parks for the masses of sightseers who scavenge the planet for entertainment and 'new experiences' and has replaced the value that heritage has for local inhabitants, participants also in this industry, into economic value. This has major consequences for cultures. Local traditions and customs, natural landmarks, antiquities, heritage sights, rituals, dances and arts are commodified and 'Disneyified'. The global market produces and celebrates, on the one hand, short distances and similarities in the 'global village' and, on the other, promotes 'originality' and 'exclusivity', leading indigenous populations to 'ethnologise' themselves and sell their cultures as commodities.[35] But, as well as the techno-bureaucratic gaze which measures 'development' and 'performance', the tourist gaze is superficial. It does not delve into cultures. D.H. Lawrence, the English novelist and essayist, would make the same point almost a century ago, when the world started already looking 'small and known':

> Superficially, the world has become small and known. Poor little globe of earth, the tourists trot round you as easily as they trot round the Bois or round Central Park. There is no mystery left, we've been there, we've seen it, we know all about it. We've done the globe, and the globe is done. This is quite true, superficially. On the superficies, horizontally, we've been everywhere and done everything, we know all about it. Yet the more we know, superficially, the less we penetrate, vertically.[36]

In other words, the fact that global capitalism pursues the levelling of all cultures under its logic does not entail that one should be studying societies and their institutions under the same logic. It is one thing to distinguish dominant significations and their effects, and it is another to view and compare societies exclusively through them. Comparative research should be avoiding deterministic accounts, and instead, it should be trying to identify the interaction (e.g., symbioses, conflicts, alterations or collapses) between the capitalist imaginary that drives globalisation and existing cultures. Societies have their own history and their own fundamental alterity, expressed by their particular world of significations, which contains now, one way or another, capitalist significations. One should, therefore, access each society's particular magma of imaginary significations, which is not homogeneous with some other, thus accessing also the transinstitutional and lifelong dimension of learning that allows one to better understand what it means to be socialised and educated in the society under inquiry. It is for this reason important, not only for comparative education but social sciences in general, to delve into the dimension of signification rather than be confined to the functional-instrumental or ensemblistic-identitary dimension of societies.

For accessing the dimension of signification in social institutions, the appropriate approach is *understanding*, rather than *explanation*. Or, as Bauman puts it simply, in his study of hermeneutics in social sciences: 'one needs to explain nature, but to understand culture'.[37] Explanation is appropriate to the ensemblistic-identitary logic, and the natural sciences that study it (physics, geology, cosmology etc.). Explanation, as noted above, entails the reduction of a phenomenon to its causes or to general laws. By applying this approach to society, the researcher seeks to establish a coherent system characterised by determinancy and objectification, which means, as Edgar Morin puts it, that he/she conceives and studies human beings as objects.[38] However, because humans and their activities and institutions are inconceivable without an imaginary dimension, the pertinent approach to their study is understanding. Understanding intends the meaning of situations or actions experienced by individuals and social groups. With regard to the individual, as again Morin notes, understanding leads to empathetic knowledge, which involves a double-bind movement: it includes a projection of the self onto the other and identification of the other with oneself, namely an *ego alter* becomes an *alter ego*.[39] With regard to society, understanding as an approach allows the researcher to access the significations created by this society and presentified in its institutions. To look for causes behind the emergence of these significations is pointless because they are creations *ex nihilo* (from nowhere) – though neither *in nihilo* (out of context) nor *cum nihilo* (with no means), in Castoriadis's terms. There may be some necessary but never sufficient conditions for the emergence of significations and meanings.[40] Thus what matters is to approach the world of significations, presentified in social institutions, which is subject to elucidation and understanding.

This presupposes that we regard the foreign society as equal, and simply as another culture, with its own haecceity, rather than as inferior or superior to ours. Looking at the other society as superior indicates a disposition to renounce one's own institutions and adopt the foreign ones. Viewing the other society as inferior (historically, the most common attitude) indicates the perception that one's own institutions are the only valid and should be adopted by the others. To see a society as simply other, it means that one is capable of reflecting on and questioning institutions at home, because they allow for it. It means also that one does not regard as meaningful only one's own representation of the world and that the effort to understand other cultures is not subjected to any sort of policy agenda or practical purpose.[41]

Acknowledging the haecceity of societies does not entail that one should abstain either from their cross-investigation or from critical reflection on their significations, institutions and practices. It entails though reconsideration of the very meaning and function of comparison. The verb 'compare' derives from the Latin *comparare*, *com-* meaning 'with' and *parare* 'to prepare', that is, to prepare a pair of things in order to identify similarities and differences. The very etymology of the verb expresses the focus of comparison on elements and properties that can be distinguished, ordered and counted as between two mathematical sets. If societies are characterised fundamentally by alterity and singularity, and if our task in studying education systems is to delve into their magma of imaginary significations while at same time exercising critical reflection, then the term 'comparison' is not accurate. It would be more appropriate to speak of *syncrisis* (*σύγκρισις*). The world means 'comparison', but it has a different etymological root. It is not associated with the adjective 'syncretic', meaning fusion of different views or forms, nor with 'crisis', as a crucial situation or traumatic change. *Syn-crisis* derives from *krinein* (*κρίνειν*), meaning to separate, decide or judge, and it is at the root of the nouns 'critique' or 'criticism'. *Syncrisis* (amongst its various meanings in Ancient Greek) indicates, not simply the quest for similarities and differences, but bringing together (*syn-*) in order to judge, namely to co-judge or co-criticise. This term would express more accurately the approach proposed here in studying education systems: accessing the magma of imaginary significations of the other society and exercising critical reflection on both its institutions and our own. In short, I am proposing a *syncritical* study of education.

The approach has its roots, as this study has shown, in Ancient Greek impartiality, expressed in Homeric poetry, in the Athenian tragedy and the Herodotean *historein* and *sēmainein*, as well as the cultural and epistemological tradition of the European Modernity. Comparative studies should be questioning taken-for-granted modes of knowledge and should be seeking to know how the society under consideration understands its own institutions, forms and activities. Again, this does not mean that one should necessarily endorse the world of significations that one studies or merely describe them, but place under critical examination both the other society and their own. The basis for this critical cross-investigation of education systems is the very idea which gave rise to comparative studies in the first place, in Ancient Greece, namely the central imaginary signification of collective and personal autonomy. Through this, Greek Antiquity acknowledged the universality and the alterity of the human condition; the multiplicity of viewpoints and of nomoi of different societies; and it valued logos as questioning of established institutions, as quest for the truth, and as pursuit of justice and freedom. And through this signification, European Modernity recognised the universality and diversity of all peoples and cultures and inspired social movements, laws and institutions around the world endorsing a host of rights and freedoms, including rights and freedoms with regard to childhood and education. This proposition has nothing to do with economic liberalism and consumer individualism celebrated by global capitalism, as the glorious pathway of progress that all countries ought to follow. The West, after all, has been systematically using the defence of human rights to open the way to transnational corporations, and governments of 'developing' countries have been mostly interested in importing Western technology and consumer culture and keep away anything that has to do with real civil freedoms. Besides, bureaucratisation, the corporate takeover of policymaking and the media, and the rise of authoritarian and exclusionist forces currently in the West render it hardly able to export anything but capitalism. Capitalism pursues normalisation, submission and unlimited expansion of production and consumption. Autonomy means democratic self-determination and self-limitation.

The project of collective and personal autonomy is incarnated in the formation of the Greco-Western comparative gaze, according to which all societies and their institutions should be viewed as equal, but, also, all are subject to critique. The same project is embedded in the Greek paideia, which in the past years has been obfuscated by the ideological squabbles between, on the one hand, 'conservatives', 'elitists' or 'Eurocentrists' and, on the other, 'liberals', 'progressives' or 'anti-Eurocentrists'. Either by ignoring the historical facts or by distorting them, the two camps tailored this important educational legacy to their ideological pursuits – the conservatives to maintain class reproduction and the progressives to 'modernise' education systems. Both sides, being averse to the possibility of real democracy, dressed up Classical Greece with all sorts of stereotypes, trying as much as possible to bury its democratic and universalistic example, as well as that of European Modernity, which they identified exclusively with capitalist domination. In the end, the political representatives of both sides, as the history of neoliberalism shows, have indeed helped capitalism to dominate education. The critical Greco-Western tradition is valuable to any effort intended to reverse the barbarism of this domination over education, society but, also, over the very life on earth.

Notes

1 Quoted in: Jones (1971: 36).
2 Hans (1949: 9–10).
3 Holmes (1984: 594).
4 Durkheim (1982: 147).
5 Ragin (1987: 26).
6 Skocpol and Somers (1980).
7 Skocpol (1979: 290).
8 See Theodoridis (2000).
9 OECD (2010: 29).
10 See Durkheim (1982: 150).
11 From comparative educationists. Holmes, for example, found this source in Plato's *Republic*. See Holmes (1984: 594).
12 See Theodoridis (2000); Hasselbladh and Theodoridis (1998).
13 See for example: Roberts (1985); Landes (1999); Ferguson (2011).
14 Ferguson (2011).
15 Hobson (2004).
16 Goody (2006: 50).
17 Goody (2006: 51).
18 McLennan (2015).
19 Go (2013).
20 Connell (2007).
21 Connell (2007: 115 and 133).
22 See: Ramirez and Boli (1987); Meyer and Ramirez (2000).
23 See Dale (2000).
24 Meyer (2004: 44).
25 Meyer and Ramirez (2000).
26 Meyer and Ramirez (2000: 116 and 130).
27 Meyer and Ramirez (2000).
28 See Hasselbladh and Theodoridis (1998).
29 Castells (2009).
30 Castells (2009: 37–38).
31 Martinelli (2012: 94).
32 Martinelli (2012: 94).

33 See Beder (2006).
34 UNWTO (2016).
35 Azarya (2004); Shepherd (2002); Gotham (2002).
36 Lawrence (1928).
37 Bauman (2010).
38 Morin (1986).
39 Morin (1986).
40 Castoriadis (2003b: 48–49).
41 Castoriadis (1991: 37–38).

Bibliography

Adam, G. (2014) *Big Bucks: The Explosion of the Art Market in the Twenty-First Century*. Surrey: Lund Humphries.

Adas, M. (1989) *Machines as the Measure of Men: Science, Technology, and Ideologies of Western Dominance*. Ithaca: Cornell University Press.

Aeschylus (1926a) *Persians*. Translated by H. W. Smyth. Cambridge, MA: Harvard University Press. Perseus Digital Library. www.perseus.tufts.edu/hopper/text?doc=Perseus:text:1999.01.0012

Aeschylus (1926b) *Prometheus Bound*. Translated by H. W. Smyth. Cambridge, MA: Harvard University Press. Perseus Digital Library. www.perseus.tufts.edu/hopper/text?doc=Perseus:text:1999.01.0010

Alexander, N. C. (2001) 'Paying for Education: How the World Bank and the International Monetary Fund Influence Education in Developing Countries'. *Peabody Journal of Education* 76(3–4): 285–338.

Anderson, B. (1983) *Imagined Communities: Reflections on the Origins and Spread of Nationalism*. London: Verso.

Arendt, H. (1969) *On Violence*. New York: Harcourt Publishers.

Arendt, H. (1999) *The Human Condition*. 2nd edition. Chicago: University of Chicago Press.

Arendt, H. (2005) *The Promise of Politics*. Edited by J. Kohn. New York: Schocken Books.

Arendt, H. (2006) *Between Past and Future*. London: Penguin Books.

Aries, Ph. (1973) *L'enfant et la vie familial sous l' Ancien Regime*. Paris: Editions du Seuil.

Aristotle (1957) *Politics*. Edited by W. D. Ross. Oxford: Clarendon Press. Perseus Digital Library. www.perseus.tufts.edu/hopper/text?doc=Perseus%3Atext%3A1999.01.0057%3Abook%3D3%3Asection%3D1275b

Aristotle (1996) *The Politics and the Constitution of Athens*. Edited by S. Everson. Cambridge: Cambridge University Press.

Aristotle (2003) *Περί Ψυχής*. Thessaloniki: Zitros Publishing House.

Aronowitz, S. and Giroux, H. A. (1991) *Postmodern Education: Politics, Culture and Social Criticism*. Minneapolis: University of Minneapolis Press.

Atwan, A.-B. (2015) *Islamic State: The Digital Caliphate*. London: Saqi Books.

Azarya, V. (2004) 'Globalisation and International Tourism in Developing Countries: Marginality as a Commercial Commodity'. *Current Sociology*, 52(6): 949–967.

Bacon, F. (1627) *The New Atlantis*. www2.hn.psu.edu/faculty/jmanis/bacon/atlantis.pdf

Bacon, F. (2010–2015) *The New Organon or: True Directions Concerning the Interpretation of Nature*. Edited by J. Bennett. www.earlymoderntexts.com/assets/pdfs/bacon1620.pdf

Ball, S. (1994) *Education Reform: A Critical and Post-Structural Approach*. Buckingham: Open University Press.

Barber, B. R. (2007) *Consumed: How Markets Corrupt Children, Infantilize Adults, and Swallow Citizens Whole.* New York: W.W. Norton and Company.

Bard, A. and Soderqvist, J. (2002) *Netocracy: The New Power Elite and Life after Capitalism.* London: Pearson Education.

Barnett, M. and Finnemore, M. (2004) *Rules for the World: International Organisations in Global Politics.* Ithaca: Cornell University Press.

Barney, D. (2004) *The Network Society.* London: Polity.

Bauman, Z. (2001) *The Individualised Society.* London, Polity.

Bauman, Z. (2005) *Liquid Life.* London: Polity Press.

Bauman, Z. (2010) *Hermeneutics and Social Science: Approaches to Understanding.* London: Routledge.

Bauman, Z. (2011) *Culture in a Liquid Modern World.* London: Polity.

Bauman, Z. and Lyon, D. (2013) *Liquid Surveillance: A Conversation.* London: Polity Press.

Bayly, C. A. (2004) *The Birth of the Modern World, 1780–1914.* Oxford: Blackwell.

Beauregard, M. (2012) *Brain Wars: The Scientific Battle Over the Existence of the Mind and the Proof That Will Change the Way We Live Our Lives.* New York: HarperOne.

Beck, U. (2005) *Power in the Global Age: A New Global Political Economy.* London: Polity Press.

Beck, U. (2013) *German Europe.* London: Polity Press.

Beder, Sh. (2006) *Free Market Missionaries: The Corporate Manipulation of Community Values.* London: Earthscan.

Bell, A. (1808) *The Madras School or Elements of Tuition.* London: T. Beneley, Bolt Court.

Bell, D. (1976) T*he Coming of Post-Industrial Society: A Venture in Social Forecasting.* 2nd edition. New York: Basic Books.

Berkman, S. (2008) *The World Bank and the Gods of Lending.* Sterling: Kumarian Press.

Bernstein, B. (2000) *Pedagogy, Symbolic Control and Identity: Theory, Research, Critique.* Revised edition. London: Taylor and Francis.

Bichler, R. and Rollinger, R. (2000) *Herodot.* Hildesheim: Georg Olms AG.

Bimber, B. (2001) 'Information and political engagement in America: the search for effects of information technology at the individual level'. *Political Research Quarterly*, 54 (1): 53–67.

Blake, D. (1982) 'The Purposes and Nature of Comparative Education: The Contribution of I. L. Kandel'. *Comparative Education*, 18(1): 3–13.

Blass, R. B. and Carmeli, Z. (2007) 'The Case against Neuropsychoanalysis: On the Fallacies Underlying Psychoanalysis' Latest Scientific Trend and Its Negative Impact on Psychoanalytic Discourse'. *International Journal of Psychoanalysis*, 88: 19–40.

Boltanski, L. and Chiapello, E. (2005) *The New Spirit of Capitalism.* London: Verso.

Bourdieu, P. (1996) *On Television.* New York: The New Press.

Boutang, Y. M. (2012) *Cognitive Capitalism.* London: Polity Press.

Bowen, J. (1981) *A History of Western Education – Volume 3: The Modern West: Europe and the New World.* London: Methuen & Co Ltd.

Brown, P., Lauder, H. and Ashton, D. (2011) *The Global Auction: The Broken Promises of Education, Jobs and Incomes.* Oxford: Oxford University Press.

Bruno-Jofré, R. and Schriewer, J. (2012) *The Global Reception of John Dewey's Thought: Multiple Refractions Through Time and Space.* London: Routledge.

Brynjolfsson, E. and McAfee, A. (2014) *The Second Machine Age: Work, Progress, and Prosperity in a Time of Brilliant Technologies.* New York: W.W. Norton & Company, Inc.

Burckhardt, J. (1995) *The Civilization of the Renaissance in Italy.* London: Phaidon Press.

Burckhardt, J. (2002) *History of Greek Culture.* New York: Dover Publications.

Burton-Jones, A. (1999) *Knowledge Capitalism: Business, Work, and Learning in the New Economy.* Oxford: Oxford University Press.

Bury, J. B. (2006a) *The Idea of Progress: An Inquiry into Its Origin and Growth*. Middlesex: The Echo Library.

Bury, J. B. (2006b) *A History of Freedom of Thought*. Middlesex: The Echo Library.

Calhoun, C. (2003) 'The Democratic Integration of Europe: Interests, Identity, and the Public Sphere'. In: Berezin, M. and Schain, M. (eds) *Europe without Borders: Re-Mapping Territory, Citizenship and Identity in a Transnational Age*. Baltimore: The Johns Hopkins University Press.

Carnoy, M. and Castells, M. (1999) 'Globalisation, the Knowledge Society, and the Network State'. Paper presented at the University of Athens International Conference on Nicos Poulantzas, September 30–October 2, 1999.

Cartledge, P. (1997) '"Deep Plays": Theatre as Process in Greek Civic Life'. In: Easterling, P. E. (ed) *The Cambridge Companion to Greek Tragedy*. Cambridge: Cambridge University Press.

Cartledge, P. (2006) *Thermopylae: The Battle That Changed the World*. London: Macmillan.

Cassirer, E. (1951) *The Philosophy of the Enlightenment*. Boston: Beacon Press.

Castells, M. (2000) *The Rise of the Network Society*. 2nd edition. Oxford: Blackwell.

Castells, M. (2004) *The Power of Identity*. 2nd edition. Oxford: Blackwell.

Castells, M. (2009) *Communication Power*. Oxford: Oxford University Press.

Castoriadis, C. (1987) *The Imaginary Institution of Society*. Cambridge: Polity Press.

Castoriadis, C. (1991) *Philosophy, Politics, Autonomy: Essays in Political Philosophy*. Oxford: Oxford University Press.

Castoriadis, C. (1993) *Political and Social Writings*. Volume 3, 1961–1979. Translated and Edited by D. A. Curtis. Minnesota: University of Minnesota Press.

Castoriadis, C. (1997) *The Castoriadis Reader*. Edited by D. A. Curtis. London: Blackwell.

Castoriadis, C. (2000) *Οι ομιλίες στην Ελλάδα*. Athens: Ypsilon/Vivlia.

Castoriadis, C. (2003a) *The Rising Tide of Insignificancy*. Translated from the French and Edited anonymously as a public service. Electronic Publication. www.costis.org/x/castoriadis/Castoriadis-rising_tide.pdf

Castoriadis, C. (2003b) *Φιλοσοφία και Επιστήμη – Ένας διάλογος με τον Γεώργιο Λ. Ευαγγελλόπουλο*. Athens: Eurasia Publications.

Castoriadis, C. (2004) *Ce qui fait la Grece, 1: D' Homer a Heraclite*. Seminaires 1982–1983. Paris: Editions du Seuil.

Castoriadis, C. (2007) *Figures of the Thinkable*. Stanford: Stanford University Press.

Castoriadis, C. (2008) *Ce qui fait la Grece, 2: La cité et les lois. Seminaires 1983–1984*. Paris: Editions du Seuil.

Castoriadis, C. (2010) *A Society Adrift*. New York: Fordham University Press.

Castoriadis, C. (2011) *Ce qui fait la Grèce, 3: Thucydide, la force et les droit. Séminaires 1984–1985*. La Creation Humaine IV. Paris: Éditions du Seuil.

Castoriadis, C. (2015) *Window on the Chaos*. Translated from the French and Edited anonymously as a public service. Electronic Publication. www.notbored.org/WoC.pdf

Charle, C. (2004) 'Patterns'. In: Rüegg, W. (ed) *A History of the University in Europe: Vol III: Universities in the Nineteenth and Early Twentieth Centuries (1800–1945)*. Cambridge: Cambridge University Press.

Cheung, C.-F. and Fan, G. (2009) 'The Chinese Idea of University, 1866–1895'. In: Mak, K. S.R. (ed) *Transmitting the Ideal of Enlightenment: Chinese Universities since the Late Nineteenth Century*. Lanham: University of Press of America.

Chomsky, N. (2016) *Who Rules the World?* New York: Hamish Hamilton.

Connell, R. (2007) *Southern Theory*. Cambridge: Polity Press.

Constant, B. (2010–2015) *The Liberty of the Ancients Compared with That of the Moderns*. Edited by J. Bennet. www.earlymoderntexts.com/assets/pdfs/constant1819.pdf

Creveld, van M. (1999) *The Rise and Decline of the State.* Cambridge: Cambridge University Press.

Cuche, D. (1996) *La Notion de Culture dans les Sciences Sociales.* Paris: Editions La Decouverte.

Dale, R. (2000) 'Globalisation and Education: Demonstrating a "Common World Education Culture" or Locating a "Globally Structured Educational Agenda"'. *Educational Theory*, 50(4): 427–448.

Dauvergne, P. and LeBaron, G. (2014) *Protest Inc.: The Corporatization of Activism.* Cambridge: Polity Press.

Davis, M. (2007) *Planet of Slums.* London: Verso.Debord, G. (1994) *The Society of the Spectacle.* New York: Zone Books.

Descartes, R. (2010–2015) *Discourse on the Method of Rightly Conducting One's Reason and Seeking Truth in the Sciences.* Edited by J. Bennett. www.earlymoderntexts.com/assets/pdfs/descartes1637.pdf

Dickinson, G. L. (1904) *Letters from a Chinese official: Being an Eastern View of Western Civilization.* New York: Doubleday.

Dijck, van J. (2013) *The Culture of Connectivity: A Critical History of Social Media.* Oxford: Oxford University Press.

Dillon, J. and Gergel, T. (ed. and transl.) (2003) *The Greek Sophists.* London: Penguin Books.

Diogenes Laertius (1925) *Lives of Eminent Philosophers.* Translated by R. D. Hicks. Cambridge: Harvard University Press. Perseus Digital Library. www.perseus.tufts.edu/hopper/text?doc=Perseus:text:1999.01.0258

Due, B. (1989) *The Cyropaedia: Xenophon's Aims and Methods.* Aarhus: Aarhus University Press.

Dufour, D. R. (2003) *The Art of Shrinking Heads: On the New Servitude of the Liberated in the Age of Total Capitalism.* Cambridge: Polity Press.

Dunn, J. (1992) *Democracy: The Unfinished Journey, 508 BC to AD 1993.* Oxford: Oxford University Press.

Durkheim, E. (1956) *Education and Sociology.* New York: The Free Press.

Durkheim, E. (1982) *The Rules of Sociological Method.* London: Macmillan.

Durkheim, E. (2009) *The Evolution of Educational Thought: Lectures on the Formation and Development of Secondary Education in France.* London: Routledge.

Eagleton, T. (1991) *Ideology: An Introduction.* London: Verso Books.

Easterling, P. E. (ed.) (1997) *The Cambridge Companion to Greek Tragedy.* Cambridge: Cambridge University Press.

Edelman, G. M. and Tononi, G. (2001) *A Universe of Consciousness: How Matter Becomes Imagination.* New York: Basic Books.

Ehrenberg, A. (2010) *The Weariness of the Self: Diagnosing the History of Depression in the Contemporary Age.* Montreal and Kingston: McGill-Queen's University Press.

Eliot, T. S. (1969) *The Complete Poems and Plays of T.S. Eliot.* London: Faber and Faber.

Ellul, J. (1964) *The Technological Society.* New York: Vintage Books.

Euripides (1938) *The Suppliants.* Translated by E. P. Coleridge. New York: Random House. Perseus Digital Library. www.perseus.tufts.edu/hopper/text?doc=Perseus:text:1999.01.0122

Ferguson, N. (2011) *Civilisation: The West and the Rest.* London: Penguin Books.

Fichte, J. G. (1873) *Popular Works.* London: Trubner & Co.

Finley, M. I. (1983) *Economy and Society in Ancient Greece.* London: Penguin Books.

Finley, M. I. (2002) *The World of Odysseus.* New York: NYRB Classics.

Foucault, M. (1986) *Power, Knowledge: Selected Interviews and Other Writings 1972–1977.* Edited by C. Gordon. Brighton: Harvester Press.

Foucault, M. (1991) *Discipline and Punish: The Birth of the Prison.* London: Penguin Books.

Friedell, E. (1940) *Kulturgeschichte Griechenlands: Leben und Legende der vorchristlichen Seele.* München: Beck.

Fulcher, J. (2004) *Capitalism: A Very Short Introduction.* Oxford: Oxford University Press.

Fusaro, D. (2015) *Europe and Capitalism: Regaining the Future.* Mimesis International.

Gellner, E. (1983) *Nations and Nationalism.* Oxford: Blackwell.

Go, J. (2013) 'For a Postcolonial Sociology'. *Theory and Society*, 42: 25–55.

Goody, J. (2006) *The Theft of History.* Cambridge: Cambridge University Press.

Gotham, F. K. (2002) 'Marketing Mardi Gras: Commodification, Spectacle and the Political Economy of Tourism in New Orleans'. *Urban Studies*, 39(10): 1735–1756.

Guibernau, M. and Rex, J. (eds.) (1997) *The Ethnicity Reader: Nationalism, Multiculturalism and Migration. London: Polity Press.*

Habermas, J. (1986) *The Theory of Communicative Action – Volume 1: Reason and the Rationalisation of Society.* London: Polity Press.

Hall, E. (1997) 'The Sociology of Athenian Tragedy'. In: Easterling, P. E. (ed.) *The Cambridge Companion to Greek Tragedy.* Cambridge: Cambridge University Press.

Hancock, G. (1989) *Lords of Poverty: The Power, Prestige, and Corruption of the International Aid Business.* New York: The Atlantic Monthly Press.

Hans, N. (1949) *Comparative Education: A Study of Educational Factors and Traditions. London*: Routledge and Kegan Paul.

Hartog, F. (1988) *The Mirror of Herodotus: The Representation of the Other in the Writing of History.* Berkeley: University of California Press.

Hartog, F. (2000) 'The Invention of History: The Pre-History of a Concept from Homer to Herodotus'. *History and Theory*, 39(3): 384–395.

Harvey, D. (2005) *A Brief History of Neoliberalism.* Oxford: Oxford University Press.

Hasselbladh, H. and Theodoridis, F. (1998) 'Social Magmas and the Conventional Explanatory Pyramid'. *Scandinavian Journal of Management*, 14(1/2): 53–76.

Hayek, F. ([1944] 2006) *The Road to Serfdom.* London: Routledge.

Hayter, T. (1982) *The Creation of World Poverty.* Bristol: Pluto Press.

Heiman, R., Freeman, C. and Liechty, M. (2012) *The Global Middle Classes: Theorising through Ethnography.* Santa Fe: SAR Press.

Henry, M., Lingard, B., Rizvi, F. & Taylor, S. (2001) *The OECD, Globalisation and Educational Policy.* Amsterdam: Pergamon.

Heraclitus. *Fragments.* Edited by R. Hoyt. www.heraclitusfragments.com/files/ge.html

Herodotus (1920) *The Histories.* Translated by A. D. Godley. Cambridge: Harvard University Press. Perseus Digital Library. www.perseus.tufts.edu/hopper/text?doc=Perseus:text:1999.01.0126

Hesiod (1914a) *Theogony*. Translated by H. G. Evelyn-White. Cambridge: Harvard University Press; London: William Heinemann Ltd. Perseus Digital Library. www.perseus.tufts.edu/hopper/text?doc=Perseus:text:1999.01.0129

Hesiod (1914b) *Works and Days.* Translated by H. G. Evelyn-White. Cambridge: Harvard University Press; London: William Heinemann Ltd. Perseus Digital Library. www.perseus.tufts.edu/hopper/text?doc=Perseus:text:1999.01.0132

Heyneman, S.P. (1993) 'Quantity, Quality and Source'. *Comparative Education Review.* 37(4): 372–388.

Heyneman, S. P. (2003) 'The History and Problems in the Making of Education Policy at the World Bank 1960–2000'. *International Journal of Educational Development*, 23(3): 315–337.

Hindman, M. (2009) *The Myth of Digital Democracy.* Princeton: Princeton University Press.

Hirst, P. and Thompson, G. (1996) *Globalisation in Question: The International Economy and Possibilities of Governance.* Cambridge: Polity Press.

Hobsbawm, E. J. (1962) *The Age of Revolution: 1789–1848.* London: Weidenfeld & Nicolson.

Hobsbawm, E. J. (1975) *The Age of Capital: 1848–1875.* London: Weidenfeld & Nicolson.

Hobsbawm, E. J. (1992) *Nations and Nationalism since 1780: Programme, Myth, Reality.* 2nd edition. Cambridge: Cambridge University Press.

Hobsbawm, E. J. (1998) *Uncommon People: Resistance, Rebellion and Jazz.* London: Abacus.

Hobson, J. M. (2004) *The Eastern Origins of Western Civilisation.* Cambridge: Cambridge University Press.

Holmes, B. (1984) 'Paradigm Shifts in Comparative Education'. *Comparative Education Review,* 28(4): 584–604.

Homer (1919) *The Odyssey.* Translated by A. T. Murray. Cambridge, MA: Harvard University Press; London: William Heinemann, Ltd. Perseus Digital Library. www.perseus.tufts.edu/hopper/text?doc=Perseus:text:1999.01.0136

Homer (1924) *The Iliad.* Translated by A. T. Murray. Cambridge, MA: Harvard University Press; London: William Heinemann, Ltd. Perseus Digital Library. www.perseus.tufts.edu/hopper/text?doc=Perseus:text:1999.01.0134

Humboldt, W. von (1854) *The Limits of State Action.* The Online Library of Liberty. http://oll.libertyfund.org/titles/humboldt-the-sphere-and-duties-of-government-1792-1854

Humboldt, W. von (1970) 'On the Spirit and Organisational Framework of Intellectual Institutions in Berlin'. *Minerva* 8(2): 242–250.

Hume, D. (1739) *Treatise of Human Nature.* Edited by L. A. Selby and M. A. Bigge. Oxford: Clarendon Press, 1896. http://michaeljohnsonphilosophy.com/wp-content/uploads/2012/01/5010_Hume_Treatise_Human_Nature.pdf

Hume, D. (1987) *Essays Moral, Political, Literary.* http://oll.libertyfund.org/titles/hume-essays-moral-political-literary-lf-ed

Hunt, J. (1863) *On the Negro's Place in Nature.* London: Trübner & Co.

Jaeger, W. (1939) *Paideia: The Ideals of Greek Culture: Vol. I, Archaic Greece – the Mind of Athens.* New York: Oxford University Press.

James, W. (1956) *Human Immortality: Two Supposed Objections to the Doctrine.* New York: Dover Publications.

Jarvis, P. (1983) *Adult Education & Lifelong Learning: Theory and Practice.* Third edition. London: Routledge Falmer.

Jepperson, R. L. (1991) 'Institutions, Institutional Effects, and Institutionalism'. In: Powell, W. W. and DiMaggio, P. J. (eds) *The New Institutionalism in Organisational Analysis.* Chicago: The University of Chicago Press.

Jespersen, K. J. V. (2004) *A History of Denmark.* New York: Palgrave Macmillan.

Jones, P. (1971) *Comparative Education: Purpose and Method.* Queensland: University of Queensland Press.

Jones, P.W. (1992) *World Bank Financing of Education.* London. Routledge.

Kant, I. (1784) *What Is Enlightenment?* Translated by M. C. Smith. www.columbia.edu/acis/ets/CCREAD/etscc/kant.html

Kant, I. (1998) *Critique of Pure Reason.* Translated and edited by Guyer, Paul and Wood, Allen. Cambridge: Cambridge University Press.

Kant, I. (2005) *Groundwork for the Metaphysics of Morals.* Edited by L. Denis. Ontario: Broadview Press.

Kerferd, G. B. (1981) *The Sophistic Movement.* Cambridge: Cambridge University Press.

Klees, S. J. (2016) 'Human Capital and Rates of Return: Brilliant Ideas or Ideological Dead Ends?'. *Comparative Education Review,* 60(4): 644–672.

Klein, N. (2007) *The Shock Doctrine: The Rise of Disaster Capitalism.* New York: Metropolitan Books.

Kolbert, E. (2014) *The Sixth Extinction: An Unnatural History*. London: Bloomsbury Publishing.

Kristeva, J. (1996) *Sens et non-sens de la révolte: Pouvoirs et limites de la psychanalyse I*. Paris: Librairie Arthème Fayard.

Kroeber, A. L. and Kluckhohn, C. (1952) *Culture: A Critical Review of Concepts and Definitions*. Cambridge: Harvard University Printing Office.

Kurzweil, R. (2005) *The Singularity Is Near: When Humans Transcend Biology*. London: Viking.

Lancy, D. F., Bock, J. and Gaskins, S. (2010) *The Anthropology of Learning in Childhood*. Walnut Creek: AltaMira Press.

Landes, D. (1999) *The Wealth and Poverty of Nations: Why Some Are So Rich and Some So Poor*. London: Abacus.

Lawler, E. (1991) 'Neohumanistic-Idealistic Concepts of a University: Schelling, Steffens, Fichte and von Humboldt'. In: Richardson, H. (ed) *Friedrich Schleiermacher and the Founding of the University of Berlin: The Study of Religion as a Scientific Discipline*. Lewiston: The Edwin Mellen Press.

Lazzarato, M. (2012) *The Making of the Indebted Man: Essay on the Neoliberal Condition*. Cambridge: MIT Press.

Le Goff, J. (2005) *The Birth of Europe*. Oxford: Blackwell.

Leibniz, G. W. (1989) 'Dialogue (August 1677)'. In: Ariew, R. and Garber, D. (eds) *G.W. Leibniz: Philosophical Essays*. Indianapolis: Hackett Publishing Company.

Lévi-Strauss, C. (1983) *Le Regard Eloigne*. Paris: Librairie Plon.

Levy, D. C. (1986) *Higher Education and the State in Latin America*. Chicago: The University of Chicago Press.

Leys, C. (2008) *Total Capitalism: Market Politics, Market State*. Monmouth: Merlin Press.

Lindenberg, M. (1975) 'The Politics of Foreign Investment in Southeast Asia from 1945–1973'. *Journal of Contemporary Asia*, 5(1): 5–18.

Lloyd, G. E. R. (1970) *Early Greek Science: Thales to Aristotle*. London: Chatto and Windus.

Louv, R. (2008) *Last Child in the Woods: Saving Our Children from Nature-Deficit Disorder*. New York: Algonquin Books of Chapel Hill.

Lovink, G. (2011) *Networks without a Cause: A Critique of Social Media*. London: Polity Press.

Macpherson, C. B. (2011) *The Political Theory of Possessive Individualism: Hobbes to Locke*. Oxford: Oxford University Press.

Mak, K. S. R. (ed.) (2009a) *Transmitting the Ideal of Enlightenment: Chinese Universities since the Late Nineteenth Century*. Lanham: University of Press of America.

Mak, K. S. R. (2009b) 'The German Intellectual Tradition, Cai Yuanpei and the Founding of Peking University'. In: Mak, K. S. R. (ed) *Transmitting the Ideal of Enlightenment: Chinese Universities since the Late Nineteenth Century*. Lanham: University of Press of America.

Makdisi, G. (1970) 'Madrasa and University in the Middle Ages'. *Studia Islamica*, 32: 255–264.

Mammone, A., Godin, E. and Jenkins, B. (eds.) (2012) *Varieties of Right-Wing Extremism in Europe*. London: Routledge.

Marrou, H. I. (1982) *History of Education in Antiquity*. Madison: University of Wisconsin Press.

Martin, H.-P. and Schumann, H. (1997) *The Global Trap: Globalisation and the Assault on Prosperity and Democracy*. London: Zed Books Ltd.

Martinelli, A. (2012) 'Global Society and Polyarchic Governance'. In: Sales, A. (ed) *Sociology Today: Social Transformations in a Globalising World*. Los Angeles: Sage.

Marx, K. (1861–1864) 'Economic Works of Karl Marx 1861–1864: Productive and Unproductive Labour'. Marx-Engels Archive. www.marxists.org/archive/marx/works/1864/economic/ch02b.htm

Marx, K. (1887) *Capital: A Critique of Political Economy*. Volume 1. Translated by S. Moore and E. Aveling, Edited by F. Engels. Marx/Engels Internet Archive (marxists.org) 1995, 1999. www.marxists.org/archive/marx/works/1867-c1/

McLennan, G. (2015) 'Postcolonial Critique: The Necessity of Sociology'. *Postcolonial Sociology*, 24: 119–144.

McMurry, Ch. A. (1897) *The Elements of General Method on the Principles of Herbart*. Bloomington: Public-School Publishing Company.

Mead, M. (2001a) *Sex and Temperament in Three Primitive Societies*. New York: Perennial.

Mead, M. (2001b) *Male and Female*. New York: Perennial.

Meier, C. (1980) *Die Entstehung des Politischen bei den Griechen*. Frankfurt: Surkamp Verlag Frankfurt am Main.

Meier, C. (1988) *Die politische Kunst der griechischen Tragödie*. München: C.H. Beck'sche Verlagsbuchhandlung.

Meier, C. (2009) *A Culture of Freedom: Ancient Greece and the Origins of Europe*. Oxford: Oxford University Press.

Messner, D. (1997) *The Network Society: Economic Development and International Competitiveness as Problems of Social Governance*. London: Frank Cass.

Metzger, W. P. (1955) 'The German Contribution to the American Theory of Academic Freedom'. *Bulletin of the American Association of University Professors*, 41(2): 214–230.

Meyer, J. W. (1977) 'The Effects of Education as an Institution'. *The American Journal of Sociology*, 83(1): 55–77.

Meyer, J. W. (2004) 'The Nation as Babbitt: How Countries Conform'. *Contexts*, 3(3): 42–47.

Meyer, J. W., Boli, J. and Thomas, G. M. (1987) 'Ontology and Rationalization in the Western Cultural Account'. In: Thomas, G. M., Meyer, J. W., Ramirez, F. O. and Boli, J. (eds) *Institutional Structure: Constituting State, Society and the Individual*. Newbury Park: Sage.

Meyer, J. W., Kamens, D. H. and Benavot, A. (eds.) (1992) *School Knowledge for the Masses: World Models and National Primary Curricular Categories in the Twentieth Century*. Washington, DC: The Falmer Press.

Meyer, J. W. and Ramirez, F. O. (2000) 'The World Institutionalisation of Education'. In: Schriewer, J. (ed) *Discourse Formation in Comparative Education*. Bern: Peter Lang.

Meyer, J. W. and Rowan. B. (1991) 'Institutionalised Organisations: Formal Structure as Myth and Ceremony'. In: Powell, W. W. and DiMaggio, P. J. (eds) *The New Institutionalism in Organisational Analysis*. Chicago: The University of Chicago Press.

Michéa, J. C. (1999) *L'enseignement de l'ignorance, et ses conditions modernes*. Paris: Editions Climats.

Michéa, J. C. (2013) *Les Mystères de la Gauche. De l'idéal des Lumières au triomphe du capitalisme absolu*. Paris: Climats, Flammarion.

Mill, J. S. (1861) *Considerations on Representative Government*. London: Parker, Son and Bourn, West Strand.

Mohamedbhai, G. (2011) 'African Higher Education: The Rise and Fall in the 20th Century'. *International Higher Education*, 62: 17–18.

Montaigne de, M. (2006) *Essays of Michel de Montaigne*. Project Gutenberg. www.gutenberg.org/files/3600/3600-h/3600-h.htm#2HCH0030

Montesquieu, Ch. (1721) *Persian Letters*. Edited and Translated by J. Davidson. London: Gibbings & Company, 1899. Persian Letters Project. http://rbsche.people.wm.edu/teaching/plp/

Montesquieu, Ch. (1911) *The Spirit of Laws*. New York: Cosimo.

Morgan, T. (1998) *Literate Education in the Hellenistic and Roman Worlds*. Cambridge: Cambridge University Press.

Morin, E. (1986) *La Méthode, 3: La Connaissance de la Connaissance*. Paris: Editions du Seuil.
Morin, E. (1987) *Penser l' Europe*. Paris: Editions Gallimard.
Morin, E. (1991) *La Méthode, 4: Les Idées*. Paris: Seuil.
Morin, E. (2001) *La Méthode, 5: L' humanité de l' humanité*. Paris: Éditions du Seuil.
Mossé, C. (1989) *L'Antiquité dans la Révolution Française*. Paris: Edition Albin Michel, S.A.
Mossé, C. (1992) *Les institutions grecques a l'époque classique*. Paris: Armand Colin Editeur.
Mossé, C. (1995) *Politique et société en Grèce ancienne*. Paris: Aubier.
Mouffe, C. (2005) *On the Political*. London: Routledge.
Moutsios, S. (2009) 'International Organisations and Transnational Education Policy'. *Compare*, 39(4): 467–478.
Moutsios, S. (2010) 'Power, Politics and Transnational Policy-Making in Education'. *Globalisation, Societies and Education*, 8(1): 121–141.
Moutsios, S. (2013a) 'The De-Europeanisation of the University under the Bologna Process'. *Thesis Eleven*, 119(1): 22–46.
Moutsios, S. (2013b) 'Imaginary Significations and Education as a Social Institution'. *Academic Journal of Interdisciplinary Studies*, 2(11): 144–149.
Mundy, K. and Iga, M. (2003) 'Hegemonic Exceptionalism and Legitimating Bet Hedging: Paradoxes and Lessons from the US and Japanese Approaches to Education Services under the GATS'. *Globalisation, Societies and Education*, 1(3): 282–319.
Murphy, B. (2001) 'International NGOs and the Challenge of Modernity'. In: Eade, D. and Ligteringen, E. (eds) *Debating Development: NGOs and the Future*. Oxford: Oxfam.
Nemo, Ph. (2005) *What Is the West?* Pittsburgh: Duquesne University Press.
Nietzsche, F. (2004) *On the Future of Our Educational Institutions*. South Bend: St. Augustine's Press.
Nikoloudis, I. P. (1999) *Έρως και Λόγος*. 2nd edition. Athens: Ideotheatron.
Nordin, A. (2014) 'Europeanisation in National Educational Reforms: Horizontal and Vertical Translations'. In: Nordin, A. and Sundberg, D. (eds) *Transnational Policy Flows in European Education: The Making and Governing of Knowledge in the Education Policy Field*. Oxford: Symposium Books.
Norris, P. (2001) *Digital Divide: Civic Engagement, Information Poverty, and the Internet Worldwide*. Cambridge: Cambridge University Press.
Nye, D. E. (2013) *America's Assembly Line*. Cambridge, MA: MIT Press.
Orwell, G. (1941) *The Lion and the Unicorn: Socialism and the English Genius*. Bungay: Penguin Books.
Paasi, A. (2001) 'Europe as a Social Process and Discourse: Consideration of Place, Boundaries and Identity'. *European Urban and Regional Studies*, 8(1): 7–28.
Papadopoulos, G. (1994) *Education 1960–1990: The OECD Perspective*. Paris: OECD.
Parsons, T. (1991) *The Social System*. London: Routledge.
Pascal, B. (1652–1653) *Discourse on the Passion of Love*. The Harvard Classics. www.bartleby.com/48/3/8.html
Paz, O. (1993) *The Double Flame: Love and Eroticism*. Orlando: Harcourt.
Perkins, J. (2006) *Confessions of an Economic Hitman*. London: Ebury Press.
Pforde, M. (2009) *Desocialisation: The Crisis of Post-Modernity*. Chesire: Gabriel.
Piattoeva, N. (2014) 'Elastic Numbers: National Examinations Data as a Technology of Government'. *Journal of Education Policy*, 30(3): 316–334.
Picciano, A. G. and Spring, J. (2013) *The Great American Education-Industrial Complex: Ideology, Technology, and Profit*. New York: Routledge.
Piketty, Th. (2014) *Capital in the Twenty-First Century*. Cambridge: Harvard University Press.

Plato (1903) *Republic.* Edited by J. Burnet. Oxford: Oxford University Press. Perseus Digital Library. www.perseus.tufts.edu/hopper/text?doc=Perseus:text:1999.01.0167

Plato (1925) *Symposium.* Translated by H. N. Fowler. Cambridge, MA: Harvard University Press; London: William Heinemann Ltd. Perseus Digital Library. www.perseus.tufts.edu/hopper/text?doc=Perseus:text:1999.01.0174

Plato (1967–1968) *Laws.* Translated by R. G. Bury. Cambridge, MA: Harvard University Press; London: William Heinemann Ltd. Perseus Digital Library. www.perseus.tufts.edu/hopper/text?doc=Perseus:text:1999.01.0166

Plutarch (1927) *De liberis educandis.* Translated by F. C. Babbitt. Cambridge, MA: Harvard University Press; London: William Heinemann Ltd. Perseus Digital Library. www.perseus.tufts.edu/hopper/text?doc=Perseus:text:2008.01.0137

Polanyi, K. (2001) *The Great Transformation: The Political and Economic Origins of Our Time.* Boston: Beacon Press.

Postman, N. (1982) *The Disappearance of Childhood.* New York: Vintage Books.

Postman, N. (1993) *Technopoly: The Surrender of Culture to Technology.* New York: Vintage Books.

Postman, N. (2005) *Amusing Ourselves to Death: Public Discourse in the Age of Show Business.* London: Penguin Books.

Ragin, Ch. (1987) *The Comparative Method: Moving Beyond Qualitative and Quantitative Strategies.* Berkeley: University of California Press.

Ramirez, F. O. and Boli, J. (1987) 'The Political Construction of Mass Schooling: European Origins and Worldwide Institutionalisation'. *Sociology of Education,* 60: 2–17.

Ramonet, I. (2015) *L'Empire de la surveillance.* Paris: Editions Galilée.

Regakos, A. (2009) *Επινοώντας το παρελθόν: Γέννηση και ακμή της ιστοριογραφικής αφήγησης στην κλασική αρχαιότητα.* Athens: Gutenberg.

Reimers, F. (1994) 'Education and Structural Adjustment in Latin America and Sub-Saharan Africa'. *International Journal of Educational Development,* 14(2): 119–129.

Reisensberg, C. (1989) *Ehe, Hetärentum und Knabenliebe in antiken Griechenland.* München: Beck.

Rich, B. (1994) *Mortgaging the Earth.* Boston: Beacon Press.

Robb, K. (1994) *Literacy and Paideia in Ancient Greece.* Oxford: Oxford University Press.

Roberts, J. M. (1985) *The Triumph of the West.* London: BBC.

Robertson, S. (2010) 'The EU, "Regulatory State Regionalism" and New Modes of Higher Education Governance'. *Globalisation, Societies and Education,* 8(1): 23–27.

Robinson, W. (2001) 'Social Theory and Globalisation: The Rise of a Transnational State'. *Theory and Society,* 30: 157–200.

Romilly de, J. (1970) *La Tragédie Grecque.* Paris: Press Universitaires de France.

Romilly de, J. (1990) *La construction de la vérité chez Thucydide: Conferences essais et Lecons du College de France.* Paris: Julliard.

Romilly de, J. (1992) *The Great Sophists in Periclean Athens.* Oxford: Clarendon Press.

Rose, H. and Rose, S. (2014) *Genes, Cells and Brains: The Promethean Promises of the New Biology.* London: Verso.

Rothkopf, D. (2008) *Superclass: The Global Power Elite and the World They Are Making.* New York: Farrar, Straus and Giroux.

Rousseau, J. J. (1755) *A Discourse on Political Economy.* Constitution Society. ISN, ETH Zurich, Free Public Service. www.files.ethz.ch/isn/125495/5020_Rousseau_A_Discourse_on_Political_Economy.pdf4

Rousseau, J. J. (1762) *The Social Contact or the Principles of Political Right.* Translated by G.D.H. Cole. Public Domain. www.ucc.ie/archive/hdsp/Rousseau_contrat-social.pdf

Rousseau, J. J. (1991) *Emile or On Education*. London: Penguin Classics.

Rüegg, W. (2004) 'Themes'. In: Rüegg, W. (ed) *A History of the University in Europe: Vol III: Universities in the Nineteenth and Early Twentieth Centuries (1800–1945)*. Cambridge: Cambridge University Press.

Salecl, R. (2011) *The Tyranny of Choice*. London: Profile Books.

Savage, M., Cunningham, N., Devine, F., Friedman, S., Laurison, D., Mckenzie, L., Miles, A., Snee, H. and Wakeing, P. (2015) *Social Class in the 21st Century*. Milton Keynes: Penguin.

Scholz, T. (2013) *Digital Labour: The Internet as Playground and Factory*. New York: Routledge.

Schott, R. M. and Søndergaard, D. M. (eds.) (2015) *School Bullying: New Theories in Context*. Cambridge: Cambridge University Press.

Sennett, R. (1977) *The Fall of Public Man*. New York: Alfred Knopf.

Sennett, R. (1998) *The Corrosion of Character*. New York: W.W. Norton & Company, Inc.

Shepherd, R. (2002) 'Commodification, Culture and Tourism'. *Tourist Studies*, 2(2): 183–201.

Shils, E. and Roberts. J. (2004) 'The Diffusion of European Models Outside Europe'. In: Rüegg, W. (ed) *A History of the University in Europe: Vol III: Universities in the Nineteenth and Early Twentieth Centuries (1800–1945)*. Cambridge: Cambridge University Press.

Shivji, G. I. (2007) *Silences in NGO Discourse: The Role and Future of NGOs in Africa*. Nairobi: Fahamu, Pambazuka.

Shotwell, J. T. (1922) *An Introduction to the History of History*. New York: Columbia University Press.

Sklair, L. (2001) *The Transnational Capitalist Class*. London: Blackwell Publishing.

Skocpol, Th. (1979) *States and Social Revolutions: A Comparative Analysis of France, Russia, and China*. Cambridge: Cambridge University Press.

Skocpol, Th. and Somers, M. (1980) 'The Uses of Comparative History in Macrosocial Inquiry'. *Comparative Studies in Society and History*, 22(2): 174–197.

Sliwka, A. (2004) *Transplanting Liberal Education: The Foundation and Development of Liberal Arts Colleges in Western India*. Berlin: Peter Lang.

Smith, A. (2007) *An Inquiry into the Nature and Causes of the Wealth of Nations*. Amsterdam: *Μετα*Libri. www.ibiblio.org/ml/libri/s/SmithA_WealthNations_p.pdf

Smith, K. E. (2010) *Meaning, Subjectivity, Society: Making Sense of Modernity*. Leiden: Brill.

Sophocles (1891) *Antigone*. Edited by S. R. Jebb. Cambridge: Cambridge University Press. Perseus Digital Library. www.perseus.tufts.edu/hopper/text?doc=Perseus:text:1999.01.0186

Spring, J. (2012) *Education Networks: Power, Wealth, Cyberspace, and the Digital Mind*. New York: Routledge.

Standing, G. (2011) *The Precariat: The New Dangerous Class*. London: Bloomsbury Publishing.

Stiglitz, J. (2002) *Globalisation and Its Discontents*. London: Penguin Books.

Streeck, W. and Schmitter, Ph. (1991) 'From National Corporatism to Transnational Pluralism Organised Interests in the Single European Market'. *Politics and Society*, 19(2): 133–163.

Swift, J. (1726) *Gulliver's Travels*. Free eBooks at Planet eBook.com. file:///C:/Users/smcom/Downloads/Gullivers-Travels.pdf

Taguieff, P. A. (2001) *Résister au bougisme. Démocratie forte contre mondialisation techno-marchande*. Paris: Mille et une Nuits.

Taibbi, M. (2017) *Insane Clown President: Dispatches from the American Circus*. London: WH Allen.

Tames, R. (2002) *Ancient Greek Children*. Portsmouth: Heinemann Library.

Taylor, C. (2004) *Modern Social Imaginaries*. Durham: Duke University Press.

Taylor, K. (2012) *The Brain Supremacy: Notes from the Frontiers of Neuroscience*. Oxford: Oxford University Press.

Theodoridis, F. (2000) 'Πέρα από αναγωγικό σκέπτεσθαι/ποιείν'. *Νέα Κοινωνιολογία*, 31: 61–69.

Theodoridis, F. (2007) 'Η σημασία του έργου του Καστοριάδη για την κοινωνική και ιστορική έρευνα'. In: Association of Friends of C. Castoriadis (eds) *Ψυχή, Λόγος, Πόλις, Αφιέρωμα στον Κορνήλιο Καστοριάδη*. Athens: Ypsilon/Vivlia.

Thucydides (1910) *The Peloponnesian War*. London: J. M. Dent; New York: E. P. Dutton. Perseus Digital Library. www.perseus.tufts.edu/hopper/text?doc=Perseus:text:1999.01.0200

Thucydides (1972) *Pericles' Funeral Oration*. Translated by R. Warner. London: Penguin Books: 143–151. https://online.hillsdale.edu/document.doc?id=355

Todorov, T. (2006) *In Defense of the Enlightenment*. London: Atlantic Books.

Toussaint, E. (2008) *The World Bank: A Critical Primer*. London: Pluto Press.

Vernant, J.-P. (1962) *Les origins de la pensée grecque*. Paris: P.U.F.

Vernant, J.-P. (1972) *Les Jardins d' Adonis*. Paris: Gallimard.

Vernart, J.-P. and Vidal-Naquet, P. (1985) *Mythe et tragédie en Grèce ancienne – II*. Paris: Editions La Découverte.

Vidal-Naquet, P. (1986) *The Black Hunter: Forms of Thought and Forms of Society in the Greek World*. Baltimore: The Johns Hopkins University Press.

Vitali, S., Glattfelder, J. B. and Battiston, S. (2011) 'The Network of Global Corporate Control'. *PLoS One*, 6(10): e25995. doi:10.1371/journal.pone.0025995.

Wallerstein, I. (2006) *European Universalism: The Rhetoric of Power*. New York: The New Press.

Walpole, H. (1757) *A Letter from Xo Ho, a Chinese Philosopher at London, to His Friend Lien Chi at Peking*. London: J. Graham.

Weaver, C. (2008). *Hypocrisy trap: The World Bank and the poverty of reform*. Princeton, NJ: Princeton University Press.

Weber, M. (1947) *The Theory of Social and Economic Organisation*. New York: The Free Press.

Weber, M. (1949) *The Methodology of the Social Sciences*. New York: The Free Press.

Weber, M. (1992) *The Protestant Ethic and the Spirit of Capitalism*. Routledge: London.

Wulf, Cr. (2002) *Anthropology of Education*. Münster: LIT.

Xenophon (February 2000) *Cyropaedia: The Education of Cyrus*. Translated by H. G. Dakyns and Revised by F. M. Stawell. The Project Gutenberg Etext of Cyropaedia. https://tripinsurancestore.com/4/cyropaedia.pdf

Young, M. F. D. (1998) *The Curriculum of the Future: Form the New Sociology of Education to a Critical Theory of Learning*. London: Falmer Press.

Websites, documents, reports, speeches and newspaper articles

Alliance for a Competitive European Industry (2010) 'Shifting Gears for a New EU Industrial Partnership: A Manifesto'. www.eurometaux.org/DesktopModules/Bring2mind/DMX/Download.aspx?TabID=57&Command=Core_Download&EntryId=189&PortalId=0&TabId=57

Anderson, D. and Johnson, R. (1998) *University Autonomy in Twenty Countries*. Centre for Continuing Education – The Australian National University. www.magna-charta.org/resources/files/University_autonomy_in_20_countries.pdf

Badiou, A., Bailly, J.-Ch., Balibar, E., Denis, C., Nancy, J.-L., Ranciere, J. and Ronell, A. (2012) 'Save the Greeks from Their Saviors'. *Public Call to Intellectuals and Artists*. 22 February 2012. https://nettime.org/Lists-Archives/nettime-l-1202/msg00079.html

Bank of America Merrill Lynch (2015) 'Creative Disruption'. *Equity Strategy, Global*, 30 April 2015. BoFAML. https://iatranshumanisme.files.wordpress.com/2015/11/11511357.pdf

BBC (2016) 'The Immortalist: Uploading the Mind to a Computer'. 14 March 2016. www.bbc.com/news/magazine-35786771

BusinessEurope (2009) 'Bologna Ministerial Conference: Reflections on the Bologna Process'. Address by Irene Seling, Social Adviser, Plenary Session I on 28 April, Leuven/Louvain-La-Neuve, 28–9 April 2009.

Credit Suisse (2016) *Global Wealth Databook 2015*. Zurich: Credit Suisse.

Cyranoski, D. (2015) 'Gene-Edited "Micropigs" to Be Sold as Pets at Chinese Institute'. www.nature.com/news/gene-edited-micropigs-to-be-sold-as-pets-at-chinese-institute-1.18448

Declaration of Independence (1776) www.archives.gov/exhibits/charters/declaration_transcript.html

ENQA (2009) *ENQA Report on Standards and Guidelines for Quality Assurance in the European Higher Education Area*. 3rd edition. Helsinki: European Association for Quality Assurance in Higher Education. www.enqa.eu/wp-content/uploads/2013/06/ESG_3edition-2.pdf

Epstein, R. (2016) 'The New Mind Control'. *Aeon*. https://aeon.co/essays/how-the-internet-flips-elections-and-alters-our-thoughts

European Commission (2002) *Education and Training in Europe: Diverse Systems, Shared Goals for 2010*. Brussels: European Commission.

European Commission (2003a) *Education & Training 2010: The Success of the Lisbon Strategy Hinges on Urgent Reforms*. Brussels, COM(2003) 685 final.

European Commission (2003b) *The Role of the Universities in the Europe of Knowledge*. Communication from the Commission. Brussels, 5/2/2003 COM (2003) 58 final.

European Commission (2005) *Mobilising the Brainpower of Europe: Enabling the Universities to Make Their Full Contribution to the Lisbon Strategy*. Communication from the Commission. Brussels 20.4.2005 COM(2005) 152 final.

European Commission (2006) *Delivering on the Modernisation Agenda for Universities: Education, Research and Innovation*. Communication from the Commission to the council and the European Parliament. Brussels, 10.5.2006 COM(2006) 208 final.

European Commission (2007) Improving Knowledge Transfer between Research Institutions and Industry Across Europe. Brussels: European Commission.

European Commission (2008) *Geographic Mobility in the European Union: Optimising Its Economic and Social Benefits*. Final Report. Brussels: DG Employment, Social Affairs and Equal Opportunities.

European Commission (2009) *GDP and Beyond – Measuring Progress in a Changing World*. Communication from the Commission to the Council and the European Parliament: Brussels, 20.8.2009, COM (2009) 433 final.

European Commission (2010a) *Europe 2020 Flagship Initiative: Innovation Union*. Communication from the Commission to the European Parliament, the Council, the European Economic and Social Committee and the Committee of the Regions. Brussels, 6.10.2010 COM(2010) 546 final.

European Commission (2010b) *The EU Contribution to the European Higher Education Area*. European Union. http://ec.europa.eu/education/pub/pdf/higher/ehea_en.pdf

European Commission (2010c) *Assessing Europe's University-Based Research*. Expert Group on Assessment of University-Based Research. European Commission: Brussels.

European Commission (2015) 'Trade in Services Agreement (TiSA)'. http://ec.europa.eu/trade/policy/in-focus/tisa/

European Commission 'Transparency Register'. http://ec.europa.eu/transparencyregister/public/homePage.do

European Council (2007) *Council Resolution on Modernising Universities for Europe's Competitiveness in a Global Knowledge Economy*. Adoption of Council Resolution. Council of the European Union, Brussels.

Freedom House (2016) *Anxious Dictators, Wavering Democracies: Global Freedom under Pressure.* New York: freedomhouse.org.

Haldane, A. G. (2015) 'Labour's Share'. Speech given by Andrew G Haldane, Chief Economist, Bank of England, Trades Union Congress, London, 12 November 2015. www.bankofengland.co.uk/publications/Pages/speeches/2015/864.aspx

Hilary, J. (2015) *The Transatlantic Trade and Investment Partnership: A Charter for Deregulation, an Attack on Jobs, an End to Democracy.* Brussels: Rosa Luxemburg Stiftung. www.waronwant.org/sites/default/files/TTIP%20booklet%20for%20RLS,%202015%20update.pdf

Hooton, C. (2015) '"Humans Could Probably Live Forever as a Machine, Potentially" Says Vague Neuroscientist'. *Independent* (26/5/2016). www.oecd.org/document/60/0,2340,en_2649_33723_37969852_1_1_1_1,00.html

Huang, Z. (2015) 'China Plans to Clone Everything from Beef Cattle to the Family Dog in This Giant Factory'. http://qz.com/556974/china-is-building-the-worlds-largest-cloning-factory-to-copy-everything-from-beef-cattle-to-the-family-dog/

Hugo, V. (1849–1869) 'Addresses to the International Peace Congress'. www.gavroche.org/vhugo/peacecongress.shtml

ICM (2014) 'New EU Members Survey – Combined/CATI Fieldwork: 11th–13th July 2014'. www.scribd.com/document/237219379/New-EU-Members-Combined-July-2014

IOM [Organisation for Migration] (2015) *World Migration Report 2015: Migrants and Cities: New Partnerships to Manage Mobility.* Geneva: IOM.

IPCC [Intergovernmental Panel on Climate Change] (2013) *Climate Change 2013: The Physical Science Basis.* Cambridge: Cambridge University Press.

Knight, W. (2013) 'Facial Analysis Software Spots Struggling Students'. *MIT Technology Review* (1/7/2013). www.technologyreview.com/s/516606/facial-analysis-software-spots-struggling-students/

Lawrence, D. H. (1928) 'Manvotional: The Know-It-All State of Mind – from "New Mexico"'. www.artofmanliness.com/2011/06/26/manvotional-the-know-it-all-state-of-mind/

OECD (2001a) *Understanding the Digital Divide.* Paris: OECD.

OECD (2001b) *The Well-Being of Nations: The Role of Human and Social Capital.* Paris: OECD.

OECD (2002) *Education Policy Analysis.* Paris: OECD.

OECD (2006) 'Sustaining Economic Growth: Outlook and Challenges'. Presentation at the Bank of Greece by the Secretary-General Ángel Gurría. Athens, June 2006. www.oecd.org/dataoecd/55/2/37007533.pdf

OECD (2007a) *Employment Outlook.* Paris: OECD.

OECD (2007b) 'OECD Education Ministers Call for Strengthening Vocational Education and Training at Meeting in Copenhagen'. 22–23 January 2007. www.oecd.org/document/60/0,2340,en_2649_33723_37969852_1_1_1_1,00.html

OECD (2007c) 'Istanbul Declaration'. www.oecd.org/newsroom/38883774.pdf

OECD (2007d) 'Measuring and Fostering the Progress of Societies'. www.oecd.org/site/worldforum06/knowledgebase-measuringprogressaroundtheworld/

OECD (2010) *PISA 2009 Results: What Makes a School Successful? – Resources, Policies and Practices.* Volume 4. http://dx.doi.org/10.1787/9789264091559-en

OECD (2013) *Assessment of Higher Education Learning Outcomes (AHELO): Feasibility Study.* Volume 2. Paris: OECD.

OECD (2015a) *In It Together: Why Less Inequality Benefits All: Overview of Inequality Trends, Key Findings and Policy Directions.* Paris: OECD.

OECD (2015b) Students, Computers and Learning: Making the Connection. Paris: OECD.

Orwell, G. (1945) 'Notes on Nationalism' (First published: *Polemic.* – GB, London. – May 1945). http://orwell.ru/library/essays/nationalism/english/e_nat

Pain, S. (1997) 'Business Calls the Tune in Research'. *Mail and Guardian* (14/3/1997). www.mg.co.za/article/1997-03-14-business-calls-the-tune-in-research

Pollock, D. (2014) 'ISIS Has Almost No Popular Support in Egypt, Saudi Arabia, or Lebanon'. *The Washington Institute.* www.washingtoninstitute.org/policy-analysis/view/isis-has-almost-no-popular-support-in-egypt-saudi-arabia-or-lebanon

Quinn, J. (2015) 'The Tragedy of Classical Languages Being for the Privileged Few'. *The Guardian* (16/3/2015). https://www.theguardian.com/commentisfree/2015/mar/16/tragedy-classical-languages-privileged-few-state-schools

Reporters without Borders (2016) 'World Press Freedom Index'. rsf.org

Rikowski, G. ([2002] 2003) 'Schools: The Great GATS Buy'. *Information for Social Change*, 16 (Winter). http://libr.org/isc/articles/16-G.Rikowski.html

Sadler, M. (1900) 'How Far Can We Learn Anything of Practical Value From the Study of Foreign Systems of Education?'. An Address given at the Guildford Educational Conference on Saturday, 20 October 1900. http://home.dpe.uevora.pt/~casimiro/michaelsadler1900.pdf

Truman, H. (1949) 'Truman's Inaugural Address, January 20, 1949'. *Harry S. Truman Library and Museum.* www.trumanlibrary.org/whistlestop/50yr_archive/inagural20jan1949.htm

Tuning www.unideusto.org/tuningeu/

UNHRC [United Nations High Commissioner for Refugees] (2016) *Trends at a Glance: 2015 in Review.* Geneva: UNHRC.

UNWTO [United Nations World Tourism Organisation] (2016) *Tourism Highlights – 2016 Edition.* www.e-unwto.org/doi/pdf/10.18111/9789284418145

Urthecast www.urthecast.com/

Walker, S. (2016) 'Face Recognition App Taking Russia by Storm May Bring End to Public Anonymity'. *The Guardian* (17/5/2016). https://www.theguardian.com/technology/2016/may/17/findface-face-recognition-app-end-public-anonymity-vkontakte

WHO [World Health Organisation] (2012) 'Depression in Europe: Facts and Figures'. www.euro.who.int/en/countries/tajikistan/news/news/2012/10/depression-in-europe/depression-in-europe-facts-and-figures

World Bank (2007) *K4D – Knowledge for Development: The World Bank Institute's Program on Building Knowledge Economies.* Washington, DC: World Bank Institute.

World Bank (2008) Measuring Knowledge in the World's Economies: Knowledge Assessment Methodology and Knowledge Economy Index: Knowledge for Development Program. Washington, DC: World Bank Institute.

World Bank (2010) *World Bank Education Strategy 2020: Learning for All: Investing in People's Knowledge and Skills to Promote Development.* http://siteresources.worldbank.org/EDUCATION/Resources/ESSU/Education_Sector_Strategy_draft_for_comment.pdf

WTO (1998) 'Council for Trade in Services: Education Services – Background Note by the Secretariat'. 23 September 1998. www.wto.org

Notes: Bibliography accessed in Modern Greek translations is cited in the original language in which it was first published. All web addresses cited were active during 2016.

Index